Unfinished

A Personal Journey of Healing, Self-Discovery and Resilience

ISANA

Suite 300 - 990 Fort St
Victoria, BC, V8V 3K2
Canada

www.friesenpress.com

First Edition — 2016

ISBN
978-1-4602-6817-9 (Hardcover)
978-1-4602-6818-6 (Paperback)
978-1-4602-6819-3 (eBook)

1. Biography & Autobiography, Personal Memoirs

Distributed to the trade by The Ingram Book Company

Jeanne Hill

Author's Note

My original intent, when writing this memoir, was to find personal healing; I had no wish to hurt those that I feel did me wrong. From the start, I was determined to be honest and to dig deep within myself. Otherwise, why bother?

I have described the events as accurately as I remember and my comments are based on my honest opinion of those events. Names have been altered to protect the identities of all parties involved, including my own.

"Isana" means strong-willed, tenacious: aspects that comprise my life as I have lived it.

We all have a story to tell & this one is mine! Wishing you a life full of adventure, lived with no regrets.

Keri

For my husband:
my rock, my constant, my everything.

Prologue

I reached the edge of the field on my trusty red bicycle and felt the sweat running down the middle of my back. The gentle breeze caused the long grass to wave and bend like graceful dancers. I quickly found the well-worn path and steered my bicycle down the steep slope. A startled, slithery garter snake glided off the path where it had been relishing the warm sun. Before long, I reached the small glade of maple and poplar trees. The large branches of the red maples blocked out the sun's rays, producing a tunnel of cool air. Goose pimples sprung out on my damp skin.

Suddenly, I was back into the heat of the sun covering me like a warm blanket. I expertly maneuvered my bike around the sharp bend that brought me to my destination. The lukewarm water from the pond lapped gently over my bare feet while the muddy bottom oozed between my toes. Bullfrogs chirped in unison and red-winged blackbirds angrily protested my arrival. There they were! Meshed into the long grass that had surrendered to the pond were hundreds of transparent frog eggs with a small black dot in the very middle. The smell of the warm stagnant water filled my nostrils while the clusters of eggs bobbed up and down to the rhythm of the rippling water.

My gaze wandered a little ways away catching sight of swarms of tiny little tadpoles, the size of my baby fingernail. Carefully, I ventured into the deeper part of the pond, the cooler waters refreshing my tanned legs. Here were the big ones! They were no longer jet black, rather shades of mossy green and dark grey. Their back legs had begun to form and their wiggly tails were getting shorter. The feel of them against my legs tickled, making me giggle. Slowly, I backed up to the edge of the pond being careful not to step on my new friends. *Splash!* Looking quickly, I spotted a big painted turtle just before it disappeared into the murky waters.

I decided to go and sit on my favourite rock at the pond's edge. I dipped my feet into the water and then onto the warm rock, watching my wet footprints eaten up by the sun. Closing my eyes, I listened. I picked out the tweet of a robin, the sweet song of the goldfinch and, drowning out all of them, the caw, caw of the crow. Crickets were in abundance but their chirps were outdone by the deep throaty belches from the bullfrogs. The soft soothing breeze rustled the long grass and fluffy milkweeds creating a sense of calmness.

I breathed in deeply, wanting to capture everything so that I could take it all with me, and so wishing that I could just stay . . .

PART I

Chapter 1

Dream: A very small baby with tiny little feet. Fingers running up and down its body, causing it to giggle.

It was Friday, November 16, 1956. Snow and strong winds raged, blasting anyone who dared to venture out into its elements. However, as the day progressed the weather improved and by late evening the winds had diminished and the sky was mainly clear.

On the maternity ward of a local hospital, a thirty-five-year-old woman progressed through the painful stages of labour. At 10:28 p.m. a healthy baby girl was born, weighing in at six pounds, seven ounces.

I was named Frances Marie, the youngest of three other siblings. Karl was the eldest, followed by Irene and then Ron. I was the final piece that allowed the dance to begin.

I don't know much about the first few months of my existence. Bits and pieces have revealed that my mother suffered from postpartum depression. In those days, this was not recognized—mothers simply had to suck it up and cope as best they could. I was told that I cried relentlessly through the nights, obviously needing something but unable to express what it was. It was a theme that would repeat itself over and over for many years.

My early memories take me to the field behind our house on the crescent where we lived. From the eyes of a young child it was huge! The tall grasses were easy to hide in and an old tree was perfect climbing for the older kids on our block.

A small lake nearby stands out clearly in my mind. It was a picturesque, serene setting with a winding road surrounding it. At the north end, the river flowing into the lake passed under a big arched bridge, cutting its way back and forth over and around the rocky terrain.

The beauty of the lakes, the rugged rocky coastlines, and the distinctive smells that welcomed each season awakened my every sense. To this day, it is in nature that I find my solace.

It would be unfair of me not to mention Mr. Reynolds. He resided in a home for the elderly where the women's group from our church would visit. As a youngster, my mother would bring me along, hence my encounter with him. I remember sitting on his bed while he would peel me slices of apple with a penknife that he kept on his window ledge. He was kind and gentle; we formed an unbreakable bond. I adored him and he genuinely loved me. On our visits I would rush to his room, eagerly anticipating our time together. I will never forget him.

In 1960, my father left his current job and became a representative for a Christian organization that distributed Bibles to hotels, prisons, schools, etc. (In later years, this became a huge source of embarrassment for me, when asked, "What does your father do for a living?" Uggh!) This new job meant relocating to southern Ontario, to a city in the heartland of dairy farming. Thus, a whole new chapter of my young life was about to emerge.

Chapter 2

Dream: I was on the street outside our house. I was flying. I could feel myself swooping down then swooping up into the air. It was a wonderful feeling that I didn't want to end . . .

My father's new job entailed a lot of travel, so he would be gone for days at a time. Consequently, it left my mother the responsibility of tending to household chores and the raising of four children. As a result, Karl was often given the responsibility of watching over his younger siblings—a position of power that he relished, especially over Ron and myself. When challenged, he would report us to our mother and the result was usually the sharp sting of the brown leather strap—an object that was hated and feared.

My parents were the extreme of conservative, born again Christians. From my earliest memories, Sunday was church day. Before leaving the house at 8:30 a.m. for Sunday school, the radio would be tuned in to the "People's Gospel Hour" founded by the Rev. Perry F. Rockwood. His message was simple: accept Jesus Christ as your personal Lord and Saviour, or be sent to an eternity of hell, fire, and brimstone!

Following Sunday school was the morning worship service. Sermons were pretty much fear-based: one had to believe a specific doctrine; activities such as dancing, smoking, attending movie theatres, and drinking alcohol were sins; divorce was totally unacceptable and could be grounds for excommunication. The message to me as a child was clear: if you didn't obey God and follow the rules you would suffer the wrath and punishment of a vengeful, all-powerful God. Many times as a child I would wake up in the middle of the night, terror stricken, dreaming that I was going to hell because I hadn't done things right. Wow.

After church we would return home to the aroma of a prime rib roast, timed perfectly for our arrival. Sunday afternoons were to be spent with the family. Sports or playing with our neighbourhood friends were not allowed. Sunday was to be a day of rest.

Sunday suppers were light, normally eaten from TV trays watching Walt Disney. I was in awe of Tinkerbell lighting up the castle at Disneyland with her magical fairy dust, wishing that I could fly and be as free as she was. But alas, 6:30 p.m. came—time to leave for another 7 p.m. church service.

Mid-way through the week, it was back to church for Wednesday night prayer meeting. The men went off by themselves, and the women remained together, sending the youth off to their own quarters. The drone of people praying in clichés and sanctimonious voices was the perfect cure for consciousness. Numerous times I received my mother's elbow in the ribs reprimanding me for drifting off.

To be fair, there were many wonderful, sincere, loving people who were part of this congregation. To them I am grateful. However, my confusion as a young impressionable child grew as I witnessed the dichotomy of the teachings of the church and what was actually happening behind the closed doors of our home.

Chapter 3

Dream: I am in a room full of people and I suddenly realize that I am naked. People are pointing at me but there is no place to hide. I am all alone with no one to help me.

I was four years old when I began school. Back then, there was no junior and senior kindergarten, just simply kindergarten. My class time was every morning, five days a week. I do remember that I wanted no part of being left behind that first day of school, but all the crying and screaming got me nowhere. The teacher towered over us and spoke with a deep, dominating voice. Her grip was like a vice that propelled me to my spot on the floor for quiet time. I was a shy child and just wanted to be by myself at my desk. Joining the other kids in the circle just wasn't going to happen.

My unwillingness to join in prompted her to call my home stating that she believed me to be mentally behind my peers. "What child doesn't want to join the circle?" Me! Eventually I gave in after being bribed with the promise of a new book if I cooperated. However, I never did warm up to my first teacher. I was sensitive and impressionable and got the message quite clearly: I was not like the other children. I was different. I didn't fit in so there was obviously something wrong with me. Sadly, I believed it.

Kindergarten progressed to Grade 1 to the "big" part of the school. My teacher was warm and caring, unlike my first experience. As this year began, Ron and I were inseparable. We walked to and from school together and at recess we would seek each other out in the play yard. He was my big brother and I adored him.

In later fall, I was admitted to hospital to have an abscess removed from my neck. Nights in the hospital were terrifying. The steel rail guards on each side of the hospital bed were ice cold. The clang of metal trays and strong smell of antiseptic permeated their way into my memory bank.

When I was well enough to return to school, everything changed. Ron wanted no part of walking to school with me and would run away from me at recess. I was devastated and couldn't understand why all of a sudden I felt like he hated me. I thought that it was my entire fault. Obviously, I had done something very bad and this was my punishment. (Note: I found out many years later what really happened. My teacher was concerned that all my free time was spent with Ron and she felt I was not socializing enough with my own peers. So she pulled my brother aside and asked him not to spend so much time with me. Being a kid, he took it literally, thinking that he was not to be anywhere near me and therefore avoided me.)

From then on as kids growing up, we had nothing to do with each other. Other than verbal confrontations, we never spoke. I felt betrayed and hurt. My guard was up. I would not give him the chance to hurt me again.

We lived in the heart of the snowbelt region so it was customary that kids wore snow pants to school. I had been told that when we came in from recess I was to remove them. For whatever reason, I decided I didn't want to and kept them on. Somehow, my mother was suspicious that I wasn't obeying the rule, so she had Ron check up on me. It was a Friday and I had just gotten home from school. My mother asked me if I had taken my snow pants off and I replied that I had. The more she asked, the more I kept to my story. She was furious and out came the infamous brown leather strap.

By now I was crying, sobbing out of control. I was seated on a kitchen chair being hit across the legs, while my siblings surrounded me, seemingly enjoying the show. I couldn't breathe; snot was pouring out of my nose and I was choking. I was terrified of my mother's anger but what was even worse was the feeling of such aloneness. No one seemed to want to help me. I believed that if I confessed to the "crime" the punishment would become even more severe.

When the episode was over and I recovered, the hurt and shame shifted to another emotion: intense, deep-rooted anger. The flame was lit. For decades I would continue to stoke the fire within.

Chapter 4

Dream: A female: one part adult, the other a little girl. A man followed her and wouldn't leave her alone. He wanted to touch her and put his hands down her pants. She was afraid and wanted someone to tell him to stop. Another adult came by and saw what was happening. Instead of helping her, he said to the man, "Do whatever you want to her." The man, groping the genitals of the adult/child, left her feeling powerless and numb. She woke up crying, feeling very little.

From my earliest memories, I was absolutely obsessed with horses. My appetite for them was insatiable.

One of the local shoe stores in the downtown core had a spring rocking horse located at the rear of the shop. Whenever I went there I couldn't get to it fast enough. One time there was a child already on it and I was so upset—it was MY horse!

Every year at the local fair there were always pony rides for children. I do recall refusing to get off when the ride was over; I just wanted to keep going.

Our local library carried the *Black Stallion* series by author Walter Farley. I devoured those books. My vivid imagination allowed me to escape into every page to the point that I could feel myself on the back of this magnificent stallion, galloping at breakneck speed, my fingers clutching its thick black mane.

I collected china horses—big ones, small ones,—it didn't matter. I had names for all of them.

People from our church owned a farm on Miners Road. My mother frequently took Ron and I there. While she visited with the woman, I beelined it to the barn, my attraction being a pair of big, powerful Clydesdale horses.

They had a hired farm hand named Ivan who would let me sit on the back of these horses. He knew how horse crazy I was and would always accommodate my desire to be around them. He was kind to me and I adored him. He also attended our church and sometimes after a service he would be invited to our house to visit. I would run and jump on his lap, so happy that he was there. He was loving and caring and I soaked it up like a dry sponge.

One summer day, when I was about seven years old, we were visiting at the farm. I, of course, was in the barn with Ivan and the horses. I was totally unprepared for what was going to happen. My naïve childhood trust was about to be shattered.

I vividly recall squatting in the hay, observing something that had caught my interest. Ivan came up behind me and knelt down. My inner red flag reacted but I froze—I couldn't move. I felt his hand slide under the elastic waistband of my shorts and his rough calloused hand sought out the area of my genitals. I could feel his hot breath on the back of my neck and in a hoarse whisper he said, "Now that feels good, doesn't it?"

I have no idea of what happened after this. I do remember my legs feeling like rubber and that something really wrong had just occurred. I didn't know until years later that Ron saw me come out of the barn that day. He told me that I looked like I was in a trance and he knew instinctively that Ivan had done something to me. Apparently, even my mother and the owners of the farm knew that he had been inappropriate towards me but no one ever spoke to me about it. I never considered for a moment of going to my mother to try to explain what had happened. I would not have had a clue of how to even try to put it into words. Somehow it was my fault, that I had done something to make him do it. This was my message to myself and I believed it.

We continued to frequent the farm but it was never the same. I managed to shut out all feelings and all memories of Ivan—at least so I thought.

Chapter 5

Dream: In the darkness, a little girl lay huddled up in the blankets on her bed. The closet door was open and a large shoe bag hung there. An evil presence seemed to fill the room and a woman appeared. She cursed the little girl to hell and the devil by waving her hands over the shoe bag. The young child was very frightened.

Growing up in the '60s was such a far cry from today's fast-paced, technology-crazed society. Owning a black and white television was a luxury. Looking back on the different families that shared our neighbourhood, there was a pretty clear standard. Routinely, mothers were stay-at-home housewives taking care of kids, meals, and household chores. Fathers were the breadwinners, arriving in time for the evening's home-cooked meal where everyone ate together, at least for the most part.

Television shows were family oriented, like *Leave it to Beaver*, *My Three Sons*, *Beverley Hillbillies*, and on and on. They were the "make you feel good" kind, with a blend of humour and wholesomeness.

After supper, kids took to the street to play. Summer months brought out games of road hockey; hide and go seek;

double dutch skipping contests; back yard baseball games with garbage can lids as the bases. Remember the roller skates that clamped on to the frame of your running shoes? How we didn't get seriously hurt is anybody's guess.

I have no idea of who made up the rule but it was universal. When the streetlights came on it was time for kids to make their way home, and we did. There was another universal rule of that era: what happened behind the closed doors of every family was no one else's business, whether it was right or wrong. No one told.

As previously stated, God was brought into all aspects of our life. "Spare the rod, spoil the child" (taken from Proverbs 13:24) was quoted to us often as out came the strap. I recall a plaque that hung above the arched doorway of our living room. It stated, "The family that prays together stays together," and so, another rule to be followed. We could not leave the table after supper until we had family devotions. For me it was torture. The Bible would be passed around the table as each of us read portions of whatever passage had been chosen. Following the scripture reading it was someone's turn to pray out loud. I dreaded the nights when it was my turn. It was always a test. You had to pray right. Eyes had to be closed and you had to choose the proper words.

As a young child I heard the adults praying in church and so I added to my prayer the phrase that I thought I had heard: "Dear God, please bless the missionaries in the corn fields," (which was actually, "… in the foreign fields"). This brought much laughter after which came the lecture. I felt such shame. Eventually I came up with my memorized prayer of the proper length and stuck to it.

When I reflect back on that time period I can still feel the humiliation of being laughed at and mocked. I felt hunted; the vultures were there, ready to pounce when I messed up. The intention of my mother was to have this be family time. I do believe her wish was sincere but the delivery sucked.

As tedious as this time was, what I really dreaded was that my friends would come calling for me before devotions were over. My mother would not hesitate to tell them that we were praying together as a family and that I couldn't come out to play until we were finished. That was so embarrassing for me. I had no idea of how to explain this to my peers.

When devotions were over and the dishes were done it was such a welcome relief to charge out the front screen door and hear it slam behind me. *Free!* At least until the streetlights came on.

Chapter 6

Dream: The basement of our house: cold cement floor and very dim light. Karl. I tried to stop the dog from eating what Karl had given him—it wouldn't be good for him. He overpowered me. I was angry. He controlled me because he was bigger and was allowed to.

Around the same time that Ivan assaulted me, other dynamics were taking shape between the relationships of my siblings and me. When we were all alone in the house with no parental presence, Karl ruled. I vividly recall him going after Irene, pinning her down on his bed with his body on top of hers and trying to kiss her. She repeatedly begged him to stop, and the more she struggled, the more he persisted, laughing at her inability to stop him. I watched from the shadows of that basement bedroom, afraid, watching my sister crying and her being powerless to make him stop. Ron would try to intervene but did not have the physical strength to compete against Karl, who would just fling him aside.

His abuse of me was much more subtle. It would occur when I arrived home from school in the afternoon. Karl would tell me to come downstairs and would then take me to the basement bathroom. The door would be closed and latched.

The mind is an incredible protector, knowing what an individual can and cannot handle. For the most part I blocked out a lot of what transpired behind that closed door, however I do remember some specifics.

This time period, after school, was when Karl liked to do his business. He would be seated on the toilet, pants around his ankles and he would have me sit on his lap. It was during this time that I developed a skill:—I learned to disassociate from what was happening and simply "leave." The door of that bathroom is as clear to me now as it was then. It was a heavy wooden door that had the old-style keyhole made for a skeleton key. It wouldn't shut and stay closed by itself so it was locked from the inside by a latch, leaving a small space. The sun shone through the basement window just outside of the bathroom. In turn, it shone through the opening of the brass keyhole. I watched dust particles floating in the streaks of sunlight.

Writing this is difficult. I feel myself become again that little girl, —helpless, —not having the right or knowledge of how to say no, —just having to wait until it was over. I remind myself now that I am okay. I survived. It wasn't my fault.

When he was finished we would look in the toilet to observe the size of his turd. "Wow," he would say. "That was a whopper, wasn't it?" And we would go upstairs like everything was normal.

There was another victim of those after-school episodes: Ron. I didn't know at the time that he would sneak outside the bathroom to try to observe what was happening. He saw. Years later I found out that he went to our mother and told her that it wasn't right what Karl was doing to Frances. She replied to him to mind his own business; she had bigger things on her plate to deal with. Okay. However unintentional, the message was clear: Frances didn't matter.

Throughout this time my report cards carried an ongoing theme: "Frances has a hard time paying attention in class. She likes to daydream." Off I would go into my own little world, leaving the unpleasantness behind; returning on my own volition. Without knowing any other way to cope at that time, it was a skill that served me well for many years.

As I got older, the bathroom episodes ceased but my relationship with Karl took on another dynamic:—it became a combat of physical dominance. He would grab my wrists and I would try to twist out of his grip. He told me that if I would just say "uncle" he would let me go. I was stubborn, feisty, and angry. I would only give in when I felt my wrist bone was about to break from being bent the wrong way.

However, he didn't always win. Sometimes I was able to break free, which gave me a great sense of satisfaction.—I won. This kept me coming back for more,—just to experience the gratifying feeling of beating him.

It seemed like everything in our household was a competition and not just between siblings. Winning was everything. If you lost, it was because you weren't good enough, smart enough, fast enough, you name it—you were the loser, period.

Chapter 7

Dream: A little girl in her bedroom. She hears her father come home and thinks she can hide from him in the closet. Quickly, she crawls in but makes some noise. He is at the door coming into the bedroom and the clothes in the closet are swinging on the rack. He and her mother come to the closet door and open it. She is found. She feels sick inside.

As I stated earlier, my father's job involved travel. When he did come home I felt no excitement upon his return; rather, I felt disdain. I did not know him. I did not like him. He would smother me, not letting me go, forcing kisses on me that I wanted no part of. The smell of too much *Old Spice* aftershave sickened me. I was not given the right to say no.

It was actually easier when he wasn't there. Arguments between my parents were frequent and, knowing no other way, my mother controlled him by manipulation and guilt. Sometimes the silent treatment would go on for days, the tension so thick you could taste it.

He could do nothing right in the eyes of my mother and was continually berated in front of us, so we followed suit. Many times during the supper hour he would be the brunt of jokes, just sitting there, taking it, not saying a word. He was given no respect.

One of my most embarrassing episodes surrounding my father occurred when I was in the fifth grade. It was customary that all Grade 5 students receive the New Testament portion of the Bible from my father's organization. He requested that he be the one to come to my Grade 5 classroom. I was sick. He was not like other fathers who had normal jobs. I so wanted to fit in with my peers and this experience only further isolated me from that. I hated him. My feelings did not count. I was singled out, forced to have my picture taken with my father presenting me with my Bible. In front of all my classmates he put his arm around me, pulling me in close, knowing how much I hated it. I was so humiliated, so intensely angry, wanting desperately to wake up and discover it was only a bad dream. But it wasn't—it was my living nightmare with no recourse.

I don't recall ever having an actual conversation with my father. He did not know how to talk to me and I had nothing that I wanted to say to him. The only time we did something together was on my twelfth birthday. My mother had harped on him that he should do something with his daughter. Okay, but what? He knew I loved to ride so it was decided that we would go horseback riding together. For me, the thrill of riding outdid the awkwardness of being in his presence. However, it was the first and last time; riding a horse really didn't appeal to him. We returned to our walls of silence.

When I was young, my father's parents lived in an area of abundant farmland. Behind their house were train tracks, and I remember hearing the whistle of the approaching train and running as fast as I could to watch it before it roared by. It was deafening and scary to be so close with only a wire fence separating us.

There was also a large apple orchard on their property where I loved to climb and hang upside down on the lower branches. It was a great place to go exploring.

However, the times that we had to stay overnight were not so fun. A narrow staircase would be lowered from a trap door in the ceiling, creaking its way down until it reached floor level. At bedtime, I had to climb up this ladder to reach the second floor where it was my place to sleep. It was dark, damp, musty, and cold. No amount of blankets was enough to instill any warmth. Mornings couldn't come fast enough.

My grandparents were anything but warm and fuzzy. My grandmother was calculating and mean. She did not like children and had no idea of how to relate to them. My grandfather, a retired educator, was of the old school—children were not respected.

Every time we visited them or they would come to visit us, there would be the mandatory greeting that I abhorred. I had to allow them both to hug and kiss me. He would inflict his kisses on my mouth and sometimes she would lick me instead, thinking it to be very funny. One time when they came to visit I went and hid in the doghouse, hoping to avoid them. Of course they found me and I could not escape from the inevitable. I hated them.

No wonder my father had no clue on how to parent or be emotionally available to his wife. He had grown up being bullied, made to feel stupid and inferior to those around him. Isn't it interesting how history and cycles repeat themselves?

Chapter 8

Memory: I was in the bathroom by the sink and my mother came in. She was intensely angry with me but I don't remember why. She grabbed my lower jaw; fingers gripping me like a vice. With her teeth clenched, she vehemently spat out, inches from my face, "Why can't I break you?"

We were always at odds, my mother and I. It seemed like she was my greatest challenge in life and I hers. She was a perfectionist and everything had to be done her way. If it wasn't, then it was simply wrong and would have to be done right. Towels had to be folded precisely so, pillowcases pressed and ironed with each fold distinct and no hint of wrinkles.

Undoubtedly, my sister was the queen in the eyes of my mother and I was constantly reminded of how I was so not like Irene. Unfortunately, this comparison blocked any chance of developing a close relationship with my sister. I was inferior and would never attain the status she held.

When I was very young, maybe three or four, Irene had bought me a stuffed doll-like toy. She was apparently so excited to bring it home to me but when given to me, I had no interest in it. I liked stuffed furry animals; dolls were boring. I recall my mother scolding me for being so selfish and how dare I hurt Irene's feelings. I was told that every girl likes dolls—it's instinctual. Clearly the message was given to me that I was strange and consequently I would never make a good mother. Ouch.

I was a tomboy through and through. Playing house and dress-up was not on my list of favourite things. I loved to catch strange-looking bugs in glass jars and watch them try to escape. I would give them names and eventually release them back to their habitat. Climbing huge oak trees was exhilarating—the higher, the better. I was a daredevil and rarely backed down.

I hated having to dress up for Sunday church. My mother would force me to wear my church hat. Easter Sunday was the worst. That was the day for Easter bonnets and frilly dresses. What was worse was that no other girls my age had to wear hats. Once again I was singled out, not allowed to just dress like everyone else. So many times I would go to my room infuriated, throwing the hat on the floor and stomping it as hard as I could, wishing I could kill it. I had to hide my tears, stifle my sobs, and swallow my fury.

Our house was run by rules—rules that demanded obedience or suffer the infliction of the strap. My mother controlled the roost. When I was put to bed, I was to stay there until morning when she got up. Getting up in the night to use the washroom was not acceptable. She had taken me to the bathroom before bed so she believed there was no reason for me to have to get up during the night. Many times my bladder would be ready to burst but I had to wait; I had to shut out a basic physical need. I remember once being so desperate that I decided to take the chance. It was a matter of relieving myself or peeing the bed. Either way there would be consequences.

It took me many years to be able to give myself permission to get up during the night if nature called. I had to reassure myself that it was okay. I had the right (and responsibility!) to listen and respond to what my body needed.

I believe that my mother's intense need to control stemmed from her own insecurities and fears. She was desperate to hold on to whatever sense of self she had left. She did not know any other way.

During grade school, I was to come home immediately following the dismissal bell. In Grade 3, I was having problems with arithmetic. One day my teacher told me I had to stay after school to work on a problem that I hadn't completed during class time. I was frantic. I was going to be late. Page 21 of my arithmetic textbook is forever etched in my memory bank. Quarters, dimes, nickels and pennies were pictured on the page and it involved figuring out a word problem. I read it over and over, trying to comprehend what I was reading, but panic had taken over. I had no idea how to solve it. My mind was blank.

I don't know how long I had to sit there. I think my teacher must have sensed my desperation and solved it for me. I ran home, crying all the way. I was met with a torrent of verbal reprimands but thankfully I was spared from the dreaded strap.

It seemed that my mother always had some physical ailment plaguing her. Being sick brought her attention and sympathy that she craved intensely. Every member of the house was manipulated into feeling sorry for her and doing a tap dance around her.

When my mother was thirteen, her mother died in their family home from a complication of Parkinson's disease. In that era, it was such a misunderstood illness and no resources were available as they are today. It would not have been a pleasant death and it obviously left my mother with an emotional wound that never healed.

She would often recall her feelings as a teenager, on Mother's Day, when she attended church. Daughters who had lost their mothers were given a white carnation corsage to wear. Whatever demons she carried around this custom found its way into the heart of our home. Mother's Day was hell. She was so angry. No card or gift that I bought for her was appropriate. I could not please her. I was so relieved when it was finally over—at least until next year.

She was always at odds with her father for reasons that were unclear. Unlike my other grandparents, I found him to be very kind and he would make me laugh. It was fun to sit on his lap and to go for walks with him. If there was this other side to him, as per my mother's account, I never saw it. My memories of Gramp are very fond.

The insatiable need for my mother to always be right rubbed off on all of us. The words "I'm sorry" were not spoken. It inferred that one had done something wrong. To speak those words were a sign of weakness that only opened oneself up for attack and criticism. It was not possible to just "be." My guard was always up, ready to fend off whatever came my way.

Chapter 9

Dream: I was in a large kitchen with family and some acquaintances. There was water and dirt all over the floor and no dry place to stand. I was being blamed for the mess. I felt like the dirt that was on the floor. I was left to clean it all up.

What I observed and experienced at home I carried with me to the playground. Kids who were younger, weaker, or just unable to take me on, I bullied. I was rough and physical.

A friend's mother from our street pulled me aside one day and told me that if I didn't stop hitting her daughter, she would not let me play with her anymore. I had no idea that she was going home with bruises on her back. I had no intent to hurt her and I felt so ashamed. I remember trying really hard not to do it again.

One of the girls I played with had a younger brother who was really small for his age. Sometimes I would catch him and take him to where there were large weeping willow trees. I would proceed to tie his hands to a limb above his head and pretend to beat him with willow branches. I guess he was terrified of me. His mother also spoke to me: "Please leave my son alone; you're scaring him." Was it the building rage within me that made me torment someone weaker or was I just acting out what I witnessed at home? I think it was probably a combination of both. Deep inside I knew it wasn't right but I just did not know how else to relate.

One day I was playing with two or three kids from the neighbourhood. One of the girls had just been given a brand-new CCM bicycle for her birthday. She was so proud of it! I don't recall causing a black mark on the seat but I was blamed for it. A girl who was a year or so older than me proceeded to tell me off. I remember it vividly. She told me that in Brownies they had been taught that when you did something wrong to someone you were to apologize. She went on to tell me that I owed Wanda an apology because it was the right thing to do. I took her words to heart and told my friend I was sorry. Wow. It was a lesson I never forgot.

I was very protective of my friends. On our walks home from school, I would lead the way wearing my black plastic Batman ring, fantasizing that we were under attack and I would be the one to save them. Although I had a tough exterior, my inner emotions were quite the opposite. I was very sensitive. Cruel words or mean actions hurt me to the core but I would try to pretend that it didn't bother me.

One day when we were walking home for lunch, my friend was angry with me for something I had said or done. When we arrived at my driveway she said something to the effect that she wasn't going to walk to school with me anymore and not to bother calling on her. I was devastated. I went inside and started to cry. My mother was there and, hoping for some comfort, I told her what had been said to me. She replied, "Well, you probably deserved it." Okay. I vowed that I would not make the same mistake again. I would not open myself up and show any vulnerability. I did not have a soft place to fall.

I had my first real crush in Grade 6. He was a blond-haired, blue-eyed boy of Dutch descent. He was smart, funny, and easy to talk to. I was smitten! One Saturday night I went ice-skating with two friends from our church and he was there. We ended up skating around the ice rink together holding hands. I was delighted but terrified that my mother would come in and catch me. I was not to have anything to do with boys. Thankfully, I was not caught and my secret remained intact.

In the same year a new girl came to our class. She was bigger than most of us and always wore jeans. Back then, girls had to wear dresses to school, so she became quite an anomaly. She and I connected immediately. She was passionate about horses and would bring me copies of the magazine *Western Horsemen*. She did not have the typical family structure of the time. Her mother was not around, and her father was a biker who liked to party and hang out with those of similar interests. It would have been a pretty rough atmosphere for a young girl with no female influence. I have no idea of the experiences she had gone through, but we were of the same mold: under the surface, scared and hurt but hiding it with the mask of toughness.

One Monday morning she came to school with the name "Dave" tattooed on the back of her hand. He was sixteen and the son of one of her dad's friends. She said they loved each other and that when she turned sixteen they were going to run away together.

I didn't see her during the summer after Grade 6, but when we returned in September we found ourselves in the same class. For the first time she was wearing a dress—clearly uncomfortable in her new attire. I guess her dad had been given a choice: either she dressed according to the rules or she couldn't attend. I felt sorry for her; she seemed sad and withdrawn. One day she didn't come back to school and we were told that she had moved. I have thought of her at times through the years, hoping that she survived and is okay.

One bright spot in my life at this time was a border collie cross that we adopted from an animal shelter. I named her Tess and she became my dog. Every day after school we escaped to an area of long grass, creeks, and great climbing trees. During these outings I would tell her about my frustrations, my fears, my secrets, knowing they were safe with her. She was my source of pleasure and comfort. We were dependent on each other; I needed her and she needed me.

Grade 7 and 8 were pivotal years: the pressure from peers to fit in was enormous and I did not have the self-esteem needed to make my own choices. I was desperate to fit in and would go to any length to do so. I hung out with the "bad" kids, giving me an air of importance, but I was terrified that my antics would get back to my mother. It didn't help that my homeroom teacher in Grade 8 attended the same church. I was busted.

During those two years, I discovered that I could run—and could run fast. I joined the local track and field club and it became my passion. My favourite distance was the 440-yard dash (prior to the distances becoming metric). I felt that I had to win or at least come close. If I didn't, I viewed myself as a failure and no good. In my mind, I would beat myself up, over and over, cursing my body for "failing" me. Prior to a race I was a nervous wreck, pacing, hyperventilating, desperate to beat my opponents. Many times at the finish line I would throw up simply from the stress I put on myself. It was a pattern that followed me throughout my entire competitive career.

My parents only saw me run one race. It was my very first race after joining the city track club. The coach had entered me in the 880-yard event rather than the 440 that I was used to. I went out too fast and ended up fading badly, finishing at the back of the pack. I was ashamed and humiliated. No comment was made. They just never came to see me run again.

My other siblings were musically inclined: Karl played the violin, Irene could sing, and Ron was proficient at the piano. When people would come to visit, my mother would have them perform for them. I remember her voicing how wonderful it was that they could use their gifts for the Lord. I couldn't compete with that. All I could do was run.

Chapter 10

Dream: I was trapped in a very narrow canal. I waded through the water, encountering obstructions and many turns. In some places, the air was hot and humid; it was hard to breathe. The water level rose and a roof came down over my head, leaving very little space to breathe. I couldn't see what was ahead or what was coming.

I was thirteen when I started high school. Karl and Irene had both attended the same school and Ron was in his final year. Our name was known so there was no chance of remaining inconspicuous.

Again, I struggled with wanting to be liked and accepted. The only problem was that I had no concept of who I was. Whoever I was, I certainly didn't like her very much. However, I did know that I was not the person my mother wanted me to be.

I gravitated to where I could receive some positive feedback: sports. I joined the cross-country team, basketball team, track team—anything to try and find a place where I could belong. With Ron around, I had to be careful that I wasn't seen doing something against the rules. I knew it would be reported when we got home.

I was not allowed to attend school dances. Dancing was a sin. I became quite creative in my excuses as to why I couldn't attend those functions. There were tight restrictions on not being allowed to socialize with friends from school, apart from school hours and sports-related events. Consequently, my real circle of friends became those from our church. I have fond memories of us driving to Skateland on weekends for indoor roller-skating. It was a great time! The faster I could whip around the rink, the better. I was in my element.

However, the tighter the reins the angrier I got; the feeling of being different from everyone else was only accentuated by what I was not allowed to do.

Somehow I survived that first year of high school. I did what I needed to pass, but beyond that I couldn't have cared less. I simply lived up to the belief that I was not smart enough to expect anything more from myself.

Prior to entering Grade 10, I expressed that I needed some school supplies. For whatever reason, my mother was unable to drive me, so she told my father, who happened to be home, to take me. He was the last person I wanted to be seen with. He had no concept of what I needed, and I felt treated like someone much younger than a fourteen-year-old, self-conscious teenager.

It was not a good scene. I was humiliated and furious and I blatantly shunned and ignored him. However, I was not the only one to become enraged. When we got home he lost it. He told me that he was going to pull my shorts down and give me a beating like never before.

At the time, I had my period, and all I knew was there was no way he was going to succeed in removing my shorts. He cornered my in my bedroom and I can still hear the sound of his belt being ripped free from his belt loops. I cringed like a dog, helpless against the torrent of lashes, hanging on to the tops of my shorts for dear life. Finally it ended and he left my room.

The physical pain was nothing compared to my anger. I was seething with rage and had no outlet to express it. Through my stifled sobs I pushed it down into the depths of my inner core. The intensity was overwhelming. I felt like I was going to literally explode.

I did have one consolation: I had held on to my shorts. I hadn't lost all my dignity.

With the start of Grade 10, I no longer had to look over my shoulder for Ron so I felt free—sort of. Our church was located right across the street from the high school, and in sheer defiance I would smoke my Export A's on the church steps, relishing the act of grinding the butts onto the cement. I never even really enjoyed smoking, but I was hanging out with the cool kids, so that's what I did. It gave me the illusion that I could control something in my life without my mother knowing.

One day, near the end of the lunch hour, I was smoking my cigarette at the side entrance to the church where the mailbox was located. The mail had just been delivered and I got this bright idea to light a match and throw it in with the mail. I quickly departed when I saw fingers of smoke creeping out from the metal gaps of the mailbox. Adrenalin made me giddy from having committed this crime against the house of God.

In retrospect, I believe I did this out of sheer frustration and anger. Everything in my life was controlled. I did not have opportunity to make choices; they were made for me. I was so controlled, so I was becoming out of control.

Later that night when I went to bed, I noted my crime in my diary kept in the nightstand beside my bed. It was only one confession of many—private things that I would never have been allowed to speak. My pen was my voice. Inwardly I felt alone and lost.

I was managing to hide my smoking from my mother but one day she asked me why my clothes smelled like cigarettes. I was totally caught off guard. My thoughts whirled, desperate to come up with an explanation. I convincingly told her that smoking was allowed in the girl's change room at school. She seemed surprised that that was allowed but she bought it. Inwardly I breathed a sigh of relief, but what I didn't know was that my relief would be short lived.

One weekend, Ron brought a friend home from university and needed a house key to come and go. I wasn't at home when my mother went searching for my key to lend to them. She found it all right, right along with half a pack of my cigarettes.

I arrived home late in the afternoon and knew immediately there was trouble. Supper was eaten in silence. It was Sunday, so of course that meant church. Before leaving, I was told emphatically that I would be going nowhere after church other than straight home. Church never seemed to end. I just wanted to get it over with—whatever "it" was going to be.

Upon arriving home, I was told to go to the living room. Shortly thereafter they came in and sat down opposite me. I was horrified with what happened next. My father pulled from his pocket my diary. I felt light-headed. Physically it was all I could do not to throw up.

They went through it page by page, demanding explanations, chastising me, shaming me over and over for how bad I was, all my private thoughts no longer private, spilled out for all to see with me completely powerless to take them back.

I had lived through episodes of my body being violated and not having the right to say no—, but this was beyond anything physical. I felt raped both emotionally and psychologically. I was ordered to flush the remaining cigarettes down the toilet. Numbly, I complied. However, it wasn't just the cigarettes that got flushed away; part of me went down with them.

Chapter 11

Let Jesus be your bridge over troubled waters
– Unknown

In the late 1960s, a new revolution was born out of California. Thousands of teenagers and young adults joined what became known as the Jesus People Movement. It was an offshoot of the hippie revolution; instead of getting high on drugs, followers sought to get high on Jesus. Jesus music also developed, a combination of rock music and gospel content. In 1971, two popular Broadway productions hit the stage: *Jesus Christ Superstar* and *Godspell*. This same year the movement became the focus of the media. The revolution had the world's attention, as well as my own.

For the first time it was considered cool to be a Jesus follower. When I look back, the course that I took over the next few years made perfect sense. It was my out from the pressures of home, incessantly on my case to conform to their rules and belief system. Did I really believe the message that was being delivered, or was it more my need to feel that I belonged to something? The latter would be most accurate. However, my participation convinced my mother that I had been born again. She was thrilled.

At school, my new identity was accepted due to the popularity that the media was giving to the movement. I sported T-shirts that read, "One Way to Jesus;" and "Jesus is Coming!" I attended the Jesus Rallies in the larger cities, getting swept up in the energy of the masses. Church moved from pews and altars to coffee houses and large outdoor stadiums.

In Toronto, a group was formed called the Catacomb Club. It grew rapidly and by 1971 a group of approximately 850 people began meeting on Thursday nights at St. Paul's Anglican Church. I attended there frequently with carloads of friends wanting to share the experience. At its peak, the group overflowed with 2500 enthusiastic teenagers and young adults.

I had longed for this sense of oneness and belonging. Although the delivery was a refreshing change, the underlying message wasn't a whole lot different. The motivation was still fear based. A book entitled *The Late Great Planet Earth* written by Hal Lindsey (an "expert" in Biblical prophecy) became a bestseller. It contained a series of sermons all proclaiming that the second coming of Christ was imminent and one had better be ready.

At the time, Larry Norman was one of the most popular Jesus music performers. He wrote a song entitled, "I Wish We'd All Been Ready" with the theme of expectation for the second coming. It portrayed two people walking together; one is taken and the other remains behind with no chance to change the outcome.

My sincerity was undisputed but I still felt like something was missing. My self-talk told me that I was obviously not doing something right. I was terrified that I would be the one left behind.

During my last two years of high school I had my share of boy crushes, however, for the most part their feelings were not reciprocated. Attention seemed to come more from the ones that I just wasn't really interested in. When they would make advances, like holding my hand or giving me a kiss, I let them. I did not feel like I had the right to say no, even though I was not attracted to them. I had to pretend that I liked them so as not to hurt their feelings. My feelings, compared to theirs, just weren't relevant.

One particular man, ten years my senior, developed a liking for me. Of course, I went along with it. He hung out with my friends and I, driving us to wherever we wanted to go. I liked him but knew that because of the age difference, it wasn't going to go very far. I guess my mother figured out that he liked me more than what she was comfortable with. As a result, she told my father to tell him to stay away from me. I found out about this conversation from a letter that he sent to me. In it he told me that he loved me but had to abide by what my father had stated.

Was it healthy for a sixteen-year-old to date a twenty-six-year-old man? No, but once again my feelings, right or wrong, were not considered. No discussion. Period.

My best friend during this time period was Karen. We had met at church many years earlier and had always hung out. Our parents were friends, so it provided us with the opportunity to spend a lot of time together. The older we got, the closer Karen and I became, to the point of being inseparable. Adults loved her. She had a charming personality on top of being pretty and smart. I got away with a lot simply because if Karen was going to be there, then it was considered to be okay.

Our favourite song was "You've Got a Friend," by James Taylor. We knew the words by heart and would belt out the lyrics, complete with our own made-up actions to accompany the words. We consoled each other through boyfriend woes; we shared our hopes and dreams; we defended and supported each other; we were each other's constant.

She completed high school a year earlier than myself and ended up going to college in Toronto. We tried to see each other as frequently as possible when either she came home or I would go and stay with her. We vowed to always be best friends.

I was seventeen when I finished high school in 1974. It had never been an option for me to go to university. The message that I had lived with was that I just wasn't smart enough; I was not university material. All I knew was that I needed to get away, but where could I go and have the approval of my parents, or at least my mother? I found out through friends, met at various rallies, about a college in Manitoba. Its major focus was theology but offered other courses as well. I knew that as long as there was "God content", my mother would approve. I applied and was accepted. I felt like I had grown wings.

High school was almost at an end. With just a few days to go I came home and saw that the gate to the backyard was open. My heart sank. I knew instinctively that my dog Tess was not going to be there to greet me. My mother had decided that since I was leaving for college she didn't want to have to take care of her, so had given her away to a family with a young girl. It was done. There was nothing I could say or do. I buried my anger and grief, refusing to acknowledge even to myself how devastated I was.

Thirty-eight years later, as I write and remember, I finally mourn the loss of my beloved pet. I guess better late than never.

Chapter 12

Dream: I am in a large train yard but no trains are moving. I can't find the people who I had come with. Many doors appear. I start going through each of them but they don't lead me anywhere. I try to come back the way I had come but it had all changed. I felt alone, lost and unwanted. I just wanted to find the people I knew.

The weeks of summer flew by. Before I knew it I was packing up a trunk full of stuff that would be put on a train to await my arrival. My parents had decided to drive me to the college to see where I would be for the next few years and to make sure I got settled in.

Final goodbyes were made to my friends and, of course, Karen. We promised to keep in touch with lots of letters. (There were no emails and texting back then!)

I will never forget the first time I saw the flat expanse of the prairies—not a tree, not a hill, just golden wheat fields swaying to the rhythm of the wind. It was spectacular.

I was excited about this new venture. I would be on my own and free from the rules that had encompassed my existence. But right behind the excitement was fear and apprehension. What if I didn't fit in? What if nobody liked me? What if I found the courses too hard? What if I failed and had to return home? All the what-ifs loomed close to the surface of my conscious thoughts.

Finally, we arrived and I was swept into the registration line for new students. Following registration it was time to find my room; time to meet my roommate; time for the campus tour; time for my parents to leave.

No doubt that it must have been difficult for them to drive away that day. I was their youngest and I was only seventeen years old. For me they represented what was familiar. Their departure left me in the wake of new surroundings, new people, and new direction. Everything that had been familiar changed instantly. I was on my own, free to make my own choices.

I quickly learned that I was in the heartland of a conservative German Mennonite culture. It was starkly different from what I had ever experienced. It was not uncommon for parents to raise families with ten-plus children. They were hardworking, many of them farmers who relied on the wheat and grain industry for their income. Husbands would work the fields alongside their sons; wives would cook and take care of the children. Girls were raised in the kitchen performing endless hours of putting together, from scratch, dozens of perogies, cabbage rolls, pies and preserves. I was introduced to farmer's sausage—a blend of ingredients that only they knew the secret to. Nothing was wasted; when feeding families of twelve or more on a daily basis frugality was essential. In short, family was everything—a concept I could not relate to. My roommate came from such a family. She was very pleasant and soft-spoken but as such we really had nothing in common.

Everyone seemed to know each other. I felt like I was on the sidelines looking in, wishing for someone to include me in their circle. Once again the old feeling of being different and unable to fit in enveloped me.

Within the first week, students were given the opportunity to go roller-skating. I was thrilled. I had even brought my own roller skates from home. Maybe this would give me the opportunity to connect with someone. Not so. No one asked me to skate. I sat alone on the bus there and back; everyone seeming to be engaged in conversation having a great time—except for me. Sadness and loneliness overwhelmed me. I had to fight back the tears. I missed Karen and I missed my friends, but undoubtedly I didn't miss my parents. It's just the way it was.

Classes began in earnest. Syllabi were distributed complete with course outlines and course objectives; term papers—seemingly endless; assigned reading; tests; exams. At first I was on overload having no idea as to how I would meet all the deadlines but eventually it all fell into place. The structure was good; it distracted me from my inward struggle.

Fridays brought about a mass exodus from the college campus. Most students lived within driving distance from their homes, leaving those of us from farther distances all to ourselves. It connected us with a commonality that we all shared.

The college had two faces: one like that of any regular post-high school facility, the other, a strict code of Biblical doctrine.

Attendance at morning chapel was mandatory. Resident assistants, to ensure that the rule was adhered to, carried out room checks. Theology-based electives were required as part of the course curriculum. Although classrooms, lecture halls and residences were all located under the same roof, visitation between male and female dormitories was not allowed. It was clear that if anyone was caught in a compromising position, it could be grounds for expulsion.

The dynamics of the Jesus People Movement was waning; it never had really infiltrated this part of the globe, largely due to the conservative culture. Without the influence of those that I had shared the experience with, my rebellious side was on the rise. Energies attract, and those of us who had similar issues gravitated to each other. We pushed the rules and butted heads with authority figures—not severely, but enough to be noticed.

PART II

Chapter 13

I love him, but I cannot show him. I want him, but he cannot know it. I need him … if only he needed me.
– Unknown

Enter Mike. I don't recall how we first connected. I remember borrowing his car to go shopping, so that was probably our first encounter.

He was from Vancouver Island—"God's country," so he claimed. I found out that he had run a lot of track, his favourite event being the 400m hurdles. This similarity gave us a lot to talk about. Conversations became frequent and for whatever reason I gravitated to him, vying for any morsel of attention that he would give me. Every waking moment I became consumed with how I could orchestrate time with him. He became my obsession.

My feelings towards him were not reciprocated. In fact, he treated me terribly and yet I kept going back for more. I craved to be loved but I chose the worst candidate to fulfill those needs. Now, as I look back and remember how unsure and confused I was, my fixation towards Mike was actually quite understandable. His treatment of me felt very familiar and was in accordance with what I believed about myself—I was not worthy, I was not loveable, I did not deserve to be treated with respect.

Since we were so often seen together, people considered us boyfriend and girlfriend but when asked about us, he flat out denied it. He would intentionally flirt with other female friends, pretending that he was interested in them. God, it hurt. I was so envious of the attention he gave them, wishing passionately that I could be the centre of his focus instead of them.

Mike claimed that he had attended the Royal Roads Military College in Victoria, B.C. and had achieved the rank of lieutenant—he even had letterhead made up with his rank and name in bold letters. He said that he had been in training with the Canadian Air Force and had flown fighter planes. His dream to continue in this field apparently came to an end due to head trauma suffered in a motor vehicle accident. Doctors had allegedly told him that if he flew again the g-force could cause him to black out and therefore he should not take the risk. Supposedly, this was what ended his military training. He was convincing and I believed him.

A lot of our time together was spent in typing term papers for other students. We both had brought our manual typewriters from home for this express reason. Somehow, he coerced the college chef into letting us set up office in a room off of the kitchen. He was even given his own set of keys to the area. We spent hours there and were never in our rooms for the 11 p.m. curfew. To this day, I have no idea of how we got away with it. Mike's friend, Henry, also occupied the office, and as long as Mike was there, he too would be. It's like it was a nightly standoff: both of us not leaving until Mike was ready to go. I had my reasons, however, for waiting it out night after night. When alone, I had the physical attention from Mike that I desperately craved. I believed that this meant he cared about me, though verbally he would deny it.

I have no idea of how I maintained a decent GPA on such little sleep and my overpowering obsession for needing to be wherever he was. Somehow, I made it through that first year. I did manage to form close relationships with other people; it was just that my priority to spend time with Mike superseded all others. I told no one about our secret. Together we never discussed our relationship and the strangeness of it; it just was.

We both went home for the summer to work. Every day I longed to hear from him either by letter or by phone. I did receive a letter within the first month; I would read it over and over, longing to pick up on any word or phrase that would lead me to believe that he missed me. He called once; his excuse for not writing more often was that he was busy with work and volunteering at a summer camp. Of course I replied that I understood and that it was okay. I couldn't bear to entertain the thought that clearly I was not on his list of priorities.

Another month or so went by and I had not heard from him. Every day I hoped to find a letter waiting for me but I was met with nothing but disappointment. My mother sensed my distress, even though she had no idea to the extent that I had become involved with Mike. One day, after I arrived home from work with, once again, no letter, she told me something that I had no knowledge of. She said that prior to dating my father, she had been engaged to another man. It was the start of World War II and he had been drafted. She received letters from him regularly but then . . . nothing. News did finally come: he had been killed in action. For the first time, I saw my mother in a different light and I genuinely felt her empathy, she having experienced it (albeit radically different circumstances). I hold on to that memory.

I finally decided to call him. In those days girls did not call boys. I didn't care, I needed to know if he was okay. I did manage to reach him but I was not prepared for what I was about to hear. He said that he had been given some tests and they discovered that he had acquired some form of cancer. He had undergone treatment, which resulted in fatigue—the reason he hadn't written or phoned. I believed him.

When we returned to college in the fall he seemed fine and never really discussed the details of his diagnosis. I didn't push for clarification, I was just relieved that he was back. So began our sophomore year.

The college had a program that helped students cut the costs of tuition: each student worked a few hours per week in various positions throughout the facility. In lieu of pay, the amount instead was credited to each student's account. My job entailed delivering mail for students into alphabetized slots. Mike, on the other hand, was put in charge of several students whose jobs were to clean offices, classrooms, etc. He was very organized and efficient at coordinating schedules. Consequently, he carried keys to virtually every locked door on campus.

We quickly settled back into our old routine, retreating to our office until the wee hours of the morning. Alan, one of my rebel friends, often joined us. We really liked each other; however, my focus remained on Mike. Many nights my standoff now not only included Henry, but Alan as well.

Our physical relationship took on a tangent of acute dysfunction. There were two spectrums: one being denial that we were involved as a couple and two, sexual involvement behind closed, locked doors (as he held the keys!). In both of our upbringings, we had been taught that sex outside of marriage was a sin. To have sexual fantasies or desires were considered to be of the devil. Consequently, the combination of raging hormones, involvement of the forbidden, and having no idea of how to communicate were ingredients that took us to another level of game playing.

It went like this: he would use ropes to tie me up under the pretense that it was only to see if I could get free. But the reality of the situation was far different. While bound, he would touch me and engage in sexual foreplay, driving me into a heightened state of sexual arousal. Once I was free of the ropes, either by Mike untying me or being able to free myself, then the game was over. Mike even kept a record of who was winning. If I couldn't get free on my own, the point went to him; if I was able to free myself, I won the point. Pretending it was a game aided in not having to discuss what was really going on. At the time, I did not understand that engaging in this warped behavior only degraded my concept of myself further. It was like I had no voice and I did not have the right to say no. He did whatever he wanted to and I would simply comply. I did not respect myself, and in turn Mike had no respect for me.

Somehow it was arranged that Mike would come home with me for Christmas break. I had very mixed feelings. I wanted him with me but I didn't want him to meet my parents, especially my mother. Her behaviour was a constant source of embarrassment to me and I felt like it was a reflection on me. Inwardly, I knew it was a set-up for disaster and I was right.

I could go into great detail of what transpired during those few days but I am choosing not to. Suffice it to say they did not like him, and I can say now their reasons were legitimate. However, their confrontation and verbal attack on Mike only humiliated the both of us. I was extremely defensive and angry, vowing to never let him or myself be put in such a situation again. We returned for our second semester, never speaking again of what had transpired.

Our charade continued for the remainder of the school year. How we were not caught during our frequent encounters and how I continued to maintain good grades is a mystery that still leaves me baffled.

Once again, I went home for the summer to work and to see my best friend Karen get married. We had stayed in close touch and I felt so privileged when she asked me to be her maid of honour. But as close as we were, I never revealed to her the truth of my relationship with Mike. The shame was too much for me to admit to myself, let alone Karen.

Chapter 14

More often, the easy part of life is finding someone to love. The hard part is finding someone to love you back.
– Unknown

Before returning for my senior year, I flew out to Vancouver Island to see Mike and to meet his family. I was introduced as just a friend from college, certainly not his girlfriend. His words stung, but I just smiled and went along with his pretend version of our relationship.

Henry came a few days later and, while there, they came up with the idea to take the second semester off and travel to Central America where Henry had grown up. His father had told him that a construction project was under way and suggested that he could use the help to get it completed.

I was sick, hoping desperately that this plan was just talk. My entire college life had revolved around Mike. Every waking hour was consumed with the need to be near him. How would I ever cope?

As first semester progressed so did their plans. It became a reality. They were leaving in December following exams and tentatively returning in April.

Before I knew it I was saying goodbye at the Greyhound bus terminal. I was overcome with raw emotion. It felt like my entire world was crashing down around me leaving a big, dark, vacant hole of nothingness. I had lost all sense of self with no idea of how to claim it back—whatever "it" was. Never had I felt so alone.

I believe my friends recognized how lost I was. They gathered around me, offering their support and company. Alan was especially present. We would go for walks and talking came easy. He even took me to his parents' farm to stay over a long weekend. He knew, however, that my heart was set on Mike. The thought of pursuing anything further than our existing friendship would have been futile.

I began to receive letters from Mike—lots of them. I was in shock and disbelief as the content radically changed. I read his words of how much he missed me and how he longed to hold me. What had happened? Suddenly I was reading everything that I had so longed to hear—that he cared about me and wanted me near. It was surreal and sounded far too good to be true. My experiences in life had left me believing that if I let my guard down and actually believed that something good was happening, it would suddenly be snatched away; the joker would win, laughing at me for having the nerve to believe that I was worthy of good things.

I was on cloud nine but fearful that I would wake up and realize it was all just a dream. The weeks marched by; midterms came and went. Before I knew it final exams were just around the corner.

I had decided not to return home to work over the summer. I landed a job as an assistant cook at a children's summer camp. Mike was going to be working as a night baker at a bakery owned and operated by a friend of ours. We could be together on weekends. I could hardly wait.

Mike surprised me by coming back from Central America a little earlier than planned. The messages in his letters held true and I was finally acknowledged as his girlfriend. We both started our summer jobs, and on Fridays after work I couldn't get back to Mike soon enough. Many nights I would crash on the floor of the bakery or at the home of his boss where Mike was staying. He and his wife didn't seem to mind that I stayed there, the only condition that I sleep in my own room. At least that's what I was led to believe.

One Friday night in August, Mike had made dinner reservations at a nightclub for when I arrived back from camp. We were seated next to the live band and had just been served our food. Suddenly the band stopped and announced that there was an engagement in the house. I looked at Mike, not having a clue that they were referring to us. Sheepishly Mike pulled out a small box from his jacket pocket. I was stunned. We had never mentioned the word marriage, but here I was, a diamond ring staring me in the face. I was in shock, disbelief, thrilled—all at the same time. He never did ask the question so there was no answer to give, it was just assumed. Even if he had asked I would never have replied, "Let me think about it." At twenty years of age I believed that this was it; no one else would ever want to marry me. Did I love Mike? I believed I did. Were we ready for the commitment of marriage? Absolutely not. There were so many issues that had been stuffed into a dark closet—issues that were too painful and threatening to address; issues that I hoped our love would cure and make go away.

It took all my nerve to make that phone call home to say, "Guess what? We're engaged!"

The first few seconds were met with an awkward silence followed by a less than enthusiastic response. My father mumbled something about the fact that Mike had not asked him if he could marry his daughter. I remember thinking that there was no way they were going to prevent me from marrying Mike. Marrying him meant that I could be free from them.

We decided to get married in Manitoba the following May, right after graduation. The months of planning that followed were brutal. My mother was furious that she was not in control nor involved due to the distance between us. That was exactly my plan.

I will not go into the details and family dynamics that surrounded the days prior to graduation and getting married. The guilt and shame heaped upon me, in particular by my mother, was immense. I was the shamed, bad little girl, all over again; still, I walked down the aisle in my white wedding dress, pretending everything was okay.

We had reserved a special suite in a higher-end hotel. I had fantasized what our first night together as a married couple would be like. Finally we could do "it" without any guilt attached. I had purchased a white, pretty negligee—perfect, I thought, for the occasion. I came from the bathroom over to the bed where Mike was reclined, eagerly anticipating our physical encounter. I moved onto him but he didn't respond. Rather, he said that he was tired and had a headache, therefore we should wait until tomorrow. Boy was I deflated. But being the good, considerate wife, I responded with understanding, offering instead to find him something to relieve his headache.

"Tomorrow" came and went and the day after that and the day after that. How do things change so drastically, literally overnight? As soon as we had that marriage certificate that apparently gave us licence to have sex with God's approval, nothing— zilch—no interest whatsoever. Did he still need to tie me up to pretend it was a game rather than for what it was? Even that would have been something. Of course I blamed myself. Obviously I was doing something wrong or not doing enough. Certainly his lack of interest was everything to do with me, at least so I thought. I begged him to let me know what was wrong and how could I make it better. Ironically, the one area where I thought we would have no problem became unresolvable. Not even once, while we were married, did we have sexual intercourse. Go figure.

Our honeymoon consisted of driving to Vancouver Island where we would live for the next several months. Mike would work in the paper mill where he had worked part time for a number of years. I became the dutiful housewife, making his lunches and preparing home-cooked meals. However I was not remotely prepared for his family. His parents, well meaning and generous, were always *there.* I was not accustomed to the daily visits and conversations. I felt suffocated, unable to escape their constant presence and intrusion. I tried to communicate with Mike how I felt but it would always end up in an argument, remaining unresolved. Knowing how to communicate was not our strong suit. The entire history of our relationship had exemplified this very fact.

As the summer wore on I became hostile and incredibly angry. How I was feeling didn't matter and the lack of sex only exacerbated my turmoil even further. During the afternoons I would escape to a quiet bay in the ocean, wishing that the salt water could heal my wounded soul and make everything better.

I decided to start running again, not that I had ever really stopped. I approached it with a new fervor. It gave me a purpose. I loved the exertion of pushing myself to run farther, faster. I could run and not feel. Here I was able to bury all the muck that I felt inside, driving it all deep below the surface into the ground upon which I ran.

Mike's experience in Central America left him wanting to return. He loved the different culture and he felt like he was contributing to people who needed his assistance. I went along with it mainly because if we did go there it would take us away from the conflict with his family, which was becoming increasingly more difficult.

In the fall of 1978, we moved back to Manitoba and found an apartment to rent. We both found jobs. Mike worked as a bookkeeper for a private company and I worked for a humanitarian organization. It was great to be back in the company of nearby friends.

Mike, however, continued to pursue plans to return to Central America. He learned of a high school located in a remote area that needed teachers. Students were housed in dormitories during the week and were bused home to their respective villages on weekends. Housing for teachers and staff was available on the property. Over the next few months plans were made. We would leave in August of 1979 in time for the start up of school in September.

I had very mixed emotions. We were both still living under the "God umbrella" that we had grown up with. One of the rules was that wives were to obey their husbands. I needed to hear that I was okay, that I was being a good Christian wife. I went along with it because it was expected and it was what I was *supposed* to do. However, deep inside, my guts were eaten up with anger and frustration. *Why should I follow Mike to this faraway place, away from my friends to God knows what? Why should I obey this man who won't even make love to his wife?* These thoughts were there but I suppressed them, too afraid to let them come to the surface where they would demand an answer.

The country was in the midst of the running boom and I enthusiastically jumped on board. I subscribed to *Runner's World* magazine, devouring every page and adhering to workouts prescribed by elite runners. Winnipeg was organizing its first marathon for May of 1979. I eagerly signed up, attending running forums for all the latest training techniques and workouts that would enable you to complete the 26.2 miles (forty-two kilometers). Training for it became my focus, shoving my inner struggle to a back corner of my mind.

The marathon came and went. I had accomplished my goal. But the positive endorphins that had been created by my successful completion disintegrated as each day, week, month passed by. Then came August. We loaded up our brand-new van, said our goodbyes, and began the long, hot drive. I choked back salty tears as the wheat fields of Manitoba became a distant speck in the rear view mirror.

Chapter 15

Sick of crying, tired of trying. On the outside,
I'm smiling but inside, I'm dying.
– Unknown

The long drive through the United States to the Mexican border, through Mexico and into Central America, provided me with an abundance of thinking time.

My relationship with my parents had disintegrated even more. My mother sent me many letters after our marriage containing a constant barrage upon my character, leaving me with feelings of anger and shame. No matter what I said or did, it was wrong and my words were twisted, taking on my mother's own interpretation. I had no one to take my side and stand up for me. I was still the bad little girl.

My relationship with Karen was also growing distant. Mike and I had seen her and her husband once after we were married. We no longer shared the ease between us that we had experienced for so many years. I have my own theory as to why this happened but it was what it was; there was no going back to what had been. I missed my friend.

The conversations between Mike and I were trivial, mainly concentrating on the travel journal that guided us through the heart of Mexico mile by mile. Neither of us knew how to dig deep within ourselves to be able to communicate on that level. I was too confused about who I even was. What did I really believe about this illusive image we called God? Whoever He was, I felt like I couldn't measure up to His standard, like I was always begging for forgiveness for not doing the right thing or thinking the right thoughts. I felt no connection with this God who loved me, as I was told. Others proclaimed and professed to feel this unconditional love. I desperately wanted to but just didn't. Frankly, I didn't feel loved at all.

As the miles clicked by, bringing us closer to our destination my feelings of trepidation mounted. Deep down, my internal awareness knew that this wasn't right for me. I was only here because it was what Mike wanted to do and it was my duty to follow him. The choice had been made for me. There was no backing out. Although I couldn't put it into words at the time, I felt trapped like a wild animal, unable to break free. And then we were there.

Crossing from Mexico into the small border town of Corozal, Belize was uneventful and we proceeded on to Orange Walk Town, one of the larger centres in Belize. British soldiers were in abundance. Belize, formerly known as British Honduras, was still a British colony, defended by the British. Guatemala continued to be a threat to this small country, hence the presence of the soldiers.

Only one main road—the Northern Highway—connected Orange Walk Town to Belize City, a distance of approximately sixty miles (96.5 kilometres). At the time, this highway was only one-and-a-half lanes wide, making it impossible for two larger vehicles to pass and remain on the asphalt (at least where there was asphalt!). The rule was simple: larger vehicles were superior to smaller ones therefore the smaller had to get out of the way. This meant dropping off onto the shoulder with sometimes the drop being quite substantial. Other times there was no shoulder at all. The highway consisted of numerous potholes, washed out sections from torrential rains and no shortage of road kill. Needless to say, accidents were frequent.

The school, which would be home, for who knew how long, was located about halfway between Orange Walk Town and Belize City. Our arrival was expected and introductions were exchanged. Our house was located at the back of the property with the jungle literally outside our back door. There was no indoor shower. Rather, rainwater was collected in large outdoor vats. The shower stall was made of cement with the ceiling being the wide-open sky. Say goodbye to long, hot showers! Whatever water was collected in the rainy season had to last until the next cycle of rain.

Cockroaches were everywhere. One did not dare crawl into bed, put on shoes or slippers, or reach for a container above eye level until all was inspected. It was not uncommon to find scorpions hanging out in these locations. Therefore being vigilant to check was crucial.

I also learned that it was not wise to stand outside without moving. Fire ants were always waiting to find a stationary target. Since they are so small, one has no idea of their presence until they start to bite—all at the same time. It happened to me once and the pain was excruciating. It felt like a fine spray of red-hot embers against bare, unprotected skin. Their name suits them well.

In total, there were six teachers plus the principal who also taught a few classes. Mike was assigned to teach mathematics to all levels; I was to teach typing and girls' physical education.

Since Belize was a British colony, their education system followed the UK structure. Instead of using grade levels, students start their first year of secondary school in Form 1, or first year. Generally they enter Form 1 at twelve years of age and finish Form 5 by the time they are sixteen. Students who want to pursue higher education have the option of continuing on at A-Levels, moving them into Form 6.

The school we were stationed at taught Forms 1–5. Not many students were able to continue on at the higher levels due to financial restrictions. Families struggled just to have food to eat and a roof over their heads. Higher education unfortunately, was a luxury for only a select few.

Our first trip to Belize City was truly an eye-opening experience. The smell from the open market was unforgettable. Putrid raw meat and large fish with bulging eyes, hung from cleavers in the hot sun, covered in flies. The market backed on to a large canal that was the recipient of feces and garbage. In this area, houses for the most part were not equipped with flushing toilets, therefore all waste emptied into water filled troughs that ran behind the rows of homes. In turn, this waste flowed into larger canals and eventually reached the main canal before running into the Caribbean Sea. I couldn't believe that they could live like this amongst the stench and filth. I found it utterly disgusting but for them it was their way of life. It was all they had.

From the market, we ventured to an enclosed grocery store. It didn't seem too bad until I noticed the expiry dates on canned goods, salad dressings and the like. Nothing was fresh. Items were not just a few months over the expiry date but rather a few *years!* Obviously I was going to have to make radical changes to our eating habits. What we took for granted at home certainly wasn't the case here.

When we returned to where we had parked our van after our shopping experience, we discovered that the side window of our vehicle had been smashed. Our camera that we had failed to conceal from view, along with other small items, was long gone. I cursed the people, the country and the fact that I was stuck in the poverty of this third world country. I wanted vengeance—badly.

I was determined to keep up my running regimen, adamant that I was going to run next year's Winnipeg marathon. Once again, running was my escape from reality.

Since there was only one road to run on, it became my everyday route—out and back; only the distances varied. Running in hot temperatures and high humidity was brutal. Water intake was essential. Unlike at home, I was the solitary runner. It was not an activity that people here pursued. They thought I was nuts but I didn't care. It just made me more determined than ever to show them!

Staff at the school had warned me that it was risky for a lone, white female to be running by herself. I brushed off their warnings, feeling quite capable of taking care of myself. No one was going to take this away from me no matter what.

My runs led me past voodoo gardens where I observed dolls hanging upside down with pins stuck in them. Some were missing limbs and others had no heads. Many times the keeper of the garden would come out of his hut yelling and cursing at me and angrily shaking his fist in the air.

The smell of marijuana in the air was a common occurrence. Crops were grown in plain view and no one thought anything of it.

Many times I ran past large Brahman cattle, the herder crossing them from one side of the road to the other to find them more to graze on. Even they looked at me with their large sullen eyes wondering what on earth was this person doing?

Shortly before we had crossed from Texas into Mexico, I had purchased pepper spray to carry with me on my runs, thinking it would come in handy for any stray dogs that might want a piece of me. It was a good choice. One particular day I set out for a longer run of ten miles or so. About three or four miles from the school, I heard a vehicle coming from behind so I moved off onto the dirt shoulder. I could tell it was slowing down and as it came alongside of me I saw that its occupants were all young Belizean males. I stopped and faced them as they yelled out, "Hey, white woman! Let us take you for a ride!"

I recall feeling fear but the emotion that superseded far beyond that was anger. I glared into the eyes of each one of them, almost hoping they would try something so I could blast them straight in the face with the pepper spray clutched in my sweaty palm. I have no idea how long I stared them down but miraculously they just left, leaving me consumed in my sweat and rage. I have no doubt today that someone was taking care of me. It could so easily have had a much different outcome than what it did.

We soon settled into the routine of lesson plans and teaching. Much to my surprise, I actually enjoyed the time in the classroom. I was even starting to catch on to Creole (a combination of English and African languages) as I listened to them talk amongst themselves.

I discovered early on that I had nothing in common with the other female staff. The wife of the principal was bossy, overbearing and knew everything about anything, at least that was my consensus. The other women were single, had never been married and it seemed they came to Belize because they didn't fit in at home. Once again, it was just my opinion.

As weeks rolled by I grew lonelier and lonelier. When I wasn't running or teaching or preparing lessons, I would sleep. Jan, the principal's wife, would come knocking on our door and I would lie there, ignoring her as she called out my name, wishing she would just go away. I didn't realize it at the time but I was in a state of depression. When I would try to express to Mike how unhappy I was, he would refuse to discuss it. I might as well have been talking to the wall.

The only social life we had was with an American couple that lived about ten miles down the road towards Belize City. They were older than us by several years but they were nice, kind people. He operated a sawmill on his property and would sell the wood to local buyers. She, on the other hand, was a terrific cook. To this day I have never tasted better southern fried chicken or her chocolate cake. It was fantastic.

They happened to own a few horses and one day I expressed how I would love to go for a ride, if it was okay with them. I was warned that they hadn't been ridden for quite some time but I was more than willing to give it a try. Off we went to the shed where saddles and riding gear were kept. One of the saddles was under some burlap and once uncovered, the ground became alive with cockroaches scurrying for cover. It should have been a clue.

Once the horses were saddled up and ready to go, off we went. It was the start of the rainy season so there were a few puddles here and there. Mike soon found out that his horse didn't like getting his hooves wet so would sidestep every one of them. I tried to get my horse to go from a trot to at least a canter but no such luck—until we turned to head back to the stable. It was great. I was back in my element, relishing the rush of adrenalin. However, my fun was shortlived. As we made a sharp turn, the girth straps of my roach-infested saddle suddenly gave way, spilling me onto the gravel-based path. Ouch. Such was the end of my horseback riding in Belize.

November brought us into the heart of the rainy season: rain, rain and more rain. The dark, wet days only dampened my spirit even more.

One weekend, right after my twenty-third birthday, Mike and I were alone on the grounds. Everyone else had left for the weekend, all to various destinations. On Saturday, around mid-morning, we heard a very loud crash followed by people screaming. We ran out of the house towards the road, oblivious to the downpour of rain that had us drenched in seconds. Just before the entrance to the school was a sharp bend in the road, which was now the scene of a serious accident. A bus carrying passengers to Belize City had collided with a pick-up truck that had lost control on the wet, slippery pavement. One of the female passengers from the truck was in bad shape; the other occupants, her parents, were injured but not as seriously. Several passengers on the bus were bleeding, mostly from facial cuts. Cell phones didn't exist and there was no convenience of dialing 911—we were their only help.

Mike ran back to get our van as I started to sort out who needed medical attention the most. The female from the truck was by far the most serious; she was put on the floor of the van and other injured passengers were crowded around her. There was an elderly man dazed and confused, unable to stand on his own. As we got him into the back, I told him it would be okay but he just looked at me with blank eyes. The vehicle was full; it was obvious there was no space for me to crowd into. The van, turned ambulance, took off and headed for Belize City.

I went back to the house and got into dry clothes, trying to calm down. I needed to get busy and do something to dispel the pulsating energy that enveloped me. For half an hour or so I paced, unsure of what to do next, so I decided to bake—something simple that didn't require too much thinking power. Suddenly, from out of nowhere, I was overtaken with panic and an overwhelming sense of having to go down the road after Mike. I even rushed out the door in the direction of my Moped and then rational thought took over—what the hell was I doing? I forced myself back into the house, puzzled, trying to figure out what had just happened. A short time later I thought I heard someone yelling my name. When I looked out I recognized one of the students racing towards our house screaming, "*Mrs. Zack, Mrs. Zack!* Mr. Zack has been in an accident!"

Then I understood. I raced for my Moped, kicked it into gear and forced it to its optimum speed.

About four miles down the road I came across the second accident of the day, this time involving Mike and the driver of a taxi. The taxi was coming towards Mike, approaching a bend in the road. Taking it too quickly for the conditions he lost control, slamming into the left front corner of the van. Mike was okay other than a large goose egg from where his head had hit the windshield. The injured occupants were hysterical, now even more traumatized from this latest event. The scene was chaotic. It had happened in a slightly more populated area so there was help on the scene to assist with the injured. Unfortunately, the elderly man that we had assisted earlier died at the side of the road, probably more from the emotional trauma than physical injuries.

It took several months to sort out insurance and payment for damages. We were fortunate: in Belize, if a white man is involved in an accident with a local, the law generally favours the Belizean, even if they're at fault. This time it worked in our favour, maybe because of the circumstances, I don't know. I do know that on that day I experienced a form of telepathic communication that did not involve words; it was powerful, unexplainable, and undeniable—period.

Chapter 16

You can only try so much until the day comes that you've had enough and you just can't take it anymore.
– Unknown

The rainy season had ended and it was back to the relentless heat and high humidity. I struggled through my runs, continuing to be harassed and threatened. For the most part, I didn't let it bother me too much.

One evening, Mike was at the main building giving extra help to a few of his math students for an upcoming exam. I didn't expect him back for at least an hour. Apart from the hum of the generator that provided lighting to the main building, the night was quiet.

At one point I thought I heard some rustling outside so I stopped and listened. It seemed to come from the back of the house that faced the jungle. I was convinced that someone/something was moving around the perimeter of the house. All the threats to the effect of, "I'm going to get you, white woman!" came rushing to the forefront. I went for the rifle that we kept on hand and quickly loaded it, making sure the safety was off. Then I strategically positioned my chair so that if someone tried to come through the door or louvers on the windows, they would be in my direct line of vision. I waited.

My heart pounded and my senses were piqued. For the first time I realized that if my life was threatened, I could and would pull the trigger. Having come to this realization actually had a calming effect.

I sat there, the minutes ticking by and finally I heard Mike come up the steps. He was startled to see me there, sitting with the loaded gun cradled in my arms. I relayed what I had heard and he wasn't overly surprised when I told him that I was more than prepared to use it, if need be.

I had had enough and Mike knew it. Reluctantly—*very* reluctantly—he went along with my plans. I would leave in May to get back in time to run the Winnipeg marathon, and he would join me after the school year was wrapped up. I knew he wanted to stay in Belize and of course I felt guilty for opposing what he wanted. Quite simply, I was done.

I don't remember much of the flight home, but I do recall the immense relief as my feet touched Canadian soil. The emotion of being back to the familiar was so overwhelming I could barely hold back the tears.

Previous to coming home, a couple that we knew invited me to stay with them until Mike arrived. The thrill of having a warm shower with unlimited water was incredible. Things I had simply taken for granted were forever changed.

Two days before the marathon, I developed an infection in one of my fingers. I was awake most of the night trying to keep it elevated to avoid the painful pulsating. It was red and hot to the touch. Finally I succumbed to the realization that it wasn't going to go away on its own but needed medical attention. The attending doctor in the emergency section of the hospital knew exactly what to do; he froze it then lanced it to drain the infection, and immediately, sweet relief! The next day I was at the starting line of the marathon, bandaged finger and all.

It was a warm, humid day—not ideal weather for running a marathon. My good friend Alan from college was my support crew and he kept tabs on my progress. At mile ten I felt terrible but I stubbornly plugged on. By mile sixteen, I had blisters and was physically and emotionally drained. Alan was waiting at the seventeen-mile mark and when I saw him I knew I was done. There was no convincing my body to run another nine miles.

For the next several days I beat myself up for not finishing, for not simply willing myself to keep going. I cursed my body and "weak" mind for letting me down. Quitting equaled failure—a belief that I carried and practiced for many, many years …

In early June, Mike drove our van and belongings back from Belize. We had to make a decision—where were we going to live? The people I had been staying with were moving to northern Ontario where he (Larry) was going to open a practice as a marriage and family therapist and become the minister of a new church that was in the planning stages. They encouraged us to move there as well. Having office experience, he suggested that once things were set up, I could possibly be hired to work as his secretary.

We made a decision. In July of 1980, we packed up all of our belongings, the van packed to the roof and $6.00 to our name—another new chapter, another choice that would be life changing.

I don't know how we made it through those first few months. Our credit card was maxed out. I started working as Larry's secretary for both his private business and the church. Not long after, Mike was hired as a cook at the Salvation Army men's shelter. Heather, Larry's sister-in-law, took us under her wing and showed us how to get around the city—especially to her favourite coffee shops.

Larry introduced us to the new members of the church and we became quite involved organizing activities for the youth of the congregation. Again, the struggle within myself ensued, striving to do what others expected of me but never quite making the mark and never feeling that I was doing it right, whatever "it" was.

By September I joined a local running club, and on Labour Day weekend I ran my first five-kilometre race. Members of the club welcomed me with open arms, inviting me and encouraging me to their social events and to the local races. I was hooked.

Mike and I carried on status quo. I had given up on begging for sex; it was pointless. I didn't at this point however ask myself if I could live like this indefinitely. It wasn't that we didn't get along—we did. It was just more like living with a roommate than a husband.

The days of fall grew shorter and colder, and before we knew it winter was upon us with no shortage of snow. I soon discovered that we lived in the mecca for winter sports—no shortage of cross-country or downhill ski areas. It helped to make the bitter cold months fly by.

Early spring of 1981 introduced a new series of local races that I enthusiastically embraced. While I was busy with training and signing up for the next event, Mike was busy elsewhere. Slowly I distanced myself from the church involvement, branching out to a world that had been held back from me. I was making new friends and for the first time I felt included and accepted.

Our first year back in Canada also brought back family connections, leaving me cringing with having to deal again with my parents. I received a call in the spring informing me that Ron was getting married in June and the family would all gather for the occasion. I was glad for my brother but I had no idea how I was going to endure this event, especially knowing how they felt about Mike. I couldn't protect myself from them let alone him as well. I was sick with the tension but I felt like I had no choice; I had to go.

Shortly before we were scheduled to leave I was at work and Larry confronted me. Unknown to me, he had been observing me over a few days noticing how withdrawn I had become and noting my nervous anxiety. Having known my parents and my struggle with them, he point blank asked if my state was because of the upcoming wedding. With that, I broke down. Thank God for him.

In a matter of fact he told me that I wasn't going—it simply wasn't physically or emotionally healthy for me. He even stated that he would make the phone call to my mother to inform her that we would not be there. The sense of relief washed over me like a tidal wave—finally, someone in *my* corner, standing up for *me*. I had never felt so grateful.

Today, as I reflect, I now realize the impact of his words. It was the first time I had been told that *I* could make a choice for what was best for *me*. The crack of insight he instilled was small but the seed was planted. It would, however, take years to evolve.

Unfortunately, my not attending prevented me from seeing Karen and her firstborn baby girl. In fact, I never saw Karen again. We might have talked once or twice on the phone after this, but time, circumstances, and distance drove us apart. I will always hold a special place in my heart for my friend.

It was a relief to miss the family gathering but the deluge of letters I received from my mother afterwards was something else. How dare I ruin Ron's special day? Every photo of the family with me not in it was the reminder of how terribly selfish I had been, so she would write. It went on and on—she was relentless. And then came fruition to one of my recurring dreams:

> *I was in a terrible hurry to get out of the house before they (my parents), came home. I'm in the car, backing out of the driveway, just as they pull in. I*

> *don't want to get out because I'll be engulfed in slobbery kisses. I feel trapped. I struggle between feelings of shame and just wanting to escape.*

One evening I was making supper so that it would be ready for when Mike came home from work. At the time, we lived on the first floor of an apartment next to the main lobby. As I made the preparations, someone in the lobby buzzed our apartment. Instead of answering from inside I went into the hallway to see who was there. I thought my legs were going to buckle underneath me and I felt sick to my stomach. There they were, in the lobby, and they had seen me. Nowhere to run, nowhere to hide—trapped.

I let them in and led them into our apartment. The tension was thick as they tried to engage in insignificant small talk. I knew the real reason for their visit was only moments away from being unleashed upon me. Inside, I felt myself shrinking into a little curled-up ball, feeling like a helpless little girl waiting for my mother to proclaim how selfish and unloving I was. And then it came: Why did I hate them after all they had done for me? What was wrong with me? Don't you know how much we love you?

Finally, I had enough. I stated that if they really wanted to talk about this then I would only do so if Larry chaired the session. They agreed but continued to blame me for all that was wrong. I was infuriated and told them to get out. They left.

Mike came home and found me pacing like a caged tiger. I had no idea what to do or how to release the inferno that raged inside me. I was frantic, inconsolable.

The meeting with Larry, my parents, and Mike and I transpired. Larry had come to my rescue before so I was hoping for a repeat. They wanted to know what they had done to make me so angry. My mind raced. How could I put into words the reasons for my years of pent-up anger and emotions that *I* couldn't even understand? I felt voiceless and had no idea as to where or how to begin.

So I started with the most raw wound that hadn't healed, the scene of reading my diary to me, page by page. I tried to convey how humiliated I felt and even stated that being raped would have been easier to take. I recall my mother gasping and proclaiming that I really didn't mean that. Again—my feelings dismissed, unimportant. Anger permeated my every cell.

Larry asked them, "After hearing how it made Frances feel by you reading her diary, if you could go back in time, would you make the same decision?" Without hesitation my mother replied that they would absolutely take the same action.

It was crushing. I knew that I was at a crossroads—either I would carry on as things had always been or I would say "enough." No longer would I allow myself to be subjected to the condemnation of my very essence. I had been berated and knocked down too many times. I wasn't going to take it anymore.

It was made very clear that they not contact me again. Rather, any contact would be from my initiative, not theirs. Before leaving, my mother drew her conclusion as to why I had turned out the way I had. Apparently it was quite simple. She told Larry that their mistake was that they had given me too much as a child growing up. The end.

Chapter 17

Memory: Driving alone at night in a relentless downpour. A popular song came on the radio that spoke of a broken relationship; of swallowing back tears while turning and leaving. I knew then, with certainty, exactly what I was going to do.

Mike took on a new job that involved working with high school age students. The more time he spent away from home, the more time I spent with my newfound running friends. I could feel the distance growing between us. Part of me wanted to maintain what we had but a bigger part was clawing to get out and break free from all the rules and image of what I was "supposed" to be.

One day Mike came home and said that he had been asked to assist at a summer camp that ran programs specifically for youth. He stated that the duration would be for approximately five weeks. It wasn't mandatory; he could choose whether or not to go. I had already volunteered to work at a major track and field event that was being held in mid-August so I told him point blank: if he decided to go, he would not be returning to the same person. With his absence and all the time for myself, I knew I was a ticking time bomb ready to come undone. He decided to go.

I know now that even if he had decided to stay home, it would only have been a matter of time. The same outcome was inevitable. Mike's decision was only the catalyst that prompted me to choose a different path, sooner rather than later.

He left and the party began. Runners love to enjoy a cold beer following a workout or a competition. I didn't just have *a* beer; I drank until I was drunk. I was unstoppable. It was like the Frances who had had her life so structured had broken free and was bent on breaking all the rules that she had grown up with. I didn't care. I felt liberated. I knew there was no going back.

For the first time, I realized that after consuming a few drinks, I could play the flirting game with men and they would respond. It gave me the illusion of power. I could bring them in so close and in a flash dismiss their advances. However, it didn't work in reverse. If they were the initiators I did not feel that I had the right to say no. I simply went along to as far as they wanted to take it.

When Mike came home at the end of August, my warning that I would be a different person was an understatement. Even I hadn't anticipated such a transformation.

In September, I quit my job with Larry and took a new position at a local institution. In my sober moments, I was stricken with guilt over what I had become. The old tapes played over and over in my head. I had rebelled against the God of vengeance and the teachings of the church. I believed with certainty that I was bound for hell.

During this time I had a very powerful dream that even to this day I remember vividly. It went like this:

> *I am with hundreds of people slowly walking to the summit of the Verrazano-Narrows Bridge in New York City. We have learned that the bridge will be*

the target of a nuclear attack. Instead of suffering a slow death from the after-effects of radiation, we have all decided to choose a fast, certain death. I fear that with my death God will judge me and sentence me to an eternity in hell. I ponder what I will say to God to justify my life. I decide that I will tell God that when I was young and accepted Jesus as my only hope of escaping the eternal fires of hell, I did so with heartfelt sincerity. If that was not good enough, then so be it. A strange calm came over me and I felt peace. Those of us who walked together observed a train full of people on the tracks below heading for the bridge. They did not know that their death was only moments away. I felt sorry that they would not have the chance to make their peace with God.

Many times over the years, when the old tapes would play over in my head about burning in hell for all eternity I recalled this dream, which provided me with some comfort.

Over the next several months, Mike and I were like ships passing in the night, each of us consumed with our own passions. I continued to party and during this time I had my first affair with a married man. I didn't care. I believed that because he wanted me sexually, then he must care about me. I craved the sex, I craved love, and I was insatiable.

By early spring, I knew I had to find my own place where I could bring home whoever I wanted, whenever I wanted. I found a furnished basement apartment that was affordable and close to my workplace. Mike really had no reaction when I broke the news; he just went along with it and didn't seem too surprised. Shortly after we filed for divorce with the reason being irreconcilable differences. No kidding. There were no lawyers involved and no fighting about material possessions. The total cost was $108.00; split two ways equaled $54.00

each—probably the cheapest divorce in history. It was official: we were legally divorced.

I felt no animosity towards Mike, in spite of what had been a sexless marriage. It was what it was and there was no going back. We remained friends and supported each other through our individual tough times, many of which lay ahead.

In 1983, I not only divorced Mike—I divorced the church, the family, and my perspective of the God that I could never please.

I was now the little divorcee—the outcast. I was even cut from my grandparents' will because of my new acclaimed status. I wanted desperately to leave my old life far behind and pretend that it never existed. I truly believed that I could just will it away. I didn't know that sooner or later our demons and secrets must be faced. They just don't go away as hard as we might try to deny their existence. They lurk everywhere, popping up when least expected, always reminding us that we can't destroy them but that we need to face them head on and make peace with the past. It would take years for me to come to this realization, but for the time being I finally felt free, free to make my own choices and deal with the consequences later.

PART III

Chapter 18

Hold me, love me, stay with me until I forget how terrified I am of everything wrong with my life.
– Unknown

I was living hard—up early for work followed by vigorous track and road workouts. Usually I could find someone to go with for a beer and something to eat, but then came the evening. I could not face returning to my basement apartment alone. I was unable to just sit with myself. It felt like the walls were closing in on me and I couldn't tolerate the silence. It became my mission to go out, try to find a party or an excuse for one, go to a friend's house—anything to avoid being alone. I only felt comfortable in returning when it was late, I was half in the bag (or just plain drunk) and I could crash, ready to resume the same for the next day and the next and the next.

One-night stands became commonplace. For the most part they were with married men who I knew through the running community, but there were also those who I would meet in a bar and they would follow me home.

During this time, I had moved on to a new job as an administrative assistant. My new boss became interested in running so I devised various running programs for him. He became hooked. If we weren't discussing work-related topics we would talk running, driving our co-workers nuts. They couldn't understand how running could be fun. Every morning before our workday started, he and I would go for our ritual twenty-minute walk. He would ask me what trouble I had gotten myself into the previous night and I would confess my sins. He would respond by saying, "Fran, Fran, Fran," followed by his distinctive chuckle. Never did I feel judged by him for my actions—actually quite the opposite. He was my sounding board and became not only my boss but also my friend.

As stated, I was living hard but I was also running hard. My name became known as one of the elite female runners in the area. In workouts I pushed myself to the extreme, ignoring the pleas from my body to take a break, recover, nurse the aching muscles and joints. I ignored all of my body's protests, cursing its weakness and then pushing and punishing it even further, blocking out its pain. I was a dichotomy, my mind and will the master over its slave, my physical body.

On race days I was a mess, waking up off and on throughout the night prior to the race, going over and over in my head who would be my competition and planning my strategy on how to beat them. If I won, I congratulated my body for doing its job; if I lost, I cursed it for letting me down, determined to push it faster, harder, and further in training sessions. My identity was determined by either winning or losing. Winning equaled worth; losing equaled being not good enough, a loser, a failure.

Road trips to various races in the States were frequent and we would attend some of the same races year after year. Americans knew how to party so I was in my element. Inevitably, too much alcohol would lead me to making out with someone in a secluded area (so I thought?) in my drunken state. Waking up the following morning, I would try to remember exactly what had happened. Sometimes I would feel incredible guilt and shame but I would push it aside, unwilling and not wanting to explore its roots—too afraid of what I would discover.

During this time, a group of us went south of the border to an area abundant in cross-country ski trails. There was a lot of drinking following a day of intense physical exertion. Inevitably, I ended up having an affair with one of the men whose wife had also come along on the excursion. I knew both of them well through running and she and I frequently competed against each other. Knowing her only enhanced the excitement of the frequent rendezvous shared by her husband and myself. (Eventually, of course, she clued in that our involvement included much more than our interest in running). One night in particular I had been at a party and was late in arriving at our pre-scheduled "date" location. Clearly, he was angry. First of all for me being late but secondly for me arriving in an intoxicated state. He said something that night that stayed with me long after our affair was over. His words to me were straight to the point: "You don't drink to enhance a good time, you drink to get drunk." He was absolutely right.

Every year, many runners would travel to a popular St. Patrick's Day four-mile road race. In 1984, race day actually landed on March 17th. The bar that hosted the post-race party was flowing with the traditional green beer. Having inherited some Irish blood, it was another excuse to party hard. It was here that I met Dan, also of Irish descent. He and a friend had decided to drive down and participate in the event, a chance for a break from each of their weekend routines.

I don't recall who introduced us but I most certainly do recall the instant chemistry between us. He was funny, attentive, and clearly interested in pursuing a sexual encounter. The details leading up to me accompanying him to his hotel room were lost in my drunken haze but I clearly recall no hesitation in deciding to spend the night with him. In the early morning I giddily made my way back to my own room that I was sharing with other runners. They didn't ask and I didn't tell. I was on a high all the way home, wondering how and when I could orchestrate our paths to cross again. I assumed he was married, even though it had not been brought up in any of our conversation. Even if it had, I know I would not have done anything differently.

Within a week or two my fantasy of running into him occurred. I was preparing to leave for a run from our training facility when I saw him. Eye contact was made, then recognition. I melted, absorbed into his infectious smile. He thanked me for our encounter and stated that he had wanted to send me flowers in appreciation but didn't know where to send them. He further exclaimed that I had made his day, rousing him out of his depressed state. I gave him my phone number and made it clear that I would love to see him again—at his convenience, of course.

And so it began: I had a connection with someone who seemed (to me) to need me, someone who I could rescue from whatever he was lacking at home, someone who I would wait for by the phone or by the door, desperate for any contact, no matter how brief, someone who confirmed my belief that what I needed was secondary . . . someone who would forever change my life.

Chapter 19

Falling in love with you was never my intention
but it became my addiction.
– Abhisheck Tiwari

I soon found out the circumstances that I had decided to become entwined with. He was indeed married, with children ranging in ages from three to thirteen years.

Dan was a teacher who taught alongside other teachers that I ran with and, in fact, had had some relationships with. But with Dan it was different. I had fallen hard and fast. It didn't take long for our joint acquaintances to figure out that we were an item. On several occasions they covered for us, relaying to his wife that Dan was with them when indeed he was with me. Although she never confronted him, it would be naïve to believe that she had no suspicion; there were just too many things that became out of sync with what had been his regular routine.

In spite of the time we did steal away with each other, it was nevertheless completely one-sided. After all, he was very much married and certainly did not want her to find out about his mistress on the side. Hence, birthdays and holidays left me feeling hollow, aching to be with him but powerless to make that happen. I somehow convinced myself that the time I was allotted made the hurting and loneliness worth it.

My internal message had not changed. I was convinced that I did not have the right to ask for or expect more. I was not his priority, and somehow I rationalized that that was okay. The feelings were all too familiar; I simply had to suck it up and pretend that everything was fine. However, the real truth was that inwardly I was torn up with heartache and longing just to be loved.

One of our first getaways was to a conference in May of 1984, his cover for going away. Although he did attend a few sessions to have on record that he was in fact there, for the most part we spent a large amount of the time together, booked in at a brand-new luxurious hotel. I recall the feeling of it being too good to be true, never wanting it to end. I desperately wanted to hold on to the fantasy of staying together; not wanting to face the harsh reality that he *was* returning home to a wife and kids, and I was going home alone.

Upon our return home my aloneness was accentuated by the emptiness and silence of my apartment. I struggled to convince myself that I would be okay. I would survive—I was tough, remember?

During the days that followed, I settled back into my routine of waiting for his next call, eagerly anticipating any chance to be together, no matter how brief.

Years earlier, Dan had built a camp on an inland lake. His wife rarely spent any time there, not caring for its lack of amenities. Often he would come up with reasons for having to go there alone without his kids, providing us with temporary seclusion from the outside world. I loved the remoteness, the rustic surroundings, and the constant sound of water lapping against the shoreline. Nights were spectacular, huddling close to the warmth of bonfires, staring in awe at the northern lights dancing across a star-filled sky. Of course, all too soon it would end, and I would be ushered back into the grim reality of my situation.

I continued to run and train with intensity, feverishly attempting to block out the fact that I was in love with a man who simply was not available. I did not allow myself to ponder the fact that he might never be; I somehow had to make him want me over her.

These pages would not be complete without the mention of Chad, a dear friend who I had the privilege of knowing. He was friends with Dan and was also involved with running local races. Chad was a man with many interests—however, I would have to say that sailing was at the top of his list. He owned a sailboat that was his pride and joy. Many times he invited Dan and I along to help crew in the local Wednesday night dinghy races. This provided opportunity for Dan and I to be together, but it also taught me about sailing—how to read the wind in the sails; when to jibe; when to come about and of course how to stay out of the way of the boom! It was fabulous. As a result, Chad invited us to come along with him to a weeklong sailing regatta that he had attended the year before.

Every year, during the first week of August, Americans and Canadians converged upon the infamous Lake of the Woods, a huge body of water that contains hundreds of islands, bays, and watery borders that separate our two countries. Each day was comprised of races amongst the many different categories of sailboats, all of them charting their way to a predetermined anchorage location.

The year prior, Chad had attended with his sailboat and met up with a father/son team that sailed a catamaran. They had hit if off and in their discussions they came up with an idea for next year—rent a houseboat that could serve as sleeping quarters and also a place to carry the week-long's supply of gear and food.

Chad's enthusiasm was contagious and before we knew it a plan of action was in place: a mutual friend would help Chad race his boat and Dan and I would drive the houseboat. Of course, Dan's wife did not know about that part of the equation. All she knew was that he was going away with his buddies to some big sailing regatta. I was ecstatic—an entire week with Dan. I could hardly contain my excitement in waiting for that first week of August.

Finally, all of our planning came to fruition and we were on our way. Several miles later our caravan arrived, along with many others from all parts of the US and Canada. The excitement was electrifying. We soon met up with Chad's American friends from the previous year, embarking upon the eve of great memories to be made.

After being shown how to operate the houseboat, we loaded it up with all of our supplies for the week—certainly no shortage of food or alcohol. Charts were laid out, determining what route we would take the next day to the first pre-selected anchorage. It was our job to get to these locations ASAP in order to ensure good anchorage sites, not only for the houseboat but also for the sailboats.

Chad had tried to describe to us the scene of the first race day, but nothing could have prepared us for the sight laid out before us: hundreds of sailboats with brilliantly coloured spinnakers, all weaving their way to the starting point, each category waiting for the blast of the air horn signifying that their classification was under way. It truly was spectacular.

The regatta had begun in earnest. After long days of racing, tranquil bays were turned into giant party zones; the larger sailboats lashed together in star formations taking up the deeper waters; rocky shorelines became home to all different kinds of sailboats, along with the odd houseboat. Evenings were spent around crackling bonfires, sparks exploding into a star-filled sky, unhindered by city lights. More often than not, out would come a few guitars strumming out old camp songs that everyone would join in on. Back then there were no cell phones, Blackberries etc. that kept you tied to the "real" world.

During the course of the week, our party boat attracted several others of varied backgrounds: some lived nearby and others were from as far away as California. We ended up anchoring together in the evenings and a strong bond began to form.

All too soon the week was coming to an end along with my pretend life. Before we knew it we were exchanging addresses and phone numbers with plans to return for next year's event.

As we began the drive home reality set in. Once again I would be returning home—alone. This time it was especially difficult. We had been together 24/7. The more time we spent together the harder it was for me to adjust without him there. I felt like a tortured soul, chained to my own unwillingness to turn myself loose. I was beginning to believe that I truly could not live without him. I had no idea that the hurt I had experienced up until now was only the beginning.

August turned into September and the fall road races were under way. I pushed myself relentlessly, desperately trying to numb my emotions through physical exertion. It was, however, only a temporary fix.

During this time I had the opportunity to move from my rather depressing basement apartment to the second floor of a house. The change was good. It was bright and comfortable, and the owners, who lived on the main floor, were great. I am sure they had their own conversations about my so-called boyfriend. Who was I kidding? No doubt they knew exactly what was going on, although they never asked and I never told.

Winter came early that year with an abundance of snow. Both Dan and I purchased memberships for downhill skiing, again providing us time to be together. But I soon found out that it wasn't only Dan that I would be sharing the time with.

On several occasions he brought along two of his kids. It felt awkward and I had to pretend that we were just friends happening to ski together. They weren't young enough to be fooled—especially when Dan told them not to tell their mother about the woman who skied with them. Thinking back, I could easily judge Dan for putting his children in that position, but he wasn't alone. I also put them in that predicament because of my choice to be involved with a married man. Plain and simple, it was wrong.

Part of my winter training program was to incorporate, along with running, cross-country skiing. Dan would meet up with me a couple of times during the week after work to hammer out a ten-kilometre loop on well-groomed trails. Considering the fact that he was a family man with responsibilities at home, we did spend a fair amount of time together. But for me it wasn't enough. I wanted more. I didn't want to share him and I resented the time he was with them and not me.

In our intimate moments I told him that I loved him, desperately wanting to hear him reply, "I love you, too." Instead, all he would say was "You're a good woman." Nice, but it crushed me, again confirming that I had to do more to earn his love, more to convince him to choose me over her.

The Christmas season was soon upon us, the time of year that I dreaded. All the media hype about family and romance only accentuated what I didn't have. I woke up alone on Christmas morning while his kids surrounded him, eagerly ripping open their presents.

New Year's Eve was no better. A good friend convinced me to go to a party with her and her boyfriend and another couple. I felt like the fifth wheel and what could have been a good time I instead turned it into a major pity party, feeling very sorry for myself. I watched as couples made their way to the dance floor while I sat alone feeling hollow and unloved. I drank heavily, wishing for midnight so I could just go home and pass out. Was this going to be the story of my life? Would I ever feel that I belonged and was loved? How long could I go on like this? I had no answers. I only knew I was not ready to give up on Dan and I convinced myself that some love was better than none at all.

Earlier, we had made plans to spend a couple of nights at his camp after the New Year. I couldn't wait, desperate for the physical closeness to convince myself that he must love me in spite of him not expressing it verbally. We arrived at the camp on January 2, 1985. It was bitterly cold and it took time for the fire in the woodstove to heat up the main floor to provide a source of warmth. I didn't care. I was finally with Dan and that was all that mattered. However, I was sensing that something was amiss. Dan was quiet and he seemed preoccupied while a big red flag was frantically trying to get my attention. I didn't want to go there to expose it but intuitively I knew it was inevitable.

Later in the evening it all came out—Dan was feeling guilty. He wanted to be home with his kids, wrestling with them on the floor, hugging them, tucking his little girl into bed, feeling her little arms wrapped around his neck. He said he thought that we should not see each other for a while; he needed time to try to figure out his situation and to perhaps try to mend his marriage.

I felt like the wind had been knocked out of me, hardly able to breathe. Anguish overtook me and I vomited. Desperately, I wanted to wake up and discover that it had just been a really bad dream but that didn't happen. I did not have the capacity to comprehend how to go on without him and furthermore, I truly believed that I couldn't. I was breaking. I was losing him. All my experiences of feeling rejected seemed to congeal all into this moment. I felt like I was drowning, unable to come up for air.

He had decided. We would spend the night but would leave first thing in the morning. I was inconsolable and did not sleep all night. My thoughts whirled, convincing myself that I couldn't live without him, and sadly I didn't want to. At the first sign of daylight I got up and went outside. I snapped my boots into the bindings of my cross-country skis and headed for the frozen lake. It was cold and the frigid wind had no mercy on exposed skin. I didn't care. I wanted to die. My world was ending and my heart was breaking. Unstoppable tears streamed down my face, my eyelids crusted in ice from the cold. I longed for him to come after me and say that he had changed his mind but he didn't.

Eventually, I returned to the camp. Dan was packing things up, making sure the fire was out, seemingly in a hurry to get back to his family. Few words were spoken and I was too distraught to even attempt a conversation.

We left soon after and I couldn't help but wonder if I would ever be back. This thought only created another torrent of tears that I could not turn off. Before I knew it he was in my driveway, dropping me off. There was so much I wanted to say but it was like paralysis had my voice in its clutches and nothing would come out. He kissed me goodbye and I walked away, hoping that I could reach my door without encountering my landlords. Once inside I collapsed, overcome with uncontrollable sobbing, besieged with grief that permeated to my very core.

I have no idea how long I remained in that condition; time didn't matter—in fact *nothing* mattered. I couldn't even call my closest friend, the shame being too much. I had lost him because I was flawed, I wasn't loveable. It was my fault. In desperation I called Mike, asking him to please come over, I needed to talk. He would be safe; he wouldn't judge me; instead he would patiently listen as I tried to verbalize my loss.

We began to drink, and the more I drank, the more I believed that I was at the end. I was convinced that I could not live without Dan, so I believed that my only option was to take my own life. I even asked him his opinion on what would be the easiest, quickest way. I thought an overdose would be the best way—just fall asleep and never wake up. There was silence between us and then he spoke. He told me that I could never take my own life. I was too much of a fighter and, most of all, I was a survivor, incapable of giving up. Deep down, in spite of myself, I knew he was right. They were the truest words that Mike ever spoke to me.

For a while Dan kept his word and did not contact me. However, our activities continually brought us into the same circle. He didn't attempt to avoid it, nor did I. After all my grief and tears, the end result was that nothing had changed—he was still married and I was still the mistress on the side.

Chapter 20

For once, I want to feel that I am important to you.
For once, I want to know that you are afraid of losing me.
For once, I want to know if you even love me.
– Unknown

We soon slipped back into our old routine of meeting on the side and planning future rendezvous. I didn't ask a lot of questions regarding his wife, mainly because I didn't want to hear that there was hope for their marriage. When he did complain about her, I listened patiently and would console him. Now and again he would infer about leaving, stating that he believed his issues with her could never be resolved. Hearing this gave me renewed hope and I vowed to be everything he wanted in a woman. Maybe then I would be worthy of his love.

In December, before our breakup, we had decided to train for and together run a marathon in the spring. Now that we were back together our training resumed. Dan's slow pace on our long runs pained me, but I had promised him that we would run it together, so I kept the frustration to myself. In retrospect, I believe my real motive was another attempt to try to earn his love. What would have been better for me was irrelevant.

Before we knew it it was marathon day. The weather was perfect and I felt great. Soon we were on our way and I tried to settle into Dan's pace. As other runners passed us it was all I could do to hold back. At one point I had to use one of the portable toilets provided on the course. I told Dan to keep going, I would catch up to him. Shortly thereafter I set out after him. It was effortless and all too soon I saw him up ahead. Not very often does a runner get one of those days when everything clicks. This was one of those moments for me and I let it pass, not knowing that I would never again have the opportunity to attempt a personal best.

We did complete the 26.2 miles together and he was ecstatic to have completed the event. At the very least I was hoping for a thank you, but that was just wishful thinking on my part. C'est la vie.

Summer months were soon upon us and plans were again under way to attend the sailing regatta in August. Again, Dan and I managed the operation of the houseboat navigating our way to the various anchorages.

Perhaps, if I had taken a step back and allowed myself to pay attention to the red flags that Dan presented, the outcome of our relationship might have been different. There was no compromise on Dan's part. His plans and decisions were final. It was his way or the highway. Far too often he would jokingly say, "Might is right." I would laugh along with him, not ready to accept that he was perhaps less than perfect.

Summer was coming to an end and Dan was coming to the realization that his marriage was as well. I couldn't believe that he was seriously considering leaving her. In fact, I truly didn't believe it until Labour Day weekend when he pulled up with suitcases and some personal belongings. I thought I had died and gone to heaven. It was too good to be true. I had won and she had lost. I vowed to make him happy so that he would never regret his decision.

Soon thereafter, we purchased a house that was in need of upgrades and a lot of TLC. For the most part Dan was able to do a lot of the work himself. It desperately needed cleaning and fresh paint, which I tackled, determined to make this house our home.

However I was not ready for the other equation of Dan's life: his children. I did not want to share him now that I had him. I was extremely insecure, fearing that I would wake up and he would be gone. I was selfish and needy, unwilling to consider or contemplate the needs of his children and what they must have been going through. I resented them a lot but I pretended otherwise with Dan. I had to live up to his expectations at whatever cost.

It was only a couple of months of being together that I was introduced to Dan's other side. The signs had been there but I had turned a blind eye, unwilling to acknowledge them. My make-believe, perfect world with Dan was about to come crashing down.

It was late November and I had gone out to get a few groceries. Upon my return, I came in through the front door where Dan was mopping. I was unable to set the bags down; I was tired and the groceries were heavy. I guess he didn't like the look of exasperation that crossed my face. He swore at me, kicking the bucket of water in a fit of anger. Then he grabbed the mop and hurled it at me like a javelin, striking me hard on the right forearm. For a moment I thought my arm was broken but the physical pain was quickly numbed by intense emotional hurt. Groceries were all over the wet floor. I tried to collect them as his tirade continued. I was sobbing, unable to comprehend what had just transpired. I quickly learned that it was my fault. If I hadn't given him "the look" then I wouldn't have gotten hurt. Simply put, I made it happen. I was crushed, trying to make sense of it. Obviously I would have to do better:

pretend, stuff my feelings, don't dare put the responsibility on him for his actions. Remember—"might is right."

Later that evening we attended my running club's Christmas party. Makeup concealed my puffy eyes and a long sleeved sweater hid the large bruise forming on my arm. I performed brilliantly, smiling, laughing and pretending that everything was just fine. This was just the beginning. I was living with Dr. Jekyll and Mr. Hyde.

As days progressed I became wary, slowly learning what would set him off and trying desperately to avoid his angry outbursts. I didn't always succeed.

I continued to run and train hard. Group workouts were held after work from Monday through Thursday and again on Saturday mornings. Apart from my own training regimen, I was also helping out with coaching female high school and university students. Initially, Dan went along with my busy schedule but slowly he began to try to talk me out of going to the Saturday workouts, claiming he wanted to relax and sleep in. However, I continued to go but would often come home to the silent treatment. If I attempted to try and talk about it with him, he would get angry and it would only make matters worse.

In the early spring of 1986, I became very interested in wanting to train for a triathlon event. I finally mustered up the courage to ask him if he would support my endeavour to do the necessary training. He flat out refused, stating that on weekends with the warmer weather approaching he wanted us to spend the time at camp without being delayed by my workouts.

It was another blow to my fantasy of what I had hoped for with him. I was hurt. What I wanted to achieve did not matter; what Dan wanted was the only thing that counted.

I persevered in spite of his lack of support, juggling times so that it wouldn't interfere with his plans. Unfortunately, a severe knee strain forced me to the sidelines and I had to forego my hope of completing the triathlon. I was so disappointed. I had trained so hard. He did not share in my disappointment.

Although it wasn't clear to me at the time, hindsight reveals a much clearer picture. I believe he used various tactics to slowly draw me away from what was important to me. At the same time, however, he could turn on the charm and be the Dan that I had fallen in love with. All of it left me whirling in a mishmash of emotions. I could not see the web that was slowly engulfing me, separating me from myself and entangling my identity into his.

Chapter 21

Memory: Sitting alone in the dark, feeling despair. Despair of my neediness to need him, no matter what the cost.

Apart from the physical threat that constantly loomed in the background, our relationship wasn't all negative, and that is what kept me hooked. We did share good times as long as I didn't challenge him on issues. His divorce was becoming finalized, but the amount he had to pay in support and the trade-off to keep his pension left him very bitter.

Visitation with his children was very sporadic and I never knew when to expect them. This became another source of conflict and angry outbursts, with me on the losing end. I had no control over what transpired in our home. Dan simply did what he wanted without regard for whether or not I fit into his plans; there was no discussion, no conversation, and no compromise.

The weeks turned into months and the months into another year. I have no idea how I managed to pull and keep myself together on a daily basis, considering the amount of stress I was under. I told no one, not even my closest friends, of feeling the ever-present threat of physical abuse. I could not verbalize that reality, because doing so would have made it real and

I would have been forced to see our relationship for what it was. Instead, I convinced myself that I could not live or survive without Dan.

For the last couple of years I had been employed with a government agency on a year-to-year contract. In March of 1987, I was informed that my contract was not going to be renewed due to personnel cutbacks. I was frantic. I had always prided myself in being financially independent, able to make it on my own. Dan was already bitter about his monthly support obligations so I knew this wouldn't go over well. My financial contribution to the household was not optional—it was a necessity.

At the time, my office skills were top notch, so I was able to sign up with a company that sent me to various job sites. The pay wasn't great, but at least it was something to hold me over while I looked for permanent employment.

Plans were again in the works to attend the sailing regatta. We had gone the previous year, but Dan was losing interest and he wasn't keen about attending this year's event. I knew it was just going to be another source of conflict between us. He knew how much I looked forward to it, but I honestly think he didn't want to share me with all the friends we had made there over the years. Perhaps this analysis is unfair and wrong, but I don't believe so. It fit the pattern of how he was slowly segregating me away from my interests and friends that were important to me, although I didn't recognize this at the time. Whether he was doing this consciously or unconsciously is not for me to judge.

In May we opened up the camp for the summer months. When I wasn't racing we would go there on weekends and I would do my long runs on the rough, gravel roads. Dan very much resented the time that races took me away from spending all of the time with him at the lake. Running had been a big part of my life before Dan was even in the picture and now I felt like I was being pressured to give it all up. No one, not even Dan, was going to take that away from me, but little did I know that I was on the brink of giving up much more than my running for Dan.

In early June, I entered a five-kilometre event held on a popular racecourse. Right from the start I felt lightheaded and had no energy. Runners that I regularly beat were passing me and I couldn't respond. My other gear just wasn't there so I dropped out. Of course, I lambasted myself afterwards for running so terribly, for not being mentally tough enough to ignore what my body was feeling and worst of all for quitting. How dare I!

But as I carried on the tirade against myself, I started to feel other physical symptoms. I was nauseous and to look at or smell food made me ill. I didn't even have the capacity to force myself out the door to go for a run. Not understanding what on earth was wrong with me, I finally succumbed to driving myself to the hospital to get checked out. The doctor on call was also a runner so we were known to each other. He carried out the routine examination—blood work, urine sample, etc. etc. Some time later, he called me into a private room and shut the door. This freaked me out but not nearly as much as his words that followed: "You are pregnant."

Impossible! It *couldn't* be. *Someone wake me up!* I thought. *This has to be a dream.* But it wasn't—it was very much real. How could it have happened? I had used an IUD as a form of birth control for years. The doctor simply explained it like the odds of winning a lottery, but I sure didn't feel like a winner.

The torrent of thoughts that permeated my brain left me spinning. How would I tell Dan? I knew he adamantly didn't want any more kids, so what would he say? How would he respond? In spite of being in a state of shock as I drove home, I clearly recall the strong undeniable pull in my gut—I wanted this baby.

When I arrived home Dan was upstairs in the bedroom. Tentatively, I climbed the stairs and went into the bedroom where he was lying down. All I could say was, "We need to talk."

I told him the news and he wasn't surprised. He had interpreted my physical symptoms better than I had. For a while we lay in silence, I not knowing how to tell him that I wanted to have this baby. He spoke before I did, his solution already decided: I would have an abortion. My heart sank. I was numb. When I did speak, I hinted at the possibility of going through with the pregnancy. His matter-of-fact response cut me to the core. He told me that ultimately it was my decision, but if I decided to keep the baby, he would leave me, period. He was adamant that he was not going to raise another child. I felt so betrayed, heartbroken, crushed. I was emotionally blackmailed and he was seemingly oblivious to the impact that his words had on me. I believe he knew even then that the threat of leaving me would get him his way. What Dan wants, Dan gets.

A few days later I was scheduled for an ultrasound to determine if the IUD could be removed without disturbing the fetus. I tried to resist, but my curiosity got the better of me and I glanced over at the screen. Clearly, I could see the small image moving, alive. I was informed that I was about seven weeks along and everything looked great. More than ever I wanted to protect and keep this life that was growing inside of me. I wish I had never looked.

In discussion with my doctor I informed him that Dan did not want another child so he offered to meet with us to discuss the situation. Surprisingly, Dan agreed to it. We entered his office and he motioned for us to have a seat. From behind his desk he stated to us that children are a gift. He went on to say to Dan that he could understand his apprehension about having another child, considering his circumstances. He believed, however, that Dan could adjust and would end up loving this baby just as much as the kids he already had. I glanced over at Dan and knew instantly that the doctor's words were having zero effect. Dan was not budging.

In conversation with Chad, I told him our predicament and he was excited about the prospect of me having a baby. Dan, however, did not share his enthusiasm and expressed exactly to our friend his thoughts on the matter. In response, Chad made it clear to Dan that it wasn't his decision to make—it was mine. Dan did not reply.

Days went by and we didn't talk about it; maybe I was wistfully hoping that the dilemma would magically resolve itself. Ironically, during this time, Dan treated me totally different. He opened doors for me and was more attentive to my physical needs. I so wished it could last.

Time was not standing still. In July, I wrote a letter to Dan trying to express my feelings and how important it was for me to have this baby. I also asked him how he would handle the inevitable—my anger if I went through with an abortion. The only reply I got was what had already been stated: if I had the baby he would leave.

Shortly before the regatta, which was fast approaching, Chad came over to talk to us, seriously concerned. He expressed the need for us to make a decision, quickly, one way or the other. We couldn't continue to ignore it. He was absolutely right except for the "us" equation. Dan had decided. It was squarely *my* quandary, *my* dilemma, and *my* burden.

We did end up going to the regatta, Dan very begrudgingly. However, the whole week was a blur. My mind was preoccupied with what I would have to do when we returned home.

I was thirteen and a half weeks into the pregnancy. I had missed the chance for a local abortion, their cutoff being twelve weeks or less. I searched out clinics in the States and ended up contacting a clinic in Minnesota. They told me to come immediately. If I waited any longer it would be too late.

Before I knew it, we were walking towards the entrance of the clinic. I desperately tried to avoid the pro-life picketers attempting to make me feel even guiltier for what I was about to do. Once inside, my information was taken, Dan paid the $500, and we were told to take a seat and wait to be called. We waited and waited and waited some more while I watched young girls giggling, not seeming to care in the least about their upcoming "procedure." I was sick, still hoping for a miracle, wishing that Dan would change his mind, take my hand and say, "Let's get out of here," but he didn't.

Few words were spoken between us. People who had come in after us were called in, dealt with, and leaving. Finally, I went and asked why I hadn't been called. After checking, they discovered my chart had been misfiled. I was assured it wouldn't be much longer. Could the torture of waiting get any worse? Yes, it could, and it did.

The details of what transpired in the "procedure" room will be forever engraved in my mind. I am not proud of the decision I made that day. I am ashamed that I was not strong enough at the time to stand up to Dan and emphatically say, "*No!* I will *not* do this." I am sad that I considered his feelings to be more important than my own. That day I gave him a piece of my soul. It would take many, many years for me to reclaim and take back that piece—the piece that had the power to make me whole.

The grief and guilt that followed was immense and I endured it alone. Dan was aloof and incapable of being my soft place to fall, either by his own choice or just not having the capacity within himself to offer that to me. I don't know.

Upon returning home, I was called back to work. I knew he would be planning to see his kids but I begged him to please give me a few days. I was emotionally and physically spent and needed desperately time to regroup. I did not have it in me to put on my happy face with them and pretend everything was great. They had no idea that I had been pregnant and what had transpired.

I went to work on the Monday trying to concentrate on the job, but my mind was elsewhere and I had a nagging suspicion that something wasn't right. At the end of the day I left work, anxious to get home. As I made the turn on to our street I couldn't believe what I saw before me—Dan's kids all playing in the front yard. Something inside of me snapped. I was broken, angry, unable to get out of my car. Dan came and opened the driver's door, smiling, until he saw my expression. He lashed out in anger at my obvious disapproval of their presence. "What the hell is wrong with you? What do you expect me to do?"

He slammed the car door hard, which only added another blow to my fractured spirit. I drove away not knowing where to go or who to talk to. I was coming undone.

I don't remember where I went, but at some point I stopped and called Mike. I was desperate. Shortly thereafter we met in a shopping plaza parking lot. When he got into my car I fell apart, slamming my head relentlessly against the steering wheel, screaming, sobbing, and inconsolable.

How long we sat there I have no idea, but it was a release of emotions that left me exhausted. There was nothing he could say that would fix my circumstances, but for some reason I felt safe enough in his presence to expose such rawness. If he hadn't come, I don't know what I would have done or what would have happened. Thank you, Mike.

Eventually I drove home, but I was not ready to go inside and face Dan and his kids, so I decided to walk, only returning when it began to get dark. I came in, trying to be unnoticed, immediately retreating to the bedroom, unable to face them with my red, swollen eyes.

Life went on, and eventually we resumed old routines, but there was no undoing what had been done. Every time

I watched Dan with his daughter, bouncing her on his knee and asking her, "Who's Daddy's favourite little girl?" I felt like I was being stabbed with a knife; inwardly seething, I felt a mixture of despair and intense anger.

Again, as always, I buried my emotions through running, mercilessly pushing my body to the extreme, not caring how much pain I inflicted upon myself. After all, it was what Frances deserved.

Chapter 22

Push me away if you are unwilling to change.
Pull me close if you can't live without me.
Let me go, if all you have to offer is sorrow.
– Unknown

In the spring of 1988, I acquired a contract position with a distance education organization affiliated with a community college. The pay was decent so it helped to alleviate some of the financial stress.

It was a constant struggle to push the events of the previous year to the back of my mind. There always seemed to be a barrage of triggers that would bombard me at the most inconvenient of times. It not only affected my waking hours but also through the night via my dreams. It seemed that I was in a constant state of torment, unable to make it go away. To share this struggle with Dan was simply out of the question. He did not want to hear it.

Dan had made up his mind that this year he had no interest in going to the sailing regatta. Even if I had been able to get the time off work, I knew there was no convincing him otherwise. So on weekends I joined him at the camp, wishing that the peaceful, serene surroundings would overpower the raging chaos within. For the most part our time spent on the lake was positive. We both enjoyed exploring all the facets of what nature had to offer. Bonfires on the beach under cascading streaks of pinks, violets, and greens from the northern lights were a spectacular sight to behold. But even this was not enough to dispel the inner turmoil of unresolved issues.

By late summer, I was exhausted. I was pale, my joints ached, and running was next to impossible. I continued to ignore the physical symptoms, persevering, determined to run through it, but my body had a different agenda: it had had enough. I finally saw my doctor and he ran a series of tests. A week or so later he called me at home and announced that I had tested positive for chronic fatigue syndrome. There was no running through it; the only remedy was rest. My hours at work were cut back so that I could come home and sleep in the afternoon. This was totally foreign to my lifestyle. Never had I permitted myself to sleep during the day, but this time it was my body that dictated what I could and could not do.

Slowly, my energy levels were on the rise, and by late fall I resumed my regular hours at work and, of course, my running regimen. Workdays were long and I was bored with not having enough work to fill the time. There was no challenge. In our local paper I noticed a job posting for an organization that provided services to remote northern school boards. It was full time and permanent. The job description more than suited my skills, so with nothing to lose, I applied. I was called in for an interview, and shortly before Christmas holidays I was offered the job, the starting date being the first week of January 1989. The timing was perfect. It didn't take long to fit in; the job was challenging, the people were great, and I enjoyed going to work.

Dan's children and the dynamics between us continued to be a struggle for me and I clashed with certain aspects of their personalities. My favourite was Tom, his second child whom

I observed to have a gentle soul. It was not difficult to form a special bond with him.

In early spring, Dan discovered that his two oldest were having issues with their mother that were not likely to be resolved. Discussion came up regarding the possibility of them coming to live with us. I would have welcomed Tom but I had real reservations about David, the oldest. I could not voice this to Dan as it would have erupted into an angry confrontation, something that I tried desperately to avoid. This seemed to be the pattern that developed—issues that came between us were never resolved. If I did attempt to voice my concerns or try to discuss our differences, the result would inevitably end in a physical confrontation. It was a fine line that I had to balance with great care, imperative that I didn't upset the apple cart, so to speak.

The house we were living in was small and would not have accommodated the four of us, so we began to search for something more appropriate. By May we found a house that would be suitable. Our real estate agent wrote up an offer that was accepted shortly thereafter. The plan was for David and Tom to move in once we took possession in mid-June.

During this time, I told Dan that I really wanted to get a puppy. I had grown up with dogs and missed the companionship that they provide. With the prospect of moving into a larger house, I felt that it could work. He went along with it but also made it clear that he wanted no part of the responsibility that accompanied a pet. That was fine with me. It would be *my* dog.

I went on a search and found what I wanted. He came from a litter of five pups, a cross between the breeds of a Labrador and Newfoundland. The owner brought him to my workplace and I fell in love with him at first sight. He was all black except for white markings on his chest. For a ten-week-old puppy, I couldn't help but notice his massive paws—perfect! I paid her the deposit and she agreed to hold him for me until we moved into the new house. As she was getting into her vehicle to leave, I offhandedly asked her what date the puppies had been born. Her response left me breathless. Ironically, he was born on February 6th—the very date forecasted for my delivery if I had carried my pregnancy to term.

The time passed quickly, taken up with packing and lawyer appointments to finalize the sale of one house and the purchase of the next. I was stressed out—not only from the stress of what goes along with moving, but how would I handle becoming a full-time stepmother to two teenagers? It was ground that I was totally unfamiliar with and I sensed it was not going to be a smooth transition.

We got moved in and began the process of unpacking and sorting out where to put everything. As promised, my new puppy was delivered. Dan had not yet seen him other than the picture I had taken of him at ten weeks old. He bounded into the house with the exuberance of youth. Dan's reaction was classic: "Holy shit! What did you buy, a horse?" He had grown—lots—and was still growing, a mass of black wavy fur with eyes that could melt your heart. "Boomer" was home.

Not long after, David and Tom moved in, each having their own room in the basement. The house had lots to offer—a finished recreation room with fireplace, a sauna complete with a three-piece bath, as well as an extra kitchen in the basement. I took upon myself all of the household chores—cooking, cleaning, vacuuming, laundry, and ironing. These responsibilities should have been shared, but it was the only area where I felt like I had control, and I was desperate to hold on to it.

I put myself under extreme pressure to fit everything in. Besides working full-time I continued to run and attend training sessions after work, rushing home to make supper. In my spare time I worked with Boomer, teaching him basic obedience as well as his own repertoire of dog tricks. By Sunday night I was exhausted, having to pull it all together, only to begin again Monday morning.

David was in his first year of university and, according to Dan, it was David's job to study. I observed, however, that discipline did not seem to be his forte and, in my opinion, for the most part, I found him to be lazy and self-centred. I was resentful of his presence and I am sure he knew it. One particular day there had been a series of things that he had done that had really pissed me off. The final straw was when he microwaved food for himself that I was saving for the next day's supper. I was in his face, screaming at him, hardly able to stop myself from landing my fist square into his jaw. The rage within was coming undone and he was simply the catalyst that sparked it. Dan watched from the sidelines, glaring. I was too angry to care. My actions and words that I spoke to David were absolutely inappropriate. I was at a breaking point, unable to communicate with Dan all the frustration and myriad of emotions that I held within, refusing to acknowledge them out of fear that they would consume me. I felt isolated and alone.

The tension between Dan and I was growing. My patience with David was non-existent and Dan felt like the referee in a boxing ring. We were in a cycle of dysfunction that would usually begin with an argument. I would want to talk about it, but Dan just wanted to ignore it and walk away. I felt desperate to try to resolve it and would beg him to stay and discuss it.

One afternoon, I particularly remember being at this impasse. My neck had been stiff and sore with limited range of motion. I was in the front hallway standing in front of him. Before I knew it, his hands gripped my biceps like a vice and I was launched backwards across the living room, landing against the front of the couch that broke my fall. He stormed out, and I was left behind to lick my wounds, get up, and pretend everything was fine. The next day I looked in the mirror and my arms bore the bruises from each of his fingers that had curled around them. I quickly realized that I needed to wear a long-sleeved shirt so that no one would see and no one would know.

We did not typically fit the cycle of domestic violence. What is referred to as the honeymoon phase did not exist. Never did I receive an apology from Dan for his actions. In his mind, he was convinced that he had done nothing wrong, so what was there to apologize for? We simply went from the tension-building phase to the battery phase, skipped the honeymoon stage, and went straight back to the tension-building phase.

Naïvely, I didn't think David or Tom were aware of the abuse, not until one morning when Tom came upstairs for breakfast. The night before both of them weren't home, during which time Dan and I got into some disagreement. I have no recollection of what it was even about. We were playing out our roles of him storming out and me wanting to talk.

On his way through the kitchen he smashed his fist through the wall, leaving a large hole. The next morning I was eating my breakfast when Tom came into the kitchen. His eyes immediately went to the hole in the wall then quickly averted, saying nothing, just simply going about like it wasn't there. It hit me—hard. It was no different than being in the home of an alcoholic who goes on a rampage in a drunken state, destroying furniture or whatever is in the path, and the next morning everyone goes about like nothing happened. I think this was the first time I admitted to myself, just slightly, that something was really wrong.

Through all this turmoil, Boomer became my constant. I took him everywhere, even to group workouts. He loved the attention and the exercise. It wasn't long before I didn't even need to run with him on a leash, him staying right at my side. He was my 100-pound gentle giant.

Sailing was again a topic of conversation and Chad convinced Dan to attend this summer's event; I didn't need any convincing. We had missed the last two years and I was more than ready for a break, especially from David. My only concern was for Boomer, but Tom assured me he would take care of him.

As always, I was not disappointed to be there. It was great to see everyone again as well as some new additions, one of which was Jeff. Little did I know when we were introduced the impact that he would have on me.

I was ready to let loose, and not even the disapproving looks I was receiving from Dan were going to hold me back—not this year. After one of our bonfires, several of our group retreated to the upper deck of the houseboat. I was sitting beside Jeff, laughing and having a great time. Dan was also there, observing, becoming more sullen and silent as the time went by. He finally asked me if I was coming to bed as it was late and we had to get an early start. I told him no, I was going to stay up a little longer. He wasn't happy. When he left, Jeff, being very observant, commented that Dan didn't seem too impressed that I wasn't joining him. This was only the beginning.

Jeff and I had connected and Dan knew it. He was easy to talk to and he listened. By the third day Dan was not speaking to me and at night he slept on shore in a tent. For the first time I didn't care. I continued to join in on the water balloon launches and the late-night parties. I knew Dan was seething with anger, but I also knew that for the time being I had safety in numbers. I didn't want to think about when we would eventually be alone, that would be a different story.

The tension between Dan and I was thick and everybody felt it. I avoided him and he avoided me. As the week wore on, I ended up confiding in Jeff what the reality was between Dan and I—finally admitting verbally to someone else all that had transpired. I clearly recall Jeff taking both of my hands in his, looking directly into my eyes, telling me that I did not deserve to be treated like this, and that I deserved better. To hear this from someone I hardly knew was like someone shining a spotlight into the reality of everything I had refused to acknowledge. It was suddenly clear, crystal clear, what I had to do.

The drive home was brutal. For the first part of the trip we had a passenger that needed a ride part of the way, but after that it was only Dan and I. For the remainder of the drive not a word was spoken between us.

Arriving home, we were greeted by Tom, eager to know all about our week. After seeing the look on Dan's face he knew enough to drop the subject. Boomer was overjoyed to see us, and as I gave him a big hug I silently asked for the strength that I was really going to need.

After unloading the car, I suggested to Dan that we go to a bar located not far from us. We needed to talk, and, surprisingly, he agreed.

We sat in a secluded corner of the room, an area where I hoped we would be unnoticed. Dan gripped the armrests so hard that his knuckles turned white. The expression on his face looked like he could kill.

Somehow, the conversation got started with me eventually interspersing that perhaps I should move out. At some point I spoke about the conflict between David and myself. Dan's reaction was chilling. He told me there was one point when he was so angry at the way I was talking to David that if he had had his gun—which he did possess—he would have shot me. I believed him. His words more than clarified again what I needed to do: leave, preferably sooner than later.

I have been blessed with dear friends, and one in particular, Ed, came through for me at this very precarious time in my life. I was not leaving without Boomer, so I either needed to buy or rent a house that allowed a dog. I discovered that renting a house was not cheap; in fact it would be more than a mortgage payment. Ed generously offered to cash in some of his stocks for me to use as a down payment. He insisted, with the only condition that I pay it back whenever I was able to—no interest, no timeframe. I am forever indebted to that generous, unselfish man.

Things were strained at home and I tried to stay away as much as possible. David and Tom were made aware that I was leaving. It tore me apart to leave Tom, as a strong bond had formed between us. I told him that he was not the reason I was leaving; I wanted and needed him to know that.

What made it especially difficult was that I still loved Dan, and although he didn't verbalize it, I knew he, in his own confusing way, loved me. One afternoon, as I was doing some packing, he asked me if I really needed to leave, as he didn't want me to go. Part of me wanted desperately to cave in and go along with what he was asking, but from somewhere deep within I found the courage to respond differently. I told him that I did love him and I didn't want to leave, but I also voiced that if I stayed, things would have to change. I even suggested counseling; someone who could perhaps help us work through our issues. Sadly, he refused by saying that he had no intention of seeking counsel. He was who he was and he was not going to change. My reply was simple: "Then I guess you aren't giving me any other choice." It was not brought up again.

We had been in a common-law relationship for five years. Legally, I could have taken half the value of the house and half the value of the camp. Just mentioning this caused him to go ballistic. He accused me of being a typical, greedy woman, only caring about money and wanting to bleed him dry. I knew that this was not who I was, but part of me still wanted his approval and to not disappoint him. Instinctively, I believed that if I were to pursue that to which I was entitled, my life would be in grave danger. It wasn't worth the risk.

All I asked for was that when he did sell the house, at whatever time, that I receive back, based on the selling price, a percentage of the down payment that I had put into it. Even the lawyer told Dan that I was entitled to much more, but it didn't phase him. He seemed furious that I was getting anything at all.

I found a small two-bedroom house with lots of windows that made it bright and inviting. Friends offered to help me move, which I gladly accepted. They all knew Dan, so "awkward" hardly described the scene on moving day. Dan stood in the background watching while they loaded my belongings into their vehicles. I just wanted to get it over with as quickly as possible.

I will never forget my first night alone in my new house. Boomer was anxious, unsure of his new surroundings. I assured him and myself that everything would be okay. For the first time in years I felt safe. I no longer felt like I was constantly walking on eggshells, guarding everything I said and did. I could finally relax and just be. It was my time to start over.

PART IV

Chapter 23

You see that girl—yeah, her.
She seems so invincible, right?
But just touch her and she'll flinch.
She has secrets and she trusts no one . . .
Because everyone she trusted, broke her.
– Unknown

It is necessary that I introduce you to Val, a friend who played a big part in helping me to unravel the pieces that were keeping me stuck in a cycle of self-destruction.

Shortly before my leaving Dan, she had joined our running circle and was dating a man that I had known for many years through running. Her day job was that of a counselor, counseling women who were dealing with addictions and histories of sexual abuse and domestic violence. Hence, she was quick to see through the dynamics surrounding Dan and I.

Val had also been a victim of sexual abuse within her home as a child growing up. Consequently, her view of herself had been distorted, resulting in choosing men that furthered the cycle of abuse and control. I could not hide from her. In looking at me I mirrored what had been her own experience.

We became close and the dynamics between us were unstrained, causing people to ask us if we were sisters. It was uncanny—we even looked alike.

For the first time, I had someone who validated everything that I was feeling. Slowly, very slowly, I began to understand how my self-loathing and negative view of what I believed about myself had influenced so many of the choices that I had made. However, this was only the beginning of untangling the webs of deceptions that I had adopted as my own. The old tapes that bombarded my thoughts somehow had to be silenced. Discovering more about who I was and my wounded inner child that I had refused to acknowledge, compelled me to convince Dan of the same. If I could just get him to look inside of himself at his issues, i.e., anger, then maybe he could make changes for the better. I was on a mission, buying him books on anger management, books on how to get in touch with one's inner self, etc. etc. Of course, he never read any of them. I didn't realize at the time that neither I nor anyone else could ever fix Dan. Only he and he alone had the power to do it.

Although we lived apart, I was still enslaved to old patterns of behaviour when it came to our relationship. He would come over to talk and invariably he would want to end the conversation in bed. I felt like I didn't have the right to say no, perhaps in part for feeling guilty about leaving him and hurting his feelings. I knew I couldn't go back but at the same time I had moments of trying to convince myself that maybe it wasn't as bad as I thought. Of course, I was fantasizing about what I had hoped for in our relationship, not the reality of what it had been.

As I began to acknowledge my own abuse issues, I recalled a conversation that I had years previously with one of the female high school runners that I had travelled with to various meets. One day, Megan had approached me asking if we could talk. I had good rapport with the girls and had gotten to know them quite well but I was unprepared for the bombshell that she was about to unload on me. In summary, she told me that Stan, the coach, had been supervising one of their high school dances. She had an argument with another girl at the dance that had upset her so she went to the washroom to calm down. When she came out Stan was there and he suggested they talk about what happened. Megan relayed how he led her to a small room adjacent to his classroom.

There, they gave each other a hug but it then progressed to him giving her a French kiss and caressing her underneath her shirt. She told me she then pushed him away and ran home. I asked her if anyone else knew and she said no. She knew she had to tell someone and had decided to confide in me. I knew I could not ignore what she had told me. I believed her and was not surprised.

I had always had my suspicions of Stan. His was not a typical teacher/coach relationship with the runners. He had formed a competitive running club that served to train students from the high school where he taught along with other competitive runners, myself included. He ran the workouts with them, taking on the role more of a friend than the authority figure he was. I observed his conduct with some of the female runners as somewhat questionable. On several occasions I witnessed him giving the girls leg massages following a race or strenuous workout going, in my opinion, just a little too high towards the crotch. I listened to him comment on their weight, telling them they were looking too heavy and needed to trim down. Some of the girls developed eating disorders such as anorexia and bulimia. Road trips were frequent, with him taking responsibility for booking the rooms and arranging who stayed with whom.

With Megan's approval at that time, I confided in a mutual friend who was also a teacher and socialized with Stan. When I described what had happened he also was not surprised and in fact recalled other situations where he had suspicions of what was going on. He agreed to talk to him in the hopes that Stan would realize the seriousness of these allegations and change his behaviour. Naïvely, I thought he would listen.

Now, I was still coaching but had moved from coaching high school students to the females at the university varsity level. Stan and his runners shared the indoor track facility that we used for workouts. I began to observe him more closely: his mannerisms, the conversations, and the girls' reactions to him, my every suspicion and red flags on high alert. With my own shame and painful experiences fresh in my mind, my reaction was intense. I was overcome with the need to protect this new generation of girls from him. I felt like mother bear ready to do anything and everything to stop him from taking advantage of them. No one had stepped up to be my protector and I believed that if I could save them I would, in part, be saving myself. He had to be stopped.

During these early months of self-reflection, I was also beginning to understand how alcohol had played a big part in my behaviour and how it had clouded my judgement in choices that I had made. In July of 1991, I decided that for the next six months I would not drink nor involve myself in any sexual relationship. I needed to get in touch with emotions and feelings that had been for far too long repressed. This decision also gave me my out with Dan. It no longer mattered that he understood why I was choosing this, just that he accept it.

I had a difficult time comprehending how I was going to attend parties and not drink. Isn't that what made parties fun? How could I be sober and actually have a good time? Thankfully, my current circle of friends rallied around me, giving me the support and encouragement to stick to my decision.

My biggest challenge would be the sailing regatta. Drinking was just taken for granted and I would not have the same support system as I had at home. Dan had lost interest in going, which left the door open for me to attend.

It was an enlightening experience, allowing me to realize that I could have just as much fun by remaining sober. Ironically, people who were not aware that I wasn't drinking thought I was drunk. I discovered that I was stronger than what I had given myself credit for. I stayed sober.

Following the regatta, my sister expressed her desire to meet with me since it had been awhile since we had seen each other. My relationship with her was strained. She was the good girl and I was the bad one. I had always felt compared to her perfection thereby unable to ever live up to the unattainable. However, I agreed to meet with her. We talked and I shared, what I believed to be in confidence, some of my experiences with Dan and what had prompted me to decide not to drink for six months. I would later find out that this information was relayed back to my mother. Trust is precarious, a fine line that can so easily be broken, sometimes never mended.

Once I was back to my day-to-day routine, behind the scenes I was focused on finding other girls that had been targeted by Stan during the same time period as Megan. Many of them had gotten married, pursued careers and even had children of their own. Megan herself had just come out of a short-lived marriage. A couple of the girls that I was sure had also been victims of Stan I ran with on a regular basis. It was a slow procedure. I had to be as tactful as possible in broaching the subject with them individually.

In my opinion, it seemed that Stan's method of operating was very similar: groom his targets for their first three or four years of high school then make his move during their senior year.

With Rachel, he waited for his opportunity while out of town at a cross-country meet. After she realized that I knew, she relayed to me what had happened to her in a hotel room.

Throughout the assault, she was stunned, confused, and unable to move.

Another girl confided in me with her own account and allegation of abuse. He was seemingly a predator who abused his position of authority, targeting their neediness to feel special, to be paid attention to, to be loved: perfect candidates that wouldn't tell.

In 1992, Stan's tirade was about to come to an end. Rachel was the first to decide to have him charged; the others came on board soon after. He was officially charged with two counts of sexual assault, one charge of indecent assault, and one charge of gross indecency. I spent hours gathering information that I had accumulated along with lists of other possible victims, turning it over to the detective in charge. The investigation went on for several weeks, making sure that no mistakes were made that could possibly jeopardize the outcome.

I have to this day nothing but admiration for those who found the courage to stand up and face the man that had taken so much away from them. They endured the cross-examination of the defence, attempting to make it look like it was consensual, agreed upon and no big deal. There was also anger directed towards them from those who supported Stan: his wife and family members, friends, teachers and other runners that they had trained alongside.

I could go into great detail of what was uncovered in the entire investigation but that is not necessary. What mattered was that a jury did indeed pronounce him guilty of sexual assault and gross indecency. What mattered was that he did lose his licence to teach and his position of authority, the very platform that I believe he had used to seek out his prey.

The girls unfortunately were not his only victims. His wife and family also had to pay a high price for his actions. For them, I am also sorry.

I truly believe there were other girls who, for whatever reason of their own, did not come forward. If so, I hope that they too will be able to process it and find peace and closure for themselves.

I am grateful that I was able to play a part in stopping this cycle of abuse. As the judge stated in court, Stan had many positive qualities and potential both as a teacher and a coach, however he also had a dark side that he chose to act upon. Consequently, he was sentenced to nine months in jail to serve his debt to society.

It is also my hope that this was his wakeup call, his rock bottom that provided him the opportunity to resolve his dark side—not only for his own sake but also for any potential future victims.

Chapter 24

Dream: I was in a classroom with several students when a young girl came over to me and whispered that she had something to tell me. We went outside and she told me that she was being abused and didn't want to have to go home. I comforted her and told her how sorry I was. I stood behind her and held her, both of us crying. She turned and when I looked at her, I realized that I was looking at myself.

My last contact with my brother Ron and his wife Diane had been in the fall of 1984. They were moving from the States to Alberta and on their way stopped in to see me. I had no idea of what to expect or what we would find to talk about. I knew nothing about their lives and I certainly wasn't going to inform them of my current lifestyle. I assumed that Ron probably still regarded me as the bad, selfish Frances.

Surprisingly, it went much better than what I was expecting. Although many years would go by before we connected again, a seed had been planted. Now that I was slowly opening up the chapters of my childhood, I needed clarification of the many things that had transpired. Had I made things up? Was it as negative as I recalled? I believed that Ron would be truthful and provide me with a realistic portrayal of the family dynamics that had been present. I decided to take the risk and visit them in Alberta. After all, I had nothing to lose since we had never had a relationship or any communication between us. When I contacted him about the prospect of coming to see them, he seemed genuinely delighted. So in July of 1992, despite my trepidation, I went for it.

The first night there, we talked until the early morning hours. Many of my questions were answered; misunderstandings explained; my suspicions confirmed; my feelings validated. For me it was an enormous breakthrough. For the first time I found Ron to be not just a brother I hardly knew but now an ally. I think he too realized that I was not the person that my mother had specifically portrayed me as. We both spoke from the heart, which forever changed the dynamics between us. As difficult as it was, I took the risk of being vulnerable and this time it paid off. I left feeling stronger, more confident, with more awareness of who I was and what I had lived through. It was a new beginning that set the stage for much more to come.

In February of this same year (1992) Chad was diagnosed with cancer detected in his kidneys. He underwent surgery to remove what they could but it was more widespread than what had been anticipated. Chad being Chad remained optimistic, determined to beat the odds. Chemotherapy sessions left him exhausted and caused him to lose what little hair he had left. Spring turned into summer and he persevered with his hobbies—gardening and, of course, sailing.

The regatta was just ahead and nothing was going to stop him from attending—nothing. All the friends that we had made there over the years made it a priority to come back. Although it wasn't spoken, we knew that it would be Chad's last. It was a week of savoured memories, especially of Chad taking in every moment: his exuberance and infectious love of being on the water, surrounded by friends and doing what he loved best—sailing.

On the last race day, we woke up to a day without even a hint of a breeze. There wasn't even a slight ripple to be seen as we looked out over the lake; it was pancake flat. We knew that if the wind did not pick up the race would be in jeopardy of being called. Unfortunately, especially for Chad, it was. His disappointment was evident and it was later reminisced that his comment to his crew was, "Well, I guess this is it."

At the final awards banquet, Chad was named as the recipient of one of the most prestigious awards —the one given to the individual that exemplified sportsmanship, camaraderie, and the true love of sailing. No one deserved it more—he had given it his all.

Within just a couple of days upon returning home, Chad became bedridden, exhausted. Tests were administered with results that no one wanted to hear: the cancer was literally taking over his entire body. Soon after, he was hospitalized with doctors and staff striving to control his excruciating pain.

For two months I watched Chad fight with everything he had. When I wasn't at work I was at his bedside, desperate to help him hold on but inwardly knowing that he didn't have a chance.

I had never watched someone slowly die—especially someone I loved like a brother. It was gut wrenching. I was afraid of death, the not knowing of what I would be met with on the other side. Visions of being cast into the fires of hell had plagued me my entire life. The memories and friendship that Chad gave me was a gift, but what he gave me in his last days of awareness was his greatest gift of all.

As I sat beside him, he would say to me, with eyes full of wonder, "Look at all the people—can't you see them? The light is so bright—can't you see it? I'm feeling pulled towards it—they want me to come. It's so peaceful . . ."

These were some of the last words that Chad spoke to me, and shortly thereafter he slipped into an unconscious state.

In late October of 1992, at forty-seven years young, I said my final goodbyes to Chad.

Chad's final words kindled my struggle to come to terms with the teachings that I had been indoctrinated with as a child. What did *I* really believe about God, if anything? Growing up, I was not permitted to explore other beliefs or religions. To do so would be considered blasphemy against God and at the time it just wasn't worth the backlash that I would have to endure. Inwardly I didn't understand how God, who was supposed to love us unconditionally, could send someone to an eternity of hell fire. It just didn't make sense to me.

Hence Chad's death was the catalyst that prompted me to explore other beliefs and ideas, far removed from the narrow minded thinking that I had grown up with. I delved into personal accounts of people who had died and come back. I explored the phenomena of ascended masters and angels whose purpose is to guide us through our human struggles. I studied the various karmas and energies that affect us either negatively or positively. For the next several years, I slowly redefined my image of God/higher power and my relationship to such, deliberately creating my own ideas and concepts, leaving far behind the doctrines that I had grown up with. Never again would I return to the ritual of church going; rather my place for inner reflection would come from nature itself. Ron, having confirmed my abuse issues within the home and having also witnessed it, sparked the anger and resentment that had been on slow boil for so many years. In conversation with Val, I knew it had to be addressed. I had to let the monster out of the cage before it entirely engulfed me.

I was introduced to Sharon, a former nun who had experienced her own share of abuse. She now worked as a counselor, helping women resolve their own personal histories. In my first few sessions with her I was guarded, not allowing any emotion to come too close to the surface. Humour helped to keep it at bay but of course she saw right through that tactic. I was going to be a hard nut to crack, so I was informed. Frances was on guard, too afraid to be vulnerable, too afraid to open the door even a crack to the intensity of buried emotions. I was well aware of what followed close behind the anger, that being extreme sadness—sadness that would bring me to my knees threatening to open a floodgate of tears that could not be held in check. I feared that even more than the intensity of my anger. When my anger flared, people would back off, intimidated; however, with tears, I was vulnerable, someone to be laughed at, ridiculed, and shamed for being so weak.

One day Sharon presented me with an idea to consider. In early January of 1993, she was offering twelve weekly sessions for women struggling with similar issues as mine. Enrollment was limited and she offered me the chance to take part. I was told flat out that it wouldn't be easy; it would be intense but it could also be life changing if I chose to participate. Instinctively, I knew that this was something I had to do. It was time to confront the monster.

Before I knew it, I was sitting in a roomful of eleven other women, all of us no doubt wondering what the hell we had signed up for. We were all given the opportunity to introduce ourselves and give a brief reason why we had chosen to be here. A common theme permeated the room: we were all tired of carrying around baggage that we just couldn't seem to get rid of. It poisoned our relationships, creating feelings of hopelessness and despair. Would we ever learn to value and appreciate our individual uniqueness? Would we ever believe that we mattered? It seemed so far out of reach.

As each week came and went, I heard accounts of abuse—physical, emotional, sexual—horrific situations that made mine appear trivial. I learned, however, that wasn't what mattered. Abuse is abuse that leaves every victim struggling with how to survive, how to cope, how to heal.

I witnessed women flashback to episodes that they had endured, reverting back to little girls, reliving their nightmares. I also watched them now, as grown women, comfort that little girl, vowing to protect her, to stand up for her and telling her that she was loved and did indeed matter. It was powerful.

Then there was me—still feeling stuck, still holding on, not even knowing how to just let it go, whatever "it" was.

Around about the fifth week I sat listening to various women, one at a time, confront their abusers. For the first time they expressed how they felt and demanded the abuser to stop—all the things that they were powerless to do as little children. Somewhere in the mix, I felt myself withdraw into myself, physically trying to curl up into a little ball. Voices in the room became distant. I remember someone getting Sharon's attention, pointing out that something was happening to me.

Soon after, a primal scream erupted from the depth of my core—screams that paralyzed everyone in the room. I don't know how long it lasted but when I came back I was shaking uncontrollably, sobbing as Sharon held me, consoling me, telling me I was safe now. She told me that she believed this flashback was from something that happened to me as an infant before I had the vocabulary to express myself and was totally powerless to stop it.

When I went home that night and went to bed, I returned to that place of being frozen with fear, unable to move, unable to shake it off, remaining in this state all night, clutching my favourite stuffed animal that I had had my entire childhood.

For the remaining weeks, each night when I would come home and go to bed, I experienced the same paralyzing fear, incapacitating me throughout the entire night. I struggled to understand why and where had this irrational response come from. Then I recalled something my mother had told me many years previously. One night, when I wouldn't stop crying, she grabbed me from my crib and told me that it was all she could do not to throw me as hard as she could into the wall across the room. She attributed it to the evil force of Satan. Personally, I would say it was a result of postpartum depression, but nevertheless the episode occurred. As an infant, I would have certainly instinctively known that my life was in imminent danger.

The monster was out of the cage and I learned that it had another side to it that went hand in hand with the anger and sadness: fear. I didn't ever recall living without fear. I feared ridicule, abandonment, and rejection. Even the teachings in our church were all based on fear—believe this, do that, or be sentenced to burn in hell for all eternity. However, it was clear: my biggest fear was fear of life itself.

As Sharon had promised, the twelve weeks were indeed intense and powerful, but also liberating. It started me on the journey of learning to identify the triggers that brought out old reactions and feelings of worthlessness and shame. Naïvely, I thought, *Okay, I've dealt with my issues, declare me fixed.* That was over twenty years ago and I have learned that it never goes away. There will always be life situations that occur, bringing me back to the old archived tapes that try to convince me that I am not important, I have no value, I don't matter. But I do, and *that's* what matters.

After completing the group work, I continued to have individual sessions with Sharon, homing in on my anger and sadness. She encouraged me to journal, to just write without thinking too hard, to just let my emotions flow out on paper. In doing so I came to a realization. A lot of my self-hatred was directly tied in with my name—Frances was bad; Frances was selfish; Frances wasn't important; Frances didn't matter.

I decided that I needed to change this constant barrage of negativity that I associated with my name. Why not give myself a different name? Why not give myself a new beginning that would allow me a new start—an identity that I could create positive associations around rather than the present persistent negativity?

I discussed my idea with a few close friends who were aware of the struggles I had gone through. All of them gave me their full support and encouraged me to go for it.

Hence I went through the process of having my name legally changed to Isana and said a final farewell to Frances Marie. I never would have realized the impact that it made. I literally felt brand new.

Chapter 25

Sometimes, Prince Charming rides a white horse.
Sometimes, he lives in a castle.
Sometimes, he is the person you would least expect.
And sometimes, Prince Charming isn't a prince at all.
– Celtic Quill

Throughout the weeks that I had attended the group sessions, I had continued to run and train hard, but my focus had changed. Masters track and field gave me the opportunity to return to my first love, the track. I still had speed but not quite enough for the 400m, so I trained specifically for the 800m event. I was back in my element, thoroughly enjoying the break from long runs that were necessary for running marathon distances.

Injuries had plagued me, always seeming to occur when I was reaching my peak performance level. It was frustrating and I continued to condemn my physical limitations. However, winter training had gone well and I had had a successful indoor season.

In the spring of 1993, and as the weather continued to improve, we were able to transition back to the outdoor track. On one of our scheduled training days I teamed up with Brian, a good friend and training partner. Our workout consisted of

3 x 3 sets of 200 metres run at a pace faster than what my personal best would be for an 800m race. We were consistent, clicking off each 200m between 32–33 seconds. With only one set to go I was feeling great, pleased with the pace that I was able to maintain. The first 200m was even quicker, 31 seconds and now with only 2 remaining.

Halfway through the next 200m, I felt a twang in my left ankle, the same ankle that I had sprained numerous times. I completed the workout but it left me limping away from the track back to where I had parked my car. Having experienced similar pain before, I thought nothing of it, believing that with an easy run the next day I would be fine. I wasn't. Little did I know that that workout would be my last at a competitive level.

My coach convinced me to take a break and give it a chance to recover. I knew he was right but it pained me to sit on the sidelines calling out splits for the girls I coached, unable to join in.

Not long after, I attended a planning meeting for one of our local road races. Sue and Joe, who also volunteered on the committee, brought along information about week long bike tours that were held to raise money for multiple sclerosis. There were several states to choose from but the one that caught my attention was T.R.A.M., standing for, "The Ride Across Minnesota." It consisted of five days of biking from one side of the state to the other. Each day, a different host town would arrange an area where tents could be set up for the night along with shower facilities, entertainment and food.

I didn't have to think twice about whether or not I would go; it was a given, exactly what I needed at this time in my life. During the last few months I had slugged through murky waters, trying to make peace with personal demons. I needed a break and I was determined to go, even if it meant traveling solo.

As it worked out, Sue and Joe were excited about giving it a try, as were my close friends, Barry and Christine. Long weekend runs were replaced with long bike rides, trying to condition ourselves to the hours that we would be pedaling, confined to uncomfortable bike seats. Group T-shirts were made up clearly declaring our Canadian status and our bikes displayed both countries' national flags.

On Sunday, July 18th we met early in the morning to begin our drive to Red Wing, MN. Arrangements were made for our vehicles to be left there, while buses transported us to Ortonville for the start of the ride. The air was electric with anticipation. Many riders that we spoke with had ridden in the tour previous years and their excitement of being back was contagious.

Imagine approximately 1600 riders setting up tents in a field large enough to accommodate all of us; no wonder it became known as tent city.

Registration packets contained our own personal ID numbers that we attached to our luggage and bikes. During the day, trucks transported our belongings to the next host town where volunteers unloaded and laid them out in numerical order. Bikes were left in secure compounds leaving us with no worry of them being stolen. The organization was flawless.

I will never forget the experience of our first night in the tent city. The night air amplified the chorus of people snoring at every level of intensity, accompanied by tent zippers going up and down from people needing to use the facilities. It wasn't the Hilton by any measure but at the same time it became like a large extended family—all there for the same purpose but each having to overlook and accept our diversities.

On Monday, our first day of riding, people began to stir around 5:00 a.m. I was wide awake, anxious to get going, frustrated with having to wait for my travel companions who were not as keen about such an early start. By the time we did get going, it was well after 9:00 a.m. and adrenalin was demanding my body to switch gears. Finally, I told my group that I would go ahead and save us tent spots in Montevideo, the next host town. They readily agreed, no doubt sensing my frustration with the slower pace. With that I was gone, feeling like a racehorse given free rein, not impelled to hold anything back.

The phrase "on your left" became part of my new vocabulary as I cruised past slower cyclists. The routes were planned to take us along secondary country roads that encompassed minimal traffic. Volunteer motorcyclists also rode the route ensuring that everyone was okay and if not, responding to whatever the rider needed.

I breathed in all the smells of the fresh open air, riding past ditches abundant with wildflowers, observing row upon row of the notorious Minnesota cornfields and acres of giant sunflowers, all steering their faces into the brilliant rays of the sun. It left me feeling more alive and free than ever before.

Since leaving Dan, and my subsequent struggle to resolve what life had dealt me, I was also trying to come to terms with living as a single person. I didn't want to be alone. I was lonely, craving companionship and that someone special to share my life with. I battled my old beliefs of being unlovable, tainted, unworthy of true love. Now, as I rode, I felt the warmth of the sun oozing through the muck and negativity, replacing it with hope that I really did deserve more. It was indeed a breakthrough; I had allowed myself to believe.

The five-day tour consisted of approximately 300 miles (483 km), making up the distance from one side of the state to the other. As I closed in on the sixty-six mile (106 km) ride to Montevideo, I was overwhelmed with the support from the town's residents. People cheered us on, visibly moved that we were riding for a good cause, the fight against multiple sclerosis. Personally, I felt like I should be the one thanking them.

As I had promised my friends, I located three great tent spots in the middle of a large baseball field that would soon be filled with the colourful displays of hundreds of tents, both large and small. I soon learned that it paid to get in early as the lineup for the showers grew increasingly longer as the afternoon wore on.

Volunteers had also constructed a large beer garden, a perfect remedy to replenish all those lost electrolytes from the physical exertion. As I relished each sip of the refreshing, ice-cold beer, I heard a voice behind me say, "Canada, eh?" I turned, realizing that the tall gentleman was talking to me. He introduced himself as Gary, and conversation between us was easy, his soft brown eyes captivating me. I learned that he was from Montevideo but was also riding in the T.R.A.M. as part of a challenge amongst a few of his friends.

All too soon he had to be on his way and I had to try to locate my group. As I wandered through the maze of bone-weary cyclists, I couldn't get Gary out of my mind. Inwardly, I chastised myself for thinking that our conversation could possibly lead to anything else. *It was just a conversation, so leave it at that,* I told myself. Besides, the chances of running into him again with 1600 cyclists milling around was remote.

Not long after, I located my friends and we all talked about our experiences of Day 1. It had been pleasantly positive for all of us and a snack of fresh, sweet Minnesota corn brought the day to a perfect end. I crawled into my tent, content and eager for the next day's ride to Redwood Falls. As I began to doze off, I entertained whimsical thoughts that maybe, just maybe, Gary and I would cross paths once again.

The next morning, I again woke early to the sounds of hushed whispers and the steady drone of tent zippers releasing their occupants into the damp morning air. My four companions wanted nothing to do with my early start, so we agreed that I would go ahead and reserve our tent spots as I had done the previous day.

I was on the road by 6:00 a.m., the sun just beginning to illuminate the horizon with shades of orange, reds, and pinks dissolving the darkness. Many had started earlier than myself, but I was still able to relish the solitude of the road and the refreshing cool morning air as I settled into a comfortable pace. Today's ride would be slightly shorter than yesterday's and I was eagerly anticipating each segment of the ride. Every ten miles or so, rest stops were set up by local volunteers, each abundant with fresh fruit, homemade baking, ice cream—you name it—all at no cost to the riders. Some of the stops along the way even provided us with the flavour of local entertainment. I was inspired by the friendliness, generosity, and hard work of the hundreds of volunteers that were required to make this event possible. They were amazing, wonderful people.

I stopped at one rest stop and listened to a group of seniors playing wind and stringed instruments. It didn't matter that they were off key; it was just delightful to feel their enthusiasm. As I stood there taking it in, I felt a tap on my shoulder, and suddenly there he was: Gary, smiling broadly and asking how my day was going. My heart leapt and I struggled to keep my composure without looking too dumbfounded at this stroke of luck.

We talked and he asked me if I was going to go to the live band entertainment planned for us in Redwood Falls. I replied, telling him that I would be there along with my four other Canadian counterparts. He promised me that he would have something for us but I would be given first pick. With that he sauntered off to try to locate a member of his group that had fallen behind.

I got back on my bike feeling giddy, elated, recalling his words and wondering what he had for us. In giving me first pick did it mean that he was also feeling something between us, or was I just reading too much into it? I was beside myself with anticipation of what was to come, considering our chance encounter amidst the throngs of people.

I cruised into Redwood Falls, again moved by the display of flags and people welcoming us to their town. A large, grassy field had been prepared for our arrival and it was easy to find comfortable spots to set up our tents.

Barry and Christine arrived first. I eagerly told them about this guy that I had met and that he had something for us Canadians. They too were intrigued and eager to meet him.

The band set up in the town square with streets closed to traffic. With the tent city located only a few blocks away, it provided us with easy access to walk to the site. I couldn't help but search the crowd for the mystery man, hoping that he hadn't changed his mind about coming. Soon after, the band started up and people eagerly began to dance in the streets to the old familiar tunes.

The sun was starting to set around about the time that we spotted each other. He strode over, again flashing his infectious smile. Introductions were made and the conversation turned to the fact that we had come to the T.R.A.M. all the way from Canada. As a token of appreciation, he had brought us all T-shirts with various Montevideo logos. As promised, I got first pick of what logo and colour I preferred. Gary left to go and buy us all a round of local draught beer, and as soon as he was out of earshot, Christine and Sue quickly commented on his good looks and that they thought he really did like me. Not that I needed their encouragement—I could feel myself falling for this man who I had just barely met. He returned with our drinks, and we continued to talk while my friends inconspicuously wandered off to leave us by ourselves.

Sooner than I would have liked, the band called it a night. During our earlier conversation, Gary had told me that he had opted to stay in motels each night rather than tenting it; he wanted the comfort of a bed over the hard ground. Now that it was time for me to head back, he offered to walk me home so I wouldn't have to walk alone in the dark. As we walked his hand found mine; my heart leapt and I fervently hoped that my hand wouldn't break out in a nervous sweat. He told me that in our next night's stay in New Ulm, he was familiar with a really good German restaurant, and asked if I would care to join him for supper. He didn't have to ask twice! I readily agreed and told him that would be great.

We reached the edge of the field where the tents were set up and I again thanked him for the T-shirts and for walking me back. He kissed me lightly on the forehead and told me that he would see me tomorrow. I turned to walk towards my tent and, looking into the star-filled sky, the full moon shone down like a giant spotlight illuminating the ground in front of me. I was overcome with what had transpired and I knew I was on the brink of falling really hard for this guy. Inwardly, I begged God, or whoever would listen, *If it isn't meant to be, please don't let it progress any further.* However, I knew in my gut that this request was a little late. I believed that I had truly found my Prince Charming who had come to rescue me from my lonely existence.

Chapter 26

Dream: I was with Gary and a group of others that we had met in a bar. I had tried so hard to save our relationship and now, here we were, together at last. But then, he begins to drift away and I struggle to pull him back, pleading for him to stay.

The remainder of the week flew by. Each day following the ride we were together, talking over cold beer; me divulging my personal history of what I had gone through. I told him of the sexual abuse. I told him about Dan and why I had to leave him. I went on and on, him listening attentively and telling me that he would never treat me that way. I believed him.

On the day of our last ride into Red Wing, we decided as a group that we would ride it in together. Gary also joined us as we pedaled our way to the finish of the tour. It was emotional, not only from the crowds cheering and applauding our accomplishment but also that my time with Gary was coming to an end.

In the early stages of planning to attend T.R.A.M., we had decided that after the tour we would spend a couple of nights in the River District of Minneapolis—an area that offered great restaurants and live entertainment. Gary asked where we were staying and then out of the blue asked me if I would mind him joining us the next day and staying until we left for home on Sunday. I was overjoyed.

So began our long-distance relationship. In the early stage, he would call me unexpectedly, proposing that we meet in various destinations for the weekend. Even if I already had plans, I would cancel whatever it was; I only wanted to be with Gary.

We were seeing each other every couple of weeks, sometimes more. He introduced me to the Renaissance Festival held in Shakopee, MN; we went tubing down the Apple River in Wisconsin; we ate at various eateries and pubs, drinking numerous samples of locally brewed draught beer. Labour Day weekend was spent, along with another couple, at his lakefront cottage. With the start-up of school, I was back to coaching the university girls' cross-country team and he, back to teaching and coaching his school's teams. I would meet up with him at some of his meets and he with me at some of mine. I never tired of the long drives to our designated spots. I just wanted to be with Gary.

In October, I convinced him to spend our Canadian Thanksgiving weekend with me. I hosted a party, inviting my friends from T.R.A.M. along with others who I wanted him to meet.

The more time we spent together, the more I tried to express how I was feeling towards him, hoping for a similar response. But every time I broached the subject he would steer the conversation away to something else, obviously uncomfortable. When it came time for us to say goodbye, I struggled. I wanted to be together—permanently. He, on the other hand, only seemed interested in connecting sporadically, more according to his schedule than mine.

In November, the weekend of my birthday, we arranged to meet in Minneapolis. I was so excited to be able to spend it with him and couldn't help wondering what he would surprise me with. Of course I never brought it up, as there was no need to. He already knew that it was my birthday. The surprise never happened. Before I knew it we were again saying our goodbyes, him nonchalantly and me trying to pretend that it was no big deal.

I drove home trying to numb out and deny the hurt. My friends at home were eager to know what he had gotten me. It embarrassed me to have to tell them, "Nothing." The next night he called, pretending that it had slipped his mind, but went on to explain that he only bought birthday gifts for his mother. My reply? "That's okay, Gary, I don't mind." Who was I kidding?

A couple of weeks later, we met for the American Thanksgiving weekend near Giants Ridge golf resort in Biwabik, MN. Snow had come early this year and the cross-country trails were superb. Again, I brought up the subject of wanting to plan ahead for when we could meet up, even expressing that I needed longer stretches of time with him. As soon as I said it, I knew I had overstepped what he wanted to hear. His facial expression changed as well as his body language. It was too late to undo what I had said and I desperately didn't want to acknowledge to myself the reaction that I had seen.

Christmas was approaching, and in earlier discussions he had agreed to spend it with me. My workplace was closed during the Christmas break so we potentially had ten days that we could be together. Finally, a Christmas that I didn't have to spend alone feeling like odd man out. But that was about to change.

About a week before he was supposed to arrive he called me, just after I had gone to bed, stating that something had come up and he wouldn't be able to come for Christmas. Feelings of disappointment, hurt, and rejection swept over me and I didn't want to believe what I had just heard. I struggled to compose myself, tentatively asking him what had come up. Bracing myself for his response, he replied that a former student who had confided in him years earlier had contacted him. He went on, saying that she was going through a really rough time and was even contemplating suicide; consequently he needed to be there for her. He also mentioned that his sister's husband had terminal cancer and that he might have to fly to Alberta to see him—maybe for the last time.

To top it off he dealt me his final blow. He had met a woman named Pat at a party who had asked him if he was still seeing "the Canadian." Apparently her interest in him (and his in her) had him confused about our relationship. His words were a dagger, cutting me to the core. Pathetically, I still replied, "That's okay, take your time, I understand."

The conversation soon ended with me trying to convince him to reconsider and even come for just a few days so that we could try to sort things out. He said he would see what he could do. After hanging up, waves of nausea swept over me, leaving me exhausted, crushed, empty, desperately wishing that I would wake up and realize that it was just a bad dream. But it wasn't; it was very real.

A few days later, I received a package from him in the mail. Its contents included a letter and a newspaper article about men over forty who have difficulty committing to a relationship. In his letter he told me how busy he was going to be come the New Year. He even included a list of all his priorities: his ailing parents; his sister and brother-in-law; his yearly snow machine rendezvous with his buddies; school obligations; coaching, etc. etc. One item that was curiously missing from his list was very apparent—*me.* However, I still held out hope that this would blow over and I would have my fairytale ending. After all, it was meant to be, wasn't it?

All through the holidays I waited for his call, determined not to call him. Besides, he had told me that he would be going to Alberta due to the condition of his brother-in-law. At least that's what I tried hard to believe.

Christmas came and went, and before I knew it, 1994 was ushered in. Surely he would call now to at least wish me a happy new year—right? He didn't. A few days later I gave in and called him, feeling that anything was better than this deafening silence. I tried to be nonchalant, asking if he had a good Christmas and how his brother-in-law was faring. He didn't go into any details other than to say that he had been really busy—so busy that he just hadn't had time to call. I asked him if there was any chance of us seeing each other sometime in January; he didn't think so since every weekend he had obligations, and even February didn't look any better.

I was devastated. What had happened? We had had such fun and were so compatible. How could he *not* want to be together? I refused to believe that we were over. He had never said so, and in fact would intersperse comments that indicated we would get together, but that now was just a really busy time. It was enough to keep me hooked.

Friends tried to convince me to move on, to let him go, but I couldn't. I believed that fate had brought us together and we were meant to be. I refused to believe that I had been duped again.

All through February I waited for the call that never came. We were well into March when I came up with a plan. Why not drive to Montevideo and surprise him with "Hi, I'm here, let's talk." And so I did. I left early on a Sunday morning, arriving mid-afternoon. I had no idea if he would even be home, but I was certain that he would have to be at school for the next day. The entire way there my thoughts raced ahead, anticipating the sound of his voice, hoping that we could pick up where we left off, hoping for my fairytale ending, not imagining that it could end any other way.

I checked into a motel on the outskirts of town and decided to stay for two nights. My heart was in my throat as I dialed the familiar number, hoping that Gary would answer and not Bruce, his landlord. No such luck. Bruce told me that Gary had gone to the Cities (Minneapolis/St. Paul) for the weekend but would be back around suppertime. He asked if I wanted to leave a message but I simply replied that I would call back later, hoping that he didn't know who was calling.

For the next few hours I drove around Montevideo, going back to the park where we had first met; finding the school where he taught; looking for his familiar vehicle; reminiscing about the good times that we had shared.

To help pass the time I found a small diner on the main street. As I walked towards a table, men seated at the counter stared at me. People here knew each other and I was obviously not from these parts, especially with my car parked outside bearing Canadian plates. I tried to be as inconspicuous as possible, hoping that no one would try to strike up a conversation.

A newspaper had been left behind where I was seated so I casually leafed through it. For fun I sought out my horoscope, hoping that it would be along the lines of rekindled love in the air. It was anything but—rather it was a warning to stay clear of the relationship I was pursuing as it would only end in hurt. I shrugged it off but in retrospect I should have listened.

A short while later I returned to my room, ready to try calling again. My lines were rehearsed, but that didn't help alleviate my sweaty palms as I dialed his number. This time he answered. Without hesitating I told him I was here, in Montevideo, specifically to see him. He asked where I was, almost with a trace of panic in his voice as he had most certainly been caught off guard. I told him which motel and he replied that he would be there in a few minutes. I hung up, not believing that in just moments he would be walking through the door.

Then, there he was. The Gary I had fallen so hard for. We hugged, and he said it was good to see me but that I certainly had surprised him. I told him why I had come, that I needed answers; I needed to know where we were at. Why the silence, why the change? And most importantly, were we over? He thought for a moment and then replied, stating that he had certainly been a jerk in the way he had treated me. Furthermore, he had thought about calling but figured that I wouldn't want anything to do with him because of his behaviour. We talked for a good while and I even asked him if he had gone to Alberta at Christmas. Sheepishly, he said that he hadn't—in fact he hadn't gone anywhere, needing to take the time to be alone and just relax. His words stung but I pretended to understand, negating my true feelings.

It was getting late and he had to be up early for school. He said that he couldn't stay—people would recognize his vehicle; people would talk and as a teacher he had to protect his reputation. However, he assured me that he would pick me up the next day at 5:00 p.m. and would take me to a town nearby for supper. He said that the theatre there was playing the sequel to *Grumpy Old Men*—fitting, since we had seen the first one together.

He left and for a moment I considered following him, curious to see where he lived. Why had he kept me from ever visiting him? I didn't have an answer.

My sleep was restless, with me tossing and turning like a fish out of water. My intuition screamed at me to pay attention, but my need to keep our relationship alive and believe what he was telling me stifled out reason. The debate between the two lasted the entire night, only ending as daylight appeared through the opening in the curtains.

It was a long day, and the hours dragged. Again I drove to the park where we had met and decided to write Gary a letter, detailing the good times, expressing the hurt when I didn't hear from him, and hoping that somehow we could pick up where we had left off.

As promised, he arrived at 5:00 p.m. sharp, eager to leave and drive to the next town. I told him that I had written thoughts down that I wanted him to read—it was important. He said that he would, after the movie was over. Our conversation remained at a superficial level, him averting the direction of discussion when it came too close to us.

During the movie my mind was elsewhere. I just wanted to be alone with Gary, talking, resolving, getting answers to the missing pieces—we were running out of time and it felt like the movie was just his way to further delay and avoid talking.

It was close to 10:00 p.m. by the time we got back to the motel. He came in and read what I had written, commenting briefly on some of what I had expressed. Finally, I asked him the question that was ever present: "Are we over?"

He replied that he did want to start over, to go slowly, even to communicate the old-fashioned way—write each other letters. It wasn't exactly what I wanted to hear but it was a start; he had given me hope. Undoubtedly it would be hard to take a step back, but I was willing to do anything to hang onto the belief that one day we would be together.

Again, he said he couldn't stay, but offered to meet me for breakfast before school and before I headed for home. At least I had that to look forward to, come morning. But for now I was exhausted, not only from lack of sleep but the emotional drain of the uncertainty of our relationship. I tried to comfort myself before falling into a troubled sleep that we weren't over; he had said so. I just needed to be patient until he came around and realized that what we had was worth salvaging.

In the morning I packed up, paid for my room, and drove to where we had agreed to meet for breakfast. He had just arrived and was making his way to a table where I joined him. There were other teachers there and I was feeling awkward and uncomfortable, wishing that it could have been just the two of us.

I had no idea when we would see each other again, assuming that would be decided in our exchange of letters. It was so hard not to have something concrete—a date and time that I could look forward to—but nothing was mentioned and I wasn't going to ask.

Sooner than I wanted, he was paying for our breakfast; it was time for him to go to school and time for me to head home. As we reached our vehicles, I hugged him, pulling him in close, but it wasn't reciprocated. He seemed embarrassed and even commented that he didn't want to have to explain me to his cohorts. Ouch.

We drove out of the parking lot, me following him until we reached a fork in the road, him going to the right and me to the left. I watched his vehicle go up the road until it was out of sight and I continued on, overcome with emotion, tears welling up and spilling over as I tried to wipe them away so I could see the road in front of me.

I didn't know then that this would be the last time I ever saw Gary. I wrote him letters, as he had suggested, but never a reply. For months I held out hope, eagerly anticipating each day's mail delivery—but nothing, only the flood of disappointment, confusion, and hurt. Even Boomer sensed my sadness, staying close as I soaked his thick black fur with my tears.

Finally, I stopped writing; there was no point and I had nothing left to say. At Christmas I decided to send him a final farewell, stating only this: "I wish you peace."

This segment of my life transpired nearly twenty years ago but the emotions of what I went through feels like yesterday. For many years I asked myself a million times, "What happened?" I will never have a clear answer to that question; moreover, I came to realize that I didn't need to know. What I *did* need to understand was why I had accepted the way he had treated me and why I had continued to set myself up for more hurt, over and over again.

Hindsight has been my teacher. I had put all my eggs in one basket, making him the centre of my existence. I shared very personal things about myself, trusting, without ever testing him to see if he was indeed trustworthy. I refused to examine the abundance of red flags that he clearly displayed, ignoring my intuition and gut feeling. I refused to acknowledge the components of what I wanted in our relationship, downplaying my needs and putting the importance instead on what he wanted (or didn't want!).

Sadly, this relationship was another mere reflection of ones gone before: painful and life changing. But this time it was different. Never again would I so naïvely refuse to examine one's behaviour towards me. The mistakes that I had made became glaringly clear.

A few years after this relationship ended I had a reading with a renowned psychic. Near the end I was given opportunity to ask questions, so I asked her, "What about Gary? Whatever happened there?"

Her quick reply left me speechless: "My dear," she replied, "he was gay."

Indeed, my last words to him were more relevant than I realized at the time, and I can only hope that he did find peace.

Chapter 27

You can't lose what you don't have
and you can't find what you don't look for;
sometimes life is not about you waiting for something to come
but you moving towards what was waiting for you.
– Blaze Olamiday

I had continued to persevere with my running but to no avail. In spite of weekly therapy sessions, cutting back on mileage and speed workouts, my ankle had had enough; it was simply not responding. My workouts were reduced to biking, swimming, and pool running. Finally, in the early summer of 1994, my doctor determined it was time to refer me to an orthopedic surgeon.

Tests and x-rays were conducted, followed up by a consultation with the surgeon. He explained that due to the number of sprains my ankle had sustained, the support of tendons and ligaments were no longer holding the joint in place. Hence the only remedy was surgery—a method that would reconstruct the tendons and ligaments in a way that would give the joint the stability it needed. There was no other option.

I, along with Barry and Christine, Sue and Joe, had already determined that we were going to ride again in T.R.A.M., scheduled for the third week of July. Thankfully, the surgery would not take place until I was back from T.R.A.M.

As we prepared, meeting on weekends for our long rides, I couldn't help but think of Gary. Would he be back, and if so, how would I react if I saw him? Part of me hoped that would happen, but inwardly I knew that he wouldn't be back; after what had transpired he would be certain to avoid me. This year the ride would take a different route along with new host towns. I hoped that would be enough to block out the events of last year.

Before we knew it we were under way, our vehicles packed with bikes and gear. This year we were better prepared, knowing what to expect but still just as excited for the ride to begin.

I had been right: there was no sign of Gary. As it turned out, there was a street dance held the night before our first ride. The music was great, inspiring the crowd to dance to the familiar songs. A gentleman approached me, asking if I wanted to dance, and of course I eagerly agreed. Soon after I introduced Bill to my friends, and Christine's response was priceless: she rolled her eyes and under her breath stated, "Oh no, not again!"

Bill was from Minneapolis and I later found out that he was recently separated. He treated me well and we hit it off, even making plans to see each other after T.R.A.M. was over.

My surgery took place the first week of August. It had gone well, but for the first few weeks it was imperative that I refrain from putting any weight on it; hence I was introduced to my new mode of transportation—a wheelchair.

I soon gained a whole new appreciation for people with disabilities. Just to have a door held open for you can make all the difference; never again did I take my mobility for granted—it is precarious at best.

During this time, Bill took time off work to come and see me for a few days. We had talked earlier and I had expressed that I didn't want to remain single forever, hoping that someday

I would meet the right person. However, I was not prepared for the gift bag that he presented me with. One item was perfume, but it didn't take much to figure out what was in the next little box. Had I missed something? My heart was in my throat, fervently hoping that I would not find myself staring at a diamond ring. As I gingerly opened the lid, I discovered it was indeed a ring, but thankfully only that.

In spite of my relief, I had a sense of unease that he was reading more into our relationship than what I was intending, moving things along faster than what I was prepared for or even wanted. It was triggering old memories of being trapped, unable to say no or to make it stop. I shrugged it off, convincing myself that I did actually have control over what I chose or chose not to do.

After I graduated from the wheelchair I moved on to crutches, becoming quite creative in maneuvering around on one leg and carrying whatever I needed in a bag strung around my neck. Boomer, on the other hand, didn't know what to make of it all, often staring at me with his quizzical, wondering eyes. Thankfully, my friend Ed would routinely come by and take him along on his runs, both of them glad for the company.

Once I was able to drive again, Bill invited me to come and see him at his home in Minneapolis, and I agreed. We had a good time and I was able to meet several of his friends.

However, in listening to some of his conversations, I did pick up that he had gone through a rough time after his wife left him, more so than what he had let on to me. At one of the parties we attended, the minister of Bill's church was also there. Offhandedly he cautioned me to be careful with his heart, intimating that he was more fragile than I realized. I took note of his words, although I did find it a little puzzling: I was having fun with no intention of hurting anyone. Perhaps his minister friend had picked up on something that even I was not aware of.

On Sunday, I left Bill's in the late morning, having to be back for an office farewell party for Nick, my boss of almost six years. He had announced several weeks earlier that he would be retiring at the end of the summer.

Over the years, a very strong friendship had formed both on and off the job with three of my co-workers. We had many discussions about who would be picked to replace Nick, unanimously hoping and praying it wouldn't be Paul. We had dealt with him on other occasions and I found him to be manipulative and condescending, especially towards women. Frankly, he made my skin crawl.

When it was finally announced who our new director would be, my heart sank; it was Paul. Our casual, fun, and relaxed office atmosphere was in for a major alteration, never to be the same again.

Paul was also going to be at Nick's party to meet us and welcome himself aboard. When I arrived, most of my co-workers had already assembled, ready for the party to begin. Boisterously, I made my entry, hopping my way in with crutches, cast and all, still hyped from my weekend road trip, proclaiming that it was "beer time!" I looked for where my cohorts were seated and saw that they were desperately trying to refrain from breaking out in laughter, totally amused at my entrance. It felt like I had just barged into the middle of a church service. What hadn't I been told?

People appeared to be very uncomfortable in not knowing how to make conversation with Paul. He, in turn, was not making any attempt himself at conversation. He sat off to the side, sometimes conversing with Nick, but for the most part quietly analyzing each of us to determine who would soon be under his regime. I was doomed from the start.

Other areas in my life, besides my workplace, were also undergoing revision. The uncertainty of where I stood with Gary during those first few months of 1994 had left me heartbroken and angry. Consequently, close friends sometimes bore the brunt of it, Val being one of them.

I had depended on her and she had been there, helping me cope as I trudged through my unresolved issues. Once, she had even assured me that the only thing that would ruin our friendship would be if I harmed her children; she had never given me any reason to believe our friendship would end otherwise.

She, her common-law partner, and her two children were my extended family, the people with whom I celebrated holidays and special occasions.

I don't recall the details, but I do know that sometime in the fall we were at a gathering and I had reacted negatively to something she had said. I wasn't aware that I had struck a chord that deeply resonated with her.

A day or two later I found a letter from her in my mailbox. It was a few pages in length, but the underlying message was that she was done and would no longer be the recipient of my inner hostility. We had gone through a lot together and I was confident that we would be able to talk it over and resolve the issue. Unfortunately, it didn't happen, and she stopped calling. Once again I felt the shame of being the bad girl—now being rejected and punished for slipping up, for making a mistake.

I was hurt, unable to comprehend that she, of all people, would turn her back on me. It was a hard pill to swallow. A few times when I had the opportunity to speak to her alone I tried to discuss it, to understand why, but the conversation would end or be steered in another direction.

Her circle of friends changed and eventually our lives took different paths. Although it hurt tremendously to lose her friendship, I will be forever grateful for her support when I needed it the most. Maybe we just outgrew each other and it was after all, time to move on.

As anticipated, our work environment changed dramatically. Instead of looking forward to going to work, I dreaded it. Paul's team approach was anything but: what Paul wanted, Paul got. I found his treatment of women—especially those in positions of authority—deplorable. He belittled, criticized, and humiliated them in front of peers. I watched him turn women who were confident, efficient, and skilled workers into nervous wrecks, never knowing what bombshell he would surprise them with next.

Part of my job was to process internal expense reports, coding expenditures to the proper accounts. In my opinion, Paul claimed expenses (such as mileage from one destination to another) that were not legitimate, but he was not to be questioned.

My colleagues and I leaned on one another for support, each of us trying to cope in our own way, all of us hoping that we wouldn't become his next target. They were better at diplomacy when it came to dealing with Paul than I was and I refused to bestow any graciousness towards him. I despised him and he knew it. I also knew that, because of this, he would ensure that my life at work would become as miserable as possible. It was only a matter of time, and time was on his side, not mine.

I struggled, not knowing how long I could tolerate working for someone who I had zero respect for, someone who so abused his position of authority, reveling in his ideology of power. He was indeed the bully of the schoolyard.

During this turmoil, I discovered that our local police department was initiating a new hiring process, one that had been provincially designed for municipal departments. Interested candidates were encouraged to apply.

I thought back, remembering that I had applied to be a police officer in 1980. In those days there were height and weight restrictions: women had to be 5'6" or taller and men had to weigh a minimum of 160 lbs. I was one inch too short. That was then, but now those restrictions had long been lifted and no longer applied.

Come November, I would be thirty-eight years of age. Did I want to leave the comfort zone of a job that I knew (albeit the issue of Paul) to that of an entirely different career that would undoubtedly have its share of challenges? If accepted, I would also have to attend police college, and the idea of going back to school frightened the hell out of me. I was torn between my options.

After lengthy discussion with my three co-workers and close friends, I made my decision to go for it. After all, the chances of being accepted were remote at best (so I thought) but if I let the opportunity slip by I knew I would always ask myself, *What if?* I had nothing to lose.

All of this was kept from Paul's knowledge in the event that nothing transpired from my application. However, just knowing there was the possibility of getting out from under Paul's dictatorship made coming to work a little easier.

Bill and I continued to communicate both by phone and letters when we weren't together, but I was beginning to have serious doubts about our relationship. He agreed with everything I said, never expressing a different opinion or alternative way of thinking. Inwardly, I questioned if he even had his own opinion, or was he just afraid of being rejected for disagreeing? Quite simply, it just didn't feel right.

On his final visit to me later in the fall, he probably sensed me pulling away from him. He grasped at straws to keep us connected, but I knew it was not going to work between us. Shortly after his departure, my "Dear John" letter was sent, attempting to explain my misgivings, encouraging him to spend some time without being involved in a relationship, and to reflect on what he needed as an individual.

He had believed that our relationship would become permanent, so I know my words hurt him, but I had to listen to my heart; he was not going to be part of the equation. I did find out sometime later through a mutual acquaintance that he had re-married. I sincerely hope that he was able to find the happiness and love that he deserved.

In late November, I received notice that my application for the police department had been accepted, but this was only the beginning. The hiring process consisted of five stages, and it was made clear that each applicant would be notified by phone if they were to move on.

Stage 1 consisted of multiple choice questions meant to analyze personality types and suitability for the profession. I quickly discovered that I wasn't alone in my quest to be hired. Over 750 candidates nervously waited for permission to begin answering the hundreds of questions put before us. I looked out over the sea of faces, my hope fading. Really, what were my chances out of so many applicants?

I was in disbelief when a few weeks later I received a phone call stating that I had successfully passed Stage 1 and was moving on to Stage 2. I could hardly believe what I was hearing!

In the beginning, I found it easier not to get too caught up in waiting for the call, but as I continued to pass each stage, the more nervous I became and the more I wanted to make it all the way. My competitive nature was sparked, to say the least.

One of the later stages was a series of physical fitness tests, for me a breeze except for one component—the 1.5 mile run. Since my surgery in August I had not run one step, determined to give it the time it needed to heal. It was ironic that the one category that was second nature to me was now an area of concern. Could I physically even perform the task?

Shortly before I was scheduled to run, my physiotherapist taped up my ankle, hoping it would provide me with the extra support I would need to run the distance. My heart was in my throat as I paced, waiting for the all-too-familiar command, "Runners, take your mark!"

It was by no means a blistering pace, but it was enough to still earn me a gold ranking for my age group. I had done it and I was elated.

After enduring six months of testing and interviews, the call that I had been anticipating and hoping for came through: I had successfully completed all five stages and had been chosen as a candidate. It was official! I was about to engage in an entirely new chapter in my life as a police officer.

The support I received from friends and my close co-workers was enormous; they couldn't have been happier for me. I will never forget the feeling when I dropped my letter of resignation on Paul's desk. I felt vindicated and free, free of him and his abuse of authority towards those under him.

If I had known then what lay ahead, my enthusiasm would have been squelched. Little did I know I was entering an environment filled with many who were the likes of Paul—so much so, in fact, that he paled in comparison. There was no going back. My life had changed course.

PART V

Chapter 28

If your nerve deny you – go above your nerve.
– Emily Dickinson

I had been informed that my official starting date would be July 4, 1995, but until then I could relish my final four weeks of paid vacation from my former job.

Earlier, I had received word that my niece was getting married in June and I was invited to attend. Unfortunately for her it wasn't under ideal circumstances, being that she was pregnant. Growing up she had been taught that sex before marriage was taboo, so I could only imagine the shame and guilt that she would have been burdened with. Undoubtedly, she would need all the support she could get.

I was faced with hard questions: Was I ready to face my entire family? Could I be in the company of my parents and older brother Karl without reverting back and succumbing to the power that they had held over me as a child? Would I be able to establish the boundaries necessary to protect that inner little girl from being hurt and victimized again?

Ron and his family would be there, also for the purpose of supporting our niece. I discussed my uncertainties with Ron; he understood perfectly where I was coming from. He too had to remind himself when in their presence that he was an adult who had the right to voice his opinion and maintain the integrity of his true self. Knowing that he would have my back if circumstances required it, I agreed to go. It was time to face my biggest fear—the family.

There was no question that I would need to stay in a safe place away from them—a place where I could regroup and breathe easy. Ron and Diane had discovered such a place located only a few miles from where the wedding would be held: small cabins right on the lake. It was perfect.

As I began the drive, with each mile bringing me closer, I felt like I was gearing up for a major competition: them versus me. I had to win. I not only owed it to the little girl that had grown up never feeling adequate, I owed it to myself to attest to all the hard work I had put in to unravel my sordid past.

The last time I had seen my parents was in 1981 when we had met with Larry and I had made it clear that I did not want them to contact me. As for Karl, I had not seen him since 1978, the day I got married. He had attempted to meet with me when he took his sons on a road trip but I had refused; I was not ready to deal with him and the issues surrounding us.

I had rehearsed repeatedly to myself how I would play out the initial greeting with them. As a child, I was not given the right to refuse the clenching embraces from my mother and the slobbery kisses from my father. That was then, but now *I* was in control, determined to protect my personal space.

Before I knew it, it was show time and we were walking through the door into my sister's house where they were all gathered. It began, just as I knew it would, only this time I controlled the outcome: a handshake sufficed in spite of their advances. Karl barely recognized me and in disbelief he stated, "Frances, I mean, Isana?" Without any hesitation I confirmed it, replying, "Yup, that would be me."

Round one was over and I felt the applause and gratitude of one little girl. This time, I hadn't let her down.

During the course of my time there, I relayed to them what would soon be my new career. There was an apparent lack of enthusiasm so I could only surmise that my mother especially was horrified that her daughter had pursued what was traditionally a man's job. I decided to drop the discussion; it was wiser to just let it go.

At one point I found myself observing Karl, strangely unattached to any feelings towards him. Who was he anyway? I had no idea. The interaction that we had encountered as children felt like a lifetime ago. I recalled that his mannerisms seemed familiar but it was also glaringly clear that neither of us had any clue as to who we had each become. I was content to leave it at that. Clearly, we were worlds apart.

The wedding took place as planned and I wished my niece and her new husband well. They seemed so young!

At the end of the reception I was eager to return to the solitude of the cabins. I had had my fill of the all too familiar family dynamics, needing to assure myself that I was okay; I was a good person and I did matter. Ron and Diane were also ready to retreat so we decided to take our leave. Goodbyes were made and I again succeeded in maintaining the safety of my personal space.

On my drive home the next morning, I reflected on the past few days. Having not lived my experience one might consider my actions hard to understand, even possibly perceived as callous and cold. But for me it was imperative that I reclaim what I had never had: the right to say *no*, the right to have a voice. Finally, I had given myself permission to take care of *me*, which ultimately was what mattered the most.

My remaining days of freedom passed quickly bringing me to the eve of a new life. Uncertainties, mixed with excitement, bombarded my thoughts as I tried to fall asleep. It was a restless night and I was wide awake long before I needed to be.

Before leaving I gave Boomer a big hug, asking for him to wish me luck.

There were nine of us, all nervously seated around a table, name tags in front of us identifying who we were, each of us processing our first impressions of the other.

For the next month we would be involved with in-service training that was designed to give us an overview of what our job would entail. For the last month, each of us would be assigned to the unit that we would be joining upon completion of our thirteen weeks at Police College. Our role would be that of a ride-along, intended for us to simply observe how officers handled the various calls. It would also be my introduction to the midnight shift.

Each day progressed to the next and before we knew it our first month of training was completed. A few of us in the group had gelled, and at quitting time on Fridays, we celebrated our survival of another week over a few jugs of cold draught beer. This would now come to an end as we had all been assigned to our different units. I was going to a unit that worked the north side of the city and I was excited to hear that my friend Tracey, a police officer for several years, was also on this unit. We had run together for many years so I was certain that she would be very supportive and I would be able to rely on her for advice that I would undoubtedly require.

I joined up with the unit as they began their dayshift rotation comprised of six eight-hour shifts, 0800–1600 hours. Following days were afternoons, 1600–2400 hours, and lastly the inevitable midnights, 0000–0800 hours.

The unit was a mixture of relatively young officers up to those who were close to retirement. Before each oncoming shift, officers were required to attend briefing—a time when updates and other pertinent information was relayed before going on duty. I sat at the back of the room close to the doors as officers shuffled in. A few acknowledged my presence, but for the most part I was met with blank stares. The unit's sergeant welcomed me aboard and announced that I would be riding with Wayne, whose expression clearly proclaimed he was not impressed. He was young, appeared to be rather hyper and, in my opinion, full of himself. As we headed towards our area it didn't take long for him to vocalize his negative view of the hiring process that we had undergone. He expressed his opposition to the hiring of older females, stating that they were taking away positions from those who could put in a full thirty years service. He also verbalized his belief that they had no idea of the physical confrontations they would be up against. Then he asked me my age, and when I told him, his response was a stony silence. Our working relationship would only go downhill from here.

Shortly after 10:00 a.m. we met with a couple of other male officers for coffee. Their conversation centred around their camps and how many fish they had (or had not) caught over their last set of days off. It was like I was not there, with no attempt to bring me into the conversation or to even tell me their names. It was beyond rude. Finally, in an effort to make some conversation, I stated, "It sure has been quiet this morning." Suddenly, I had their attention and was matter-of-factly told to *never* use the "q word"—it was a jinx that could change the entire outcome of the shift.

Not even five minutes later the dispatcher radioed us stating that there was a call in our area that was possibly a 10-45.

With that, he spat out at me, "That's why you never use the 'q word!'" I quickly learned the meaning of a 10-45: a dead body.

Such was my introduction to police work. We found out that the body was that of an elderly gentleman who had been fighting a terminal illness. Nighttime temperatures had been extremely high and I guess he had enough. In the early morning hours he loaded his shotgun, sat on his chair in the front room, placed the barrel under his chin and pulled the trigger. A concerned relative had discovered what had occurred when he failed to answer the phone or his door.

When I surveyed the scene it felt surreal. I couldn't believe how far bone fragments and brain matter could spread. It wasn't only in the front room but out into the hallway, kitchen, everywhere. The front half of his head was gone with the rifle still lying to the side across his body. What struck me the most was the eerie silence of his physical remains. His life force, energy, soul—whatever one wants to name it, was clearly gone. For the first time I smelled death, unmistakable and unforgettable.

My first lesson had been learned: I never used the "q word" again.

As I rode with various officers I soon discovered that each had a style of their own. Some were skilled at diffusing volatile situations while others escalated placid events into hostile confrontations—all by their tone, choice of words, and attitude.

Every time I had to ride with Carol I knew it was going to be a very long eight hours. She just had a knack for rubbing people the wrong way through her sarcasm, belittling tone, and lack of discernment. One such instance left me speechless and mortified: Carol loved to hand out traffic tickets for whatever violation she could find. One particular day she decided to target the area in front of the cancer clinic. A van was stopped in a No Parking zone with its hazard lights activated. She was like a predator going in for the kill, bouncing out of the driver's seat with ticket book in hand. As she was writing out the ticket a middle-aged gentleman returned and observed what was happening. He stated, "I'm sorry, officer, I had to drop off my mother for her treatment and she is too weak to walk. I'll move my van right away."

Carol, not even looking up, finished writing out the ticket, ripped it from the ticket book, handed it to him and stated, "Too late."

My heart went out to him but there was not a thing I could do. She was the officer and I just the ride-along. Thankfully, her tactics were not the norm.

On one of the afternoon shifts, the sergeant announced that I would be riding with Terry. He was not impressed and under his breath he muttered, "Fucking rookies."

I cringed thinking, *Oh great—this is going to be a treat..*

We had barely pulled out of the parking lot when we were dispatched to a call in a lower-income housing area. Apparently, a thirteen year old was not happy with the rules that her mother was trying to enforce and wanted to file a complaint against her.

The entire way there Terry voiced how much he hated his job, how much it had changed since he started, and how I had better make sure that this is what I really wanted to do.

As I accompanied him into the residence, what I witnessed was a far cry from what I had anticipated. He showed the girl respect, listened to both parties, and offered solid, constructive advice. For someone who hated his job he never let that interfere with how he treated people. I was impressed.

My days of being the ride-along were quickly coming to an end and the departure date for police college loomed ever closer. To say I was anxious was by far an understatement. The thought of going back to school terrified me. My uncertainties of not being able to pass the required courses had my stomach in knots—in spite of reassurance from other officers that I would be fine.

My apprehensions concerning the academic segment were only part of my worries. I had to leave Boomer and that was tearing me apart. I had arranged for a young man named Sean to rent my house for the three-month period with the agreement to also take care of my dog. I felt like I was deserting my best friend and entrusting him to a stranger. Sean seemed okay, but no one would care for Boomer as I did. I just prayed that he would be okay. My good friend Ed promised me that he would check in and even take Boomer on runs with him. I was so grateful. His assurance at least gave me some consolation.

I had decided to drive to OPC so that I would have my own means of transportation once I was there. The college is located in southern Ontario, only a short distance from where I grew up. I knew I would have to visit my old stomping grounds. Some demons had to be put to rest.

On September 4, 1995, my car was packed and ready to go—more ready than I was. I hugged Boomer goodbye, promising him that I would be back, wishing that he could understand, praying that he would be okay. As I drove away, the torrent of emotions I had kept in check gave way, demolishing any chance of my ability to hold back the tears. I came undone. My positive self-talk, which I had struggled so hard to maintain, was drowned out by my wails of uncertainty, insecurity, and fear of the unknown that unrelentingly awaited my arrival.

Chapter 29

If you obey all the rules, you'll miss all the fun.
– Katherine Hepburn

I have always found solace in driving. There's just something about being on the open road, finding myself deep in thought, contemplating the turns and twists of life or just singing along to my favourite songs. This trip was no different.

As the miles clicked by, I gave myself pep talks that bolstered my self-confidence; I determined that I was where I was meant to be, that I was indeed on course. I recalled how I had progressed through each stage of testing, eventually bringing me to where I was today. In spite of my feelings of trepidation, I knew I was in exactly the right place at exactly the right time, with no reason not to go forward with confidence. I had no idea the number of times that I would repeat this to myself throughout the next three months.

I had decided to split the drive into two days that would leave only about a six-hour drive for the second day. As I crawled into bed the first night I was emotionally drained. Thoughts of Boomer crept in; I valiantly attempted to hold back the tears but to no avail. It was only day one and I missed my dog terribly.

The next morning, I took my time before getting on the road. Today would be my last opportunity to follow my own schedule; tomorrow would be a different story.

It was a beautiful fall day, and as I drove along I relished the warm breeze through my open window. Soon there were signs of places that I remembered visiting as a kid, the first being the Mackinac Bridge.

At first sight, the enormity of the structure takes your breath away. It is the fifth longest suspension bridge in the world, measuring five miles long and tethered by miles of massive cables. As I drove my compact car across, wind gusts buffeted it, unrelenting, not exactly comforting while gazing at the water far below. As spectacular as it was (and is!) I still breathed a sigh of relief upon reaching solid ground.

Four hours later, I approached the border into Canada, but before crossing I decided to stop for something to eat along with a cold mug of draught beer. With only 128 km (80 miles) to go, I felt torn: part of me just wanted to get there, but another part wanted to linger and just enjoy my view of the water and the taste of my beer. I checked my watch—it was time to get going.

I passed signs and landmarks, recognizing many of them from so many years ago. It was surreal; I had to pinch myself to confirm that I wasn't dreaming.

Finally, I made my last turn onto the country road that led to the college. I passed conservative Mennonites in their horse-drawn wagons—a culture that still formed a significant portion of the rural population. It was just as I remembered, with acres of cornfields and herds of dairy cattle. Then, in the distance, the water tower of the college loomed against the horizon, inching ever closer.

As I turned into the entranceway, my heart was pounding and my hands were sweating. This would be home for the next three months.

After registering and finding my room I began the task of unloading my car. Several trips and staircases later I was moved in. The rooms were small, containing a single bed, desk, chair, clock radio, and closet. Being a paramilitary institution, the rules and guidelines were strict: rooms were to be kept neat and clean and the bed properly made, military style, before reporting to any classes. Students were required to be quiet and in their sleeping quarters by 2300 hours. Liquor, for Basic Constable Course students, was only permitted in the licensed lounge, and no alcohol was allowed in personal rooms or common areas.

There was no shortage of rules of conduct. If a student was found in violation of the rules they could be reported to their employer for disciplinary action, or could even be dismissed from the college.

In reading through the resident handbook I felt my rebellious side creeping to the surface. Who were they to tell me what I could or couldn't do? I was an adult who had done my share of living, abiding only by my rules and code of behaviour. I felt like a teenager back in high school and it wasn't sitting well with me. However, I also knew that I had to play the game and simply suck it up for the time that I was here. I had come too far to throw it all away.

After unpacking and attempting to find a place for everything, I discovered that the room right beside mine was now occupied. I'll never forget the first time I saw my roomie. Her name was Paula and she had been hired on with the OPP detachment in eastern Ontario. She looked scared shitless, sitting on the edge of her perfectly made bed, not knowing what to do next. It would be a memory that we would both recall with much laughter. I couldn't have asked for a better person to room beside. We became close, supporting each other through the good and the bad, always helping to maintain each other's sense of humour and lifting each other's spirits when either one of us required it.

It had been a long day and I was exhausted. Being so close to where I grew up was playing havoc with old memories. Even the radio was on the station that I had listened to as a kid. When I turned out the light I was suddenly overwhelmed with loneliness, feeling like a child in desperate need of comfort. I missed everything that was familiar—my home, my friends, and most of all Boomer. I was at a loss as to how to cope with the barrage and intensity of so many emotions, eventually curling up into a ball and crying myself to sleep.

The next morning I was up early, managing to get ahead of the rush for the limited number of showers. Uniforms were required to be worn from 0630 hours to 1630 hours, Monday to Friday. I gazed at myself in the mirror, hoping that my shirt was pressed properly and my boots polished up to standard. I did a double take. Seeing myself in a police uniform still didn't seem real.

As I headed towards the cafeteria, I finally saw some familiar faces from home. We joined up, each of us vocalizing our experiences thus far and wondering what next was in store for us. At least I wasn't alone in my doubts and apprehensions.

By 0830 hours, 330 new recruits, the largest intake group to date, were assembled in the college auditorium for orientation. I looked over the sea of faces, the majority appearing to be much younger than myself. We were quickly brought to order with the command "Listen up!"

Rules of conduct were spelled out along with clear ramifications of what would happen if not adhered to. Instructors from each segment of training were introduced, all of them being police officers who had applied from various jurisdictions throughout the province. Two officers from home had also been accepted for the two-year secondment.

As the morning wore on, each area of the curriculum was reviewed along with the expectations for each. The list was extensive: police vehicle operation; fitness; defensive tactics; traffic law; provincial laws; federal laws; firearms; police procedures. The scope of what we would need to comprehend in just three months was overwhelming. I had been out of school for years and the old stigma of feeling dumb still reared its ugly head in my moments of self-doubt. The break for lunch was a welcome relief.

In the afternoon, we all reported to various classrooms where we met each member of our class and our "homeroom" instructor. There were thirty of us in total, all from varied and diverse backgrounds. I was the senior of the group with the majority of the other recruits ten to fifteen years my junior. Our instructor was Sgt. Baxter, a very pleasant and sincere individual who I learned to greatly appreciate and respect. He was special.

To start things off, each member of the class was asked to make an introduction and say a few things about themselves. Recalling those first encounters makes me laugh. We were all so nervous, trying to make somewhat of a positive impression amongst our peers. However, it didn't take much for me to figure out the personalities that appealed to me as well as those who would not be on my let's-hang-out list. Either way, we were all in this together with the singular goal of making it through to the end.

Schedules were distributed detailing where we would be each hour of the day, starting from 0700 hours right through to 1630 hours, not including intramural sports and special night-time training exercises. It was clear that I was not going to have time to sit around feeling sorry for myself. The challenge had begun and I prayed that I'd be able to keep up.

Classes began in earnest with the Criminal Code of Canada and the Highway Traffic Act editions always close at hand. It was like they were written in a foreign language requiring us to decipher codes so we could understand the lingo and complexity of all the numerous sections and acts.

Twice a week we had to report to the Drill Hall at 0700 hours. There we lined up, shoulder to shoulder, while the drill sergeant walked down the line inspecting each of us, singling out individuals for various dress infractions: boots lacking the lustre of shiny black polish; shirts that were not pressed to satisfaction; hair that infringed on shirt collars. Those of us, especially those with no military training, were more than once called to task on our imperfections.

The real fun began when learning how to march and move in unison to the various commands that had never been part of my vocabulary: attention, forward march, halt, at ease, right face, about face, fall in, fall out—on and on it went. Many times, Paula and I would make eye contact and it would be all we could do not to burst out laughing, which would certainly not have gone over well with the drill sergeant. It was his task to train 330 of us to march like we had being doing it all our life and we were expected to take it very seriously. I suspect, under his exterior gruffness and barking out of orders, he too must have seen the humorous side of our ineptness. Fridays at dismissal time was like the Daytona 500—a mass exodus of students heading home for the weekend. Those of us who had nowhere to go stayed at the college, relishing the sudden transformation into peace and quiet, having the entire campus all to ourselves.

Friday nights became our time to leave the books behind and head to popular eateries and bars. Four of us soon banded together, two from home and my classmate Kathy, to whom I had grown close. She had been hired by a municipal detachment in the southeastern part of the province but was from British Columbia and engaged to a man serving in the military. The distance between them, however, was starting to take its toll.

No meals were provided on weekends, so we became frequent patrons to the limited number of restaurants in the nearby town, only 5 km from the college. The Corner Cupboard served fabulous breakfasts, and Johnny's was renowned for its pizza. The food was great, and the owners were hardworking, wonderful people. Over the years, thousands of recruits had passed through their doors and they never tired of serving us well.

Saturday nights turned into movie night, with us fittingly taking in all six of the *Police Academy* movies from the 1980s. It was uncanny how some of the scenes actually had a close resemblance to our own experiences.

The time we spent together over the weekends created a bond between us that was very special, sharing in the difficulty of being away from loved ones and friends. We supported each other as we studied together, worried together, ate together, but most of all, laughed together.

On Sundays, as students began to return for Monday's classes, it was hard to accept their intrusion back into our space, but we hung on knowing that Friday was coming.

As mentioned, I had grown up in close proximity to the college. Ever since my arrival my sleeps were interrupted with haunting nightmares of my childhood home and the people who had contributed to my troubled past. I couldn't shake them. My demons needed closure. One Saturday afternoon I got in my car and made the drive.

Approaching the west end of the city my heart was pounding. Familiar landmarks that had remained distant were suddenly in my face, staring me down, real, bombarding me with old memories attached to them all. I drove slowly, half expecting to see the faces of people I found myself recalling—people who hadn't entered my mind in years.

It hadn't changed much, so it was relatively easy to find my way around, recognizing street names that led me to where I needed to go. Soon I was on my old street being pulled like a magnet to the house that in my dreams still held me captive.

I pulled over, letting the memories flow. In my mind it was like watching hundreds of movie clips with myself playing the main character. It was a part that I didn't have to rehearse. I knew all the lines; it had been my life. Only the scenes changed as I grew older—different places, different characters, but I had carried the old tapes of who I had been told I was, believing them, living them as the years had passed. I sat and stared, unable to move, tears of sadness and regret welling up then streaming down my face, releasing. I breathed deeply reflecting on how far I had come, comforting that little girl who had endured much.

Eventually I pulled away and drove past the elementary school I had attended, more movie clips reeling through my mind, filled with people I had been hurt by, longing for someone to stand up and defend me, feeling so alone.

I drove a few blocks more to my old high school and parked, overlooking the playing field and track, remembering all the races I had run there, never feeling good enough, puking on the infield at the finish line from the exertion but mostly from the pressure I had put on myself. I sat there, actually feeling like I could vomit.

I moved to the other side of the school that directly faced the church we attended. I felt the hostility rise up, making me want to scream, to act out, to rebel against the fear that had been instilled—fear of God and fear I would burn in hell for not doing it right. I had to remind myself to breathe, to let it go; that was then and this was now.

I drove on, finding Miners Road where the farm —and the horses, and Ivan—had been but it had all changed. Land that had been farmland was gone, developed into something else, I guess of more importance. But I didn't need to see it to remember. I had remembered my entire life, bringing its message to all of my relationships: don't trust, don't feel, always be on guard. I had been taught well.

I continued to drive, passing places that triggered so many memories and emotions, giving them permission to express themselves in whatever way they wanted or seemed fitting.

Eventually, I knew it was time to go. Emotionally I was spent, but above that I felt calmness, relief, and a sense of okayness. I made one last stop before heading back to a downtown bar for a much needed and well-deserved cold beer.

I had dared to visit the past, the past that had followed me through life holding me captive. This experience changed something within me that resulted in giving myself permission to let it go and just accept what had been. For the remainder of my time at the college, the nightmares of my childhood were gone, and I slept in peace.

Chapter 30

I know God will not give me anything I can't handle. I just wish that He didn't trust me so much.
– Mother Teresa

During our three months away we were allowed two trips home, paid for by the department. Our first trip was scheduled for Thanksgiving weekend in October. Due to flight schedules, we were given special permission to leave before classes were dismissed on the Friday but had to return on the holiday Monday.

Once in the air and on our way my excitement built, eagerly anticipating my reunion with Boomer. Ed had offered to pick me up at the airport and even arranged for me to have the use of one of their vehicles for the weekend. Sean, my house-sitter, was going away for the weekend, giving me the luxury of having my home all to myself. I couldn't wait for the much-needed break.

As I entered the terminal I caught sight of Ed, there at the gate as planned. As he drove me home, he filled me in on all the happenings since I had been gone. We made plans to meet for a run the next morning followed by breakfast at our favourite establishment, along with friends who I couldn't wait to see.

Soon my arms were around my big black dog, hugging him close, promising him a weekend of togetherness, apologizing for my absence. But what I encountered next left me speechless, not believing what I saw, unable to comprehend the condition of my back yard. Boomer's droppings were everywhere, not a square foot of clean grass. I could not fathom what my dog had gone through. He had always been very particular about where he did his business: always in the same area, always away from his dog house and play area. I was horrified, and more than anything else, livid.

Garbage that I had left in the garage before I went away was still there, in spite of my written note requesting that he put it out for collection. My mind was reeling. What else had this jerk failed to do for my dog that I had entrusted to his care? As for the yard, I hardly knew where to start. To say it was disgusting was by far an understatement.

As I slowly progressed through the task of picking up, I tried to figure out my options of what to do about Sean. What I wanted to do would have had me charged with assault. My hands were tied. I could not leave my house vacant for the next month and a half and I had no time to find a replacement. Furthermore, I had no idea of where to reach him even if I did find someone else.

On my run the next morning with Ed, I vented and he too couldn't believe how Sean had just turned a blind eye to what was more than noticeable. As always, Ed came through for me again. He assured me that he would take care of the yard and would continue to take Boomer for runs. I hated to impose on him with something that was entirely not his responsibility, but we both knew with certainty Sean wasn't going to do it.

While home, I also discovered that he had broken a glassware pot—no note, no apology. I guess he thought I wouldn't notice. However I did get a chuckle when I saw that my frozen bag of peas was missing from the freezer. Little did he know that I had used this as an ice pack, taking it in and out of the freezer multiple times and wrapping it around whatever joint was hurting. I'm sure they must have tasted simply delightful!

The trip home was a needed break and, considering the state of how I had found things, crucial. Knowing what Boomer had gone through, at least in part, made it even harder to leave him again. My only relief was found with Ed reassuring me that he would take care of things. It wouldn't happen again.

Much too soon I was back in my room feeling like I had never left, feeling the mounting pressure of midterms only one week away. My work was cut out for me with no time to spare.

As each day passed I felt the old familiar panic setting in. Exams and I had never been compatible. If I didn't understand a question or was confused by how it was worded, my self-talk would kick in telling me to smarten up; read the question, stupid; you're going to run out of time; you're going to fail! Of course this only heightened my anxiety, causing my mind to draw a blank, retreating from the barrage of criticism.

It was imperative that this time I learn to change my inner dialogue and not replicate the messages that I had fed myself. Rather, I *have* done the work; I *am* prepared; I *will* succeed, and most importantly, I *am not* stupid. In spite of my determination to change the negativity of my self-talk it still didn't prevent the pounding of my heart and clammy hands as the first exam was distributed.

However, this time I did it, not only receiving better-than-expected results, but more importantly I succeeded in being kinder to myself.

It seemed that no sooner were midterms completed that finals followed right behind, spread out over the last three weeks of November. Everyone had his or her own way of coping with the added stress, at times consumed by the pressure. Tempers ran short and sleep was disrupted with anxious thoughts of the next day's exam.

I opted out of another trip home, feeling that it would disrupt my focus, not an option now that the end was in sight. Instead, Kathy and I decided to spend the weekend in a hotel, relishing the change from the college surroundings. It proved to be the right choice. Aside from reviewing material for the upcoming exams, we ate out, did some shopping at a nearby mall and visited an Irish pub—complete with great food and entertainment.

We were into the home stretch, each exam bringing us closer to completion. The last week was the toughest: three days of exams back to back, finishing one then on to the next.

On November 29th at 11:30 a.m. I put down my pen. It was over. The feeling of relief in this moment was immense! The huge weight suddenly lifted, leaving me emotional, giddy, but most of all, free.

On Thursday, November 30th at 1400 hours, all 330 of us were assembled in the drill hall, all in dress uniform and lined up with our respective classes. We had come a long way in the last three months, bringing us to this day. Now we were ready to march past invited family members, friends and dignitaries; ready to be recognized for our accomplishment; ready to return to our respective departments; ready to become what the training had been all about—police officers.

What certainly contributed to our success was the incredible support that the seconded officers provided us with. Extra classes, on their time, were available for anyone who wanted further clarification on various subject matters. Their patience, encouragement and positive reinforcement was inspiring. They wanted to see each of us succeed just as much as we wanted it for ourselves. Furthermore, they had given us no reason to believe that we wouldn't receive the same kind of support and guidance from each of our jurisdictions. I was in for a rude awakening, having yet to learn that the camaraderie between officers was anything but all for one and one for all.

Goodbyes to those I had become close to were emotional. We knew we were embarking on a career that would put us in harm's way every time we donned the uniform. None of us knew what the future had in store, but one thing was certain: each of us would have our own story to tell.

The drive home not only provided me with the opportunity to reflect on the last three months but to also determine the kind of officer I wanted to become. I prayed that I would not regress and become cynical, hardened, callous, insensitive, and uncaring to people in need. More than anything I just hoped that I could make a difference, no matter how small or how great in the lives of those who would cross my path.

To finally be back in the comfort of my own home, with Boomer at my side, provided me with calmness and such a sense of relief. I had succeeded in what I had set out to do and now I was home, ready for the next segment of training: three months of working side by side with my coach officer whose job was to prepare me for being out on my own—an immense responsibility. Upon arriving home I was scheduled to report for dayshift on Monday, December 4th. Although we had qualified with our firearms at the police college, we now had to qualify to the standards of our own department before being permitted on the road. Gone were the days of a warm indoor range. Instead, we were confronted with the harsh outdoors, freezing temperatures, and just to make it really memorable, standing in the middle of a full-fledged snowstorm. It was unbelievable, barely discerning the targets through the wall of white. It was hard to say who had it worse: those of us under the pressure to qualify or the range instructor given the responsibility to have us pass all the various components. It took two full days for all of us to qualify, slowed down by frequent breaks in the on-site trailer while attempting to get some feeling back in our fingers. However, we did it! On one of these mornings, before heading to the range, I was at my locker in the ladies' change area along with several other female officers. The door opened and in came Tracey whom I hadn't yet seen since arriving home. I was excited to see my friend's familiar face exclaiming, "Hey Tracey, good to see you!"

Her lack of response and acknowledgement set me back, leaving me baffled, speechless, not knowing what to say next. She merely grunted something at me and totally went on as if I wasn't there.

At the time, I could not comprehend the reason for her coldness. Only later would I make my own conclusion regarding the dynamics behind her behaviour. It didn't matter that we had been friends for many years, running together, attending parties together, travelling together, even being there to celebrate the birth of her first child . . . it was irrelevant. This was a different world—a world of protecting your back and your status, specifically with male officers who could make your life a living hell. I believe that she felt that she could not openly declare our friendship until I had passed the scrutiny of those whose opinion apparently mattered. My earlier excitement of working on the same unit as Tracey quickly dissolved into hurt, disappointment, and most of all feeling betrayed and rejected by someone who I thought was my friend.

Our swearing-in ceremony was set to take place at the Provincial Courthouse on Thursday, December 7th. Anyone could attend to witness the event and I felt honoured to see in the courtroom my close friends. They had supported me from the very beginning with their "You can do it!"—listening to my doubts and apprehensions, sending cards of encouragement while I was away and now, here, celebrating my accomplishment with me. It was official! I was a sworn-in police officer, so help me God.

Chapter 31

He is your friend, your partner, your defender, your dog.
You are his life, his love, his leader. He will be yours,
faithful and true, to the last beat of his heart.
– Unknown

My assigned coach officer was Roger, who had been with the department for eighteen years. I had liked him from the start, being one of the few who would actually carry on a pleasant conversation with me. He was laid back and had a great sense of humour, but most importantly he knew how to listen and converse with people by exhibiting respect and fairness.

On our first shift together, Roger explained what he would expect from me for the next three months: hard work. He had an extensive checklist of everything that would have to be covered before the higher-ups would determine me capable of working alone. Initially, I would observe him taking the various calls that we would be dispatched to, asking the relevant questions and taking down all the necessary information in his notebook. This information would later be the content that would go into the submitted reports. Serious calls, such as domestic or sexual assaults, required detailed accounts. It was imperative that the question of who, what, where, when, why, and how were answered. If not, the report would be deemed incomplete.

Every day was different, with no two calls the same. At times, the amount of information and details that needed to be learned was overwhelming, but Roger was patient, supporting and encouraging me that I was doing just fine.

Thankfully, Roger enjoyed his coffee as much as I did, especially at the start of dayshift. Early on in my training the various personalities of the officers on our unit became very apparent. Some would only go for coffee with a select few, avoiding the less popular officers, which included Roger. He certainly did not care for the attitudes of some but he was still friendly and civil towards them.

Our most frequent coffee dates were with Terry, whom Roger had also trained when he came on the job in the fall of 1982. Like Roger, Terry knew how to treat and speak to people, as I had observed first hand as his ride-along before leaving for police college. He still made it very clear, though, that he hated coming to work. Terry had started to date a woman he had met while I was away and it was obvious that he very much cared for her. Both Roger and I were very happy for him as he had not dated since his divorce in 1991. I really hoped that it would work out for him and Liz.

The winter of 1995–96 brought us record snowfall that at one point shut down the entire city. Several people who required medical attention ended up getting transported to the hospital via snowmobiles, as even paramedics could not maneuvre ambulances through the deep snow.

Our cruisers fared no better, making it impossible to respond to calls on streets not yet ploughed. The worst of the storm occurred while we were working midnights, demanding an alternative to our current situation. Consequently, we swapped our cruisers for city-owned trucks with front-end ploughs. Roger was in his glory, seizing the opportunity to clear out both his driveway and mine in the early morning hours. Not exactly police work, but at least we could both now get in and out of our driveways. Thank God no one complained.

As the winter wore on, I became very aware that some officers were grumbling about the way Roger was training me, the ringleader appearing to be Wayne. The undercurrent of comments varied: he wasn't volunteering us to take calls out of our area; we weren't getting to dispatched calls fast enough; I shouldn't be going through my training in the winter months when calls were down, rather it should be in the warmer months when there was more action; he should be doing this rather than that. It never seemed to let up, and although Roger was responsible for my training, I clearly felt Wayne's disdain was also directed at me personally. It was obvious that I was not up to par in matching his criteria of what a cop should be. The rift would only intensify as the weeks marched on. It didn't take long to discover that there were two sets of rules: one for females and one for males. Within our group that had just returned from police college, it seemed that those of the male gender were automatically accepted among other officers. On the other hand, females were up against the old stigma that we were in a profession where we didn't belong, always under the gun having to prove ourselves. We were judged on everything, from our size and stature, to our looks, to how we drove, to how we cleared from calls—nothing was overlooked. Outlandish behaviour from male officers was considered funny, with cheers of "Atta-boy!" followed by high fives. It was a complex world that I observed to be filled with double standards and no consistency. Rather, it seemed to all just come down to who you were—or weren't.

When time permitted, we continued to meet Terry for coffee, getting updates on his relationship with Liz, which seemed to be progressing favourably. They were both excited about attending a lavish New Year's Eve party that was being put on by her bosses from her workplace. Terry even took her shopping to buy a new dress and shoes for the special event that would include dinner and a live band to follow. His anticipation was evident and both Roger and I wished him a great night.

Following our days off we returned to work for dayshift, meeting Terry for coffee as per our usual. We fully expected to hear about the great time they had had, but the look on his face clearly indicated that things had not gone well.

Terry relayed that Liz had consumed a fair amount of alcohol, revealing a side of her that he had not seen before. He went on to say how she had ignored him, pretending that he wasn't there, dancing with everyone else but refusing to dance with him when he asked. He recalled to us that finally he had had enough and left without her, feeling hurt and angry.

My heart went out to him, as it was obvious that he cared about her and did not want their relationship to dissolve. At the same time, he did not warrant or want a repeat of the treatment that she had apparently dished out.

Many times Roger and I discussed his situation, both of us hoping that their relationship could be resolved. I even told Roger that she would be nuts to let him go. According to what she had told Terry, her background was intertwined with drugs and involvement with unfavourable people, but this did not matter to him. He accepted her without judgement for who she was today, not for who and whatever she had done in the past. It seemed that this was an issue she struggled with: not knowing how to accept the respect that Terry gave her. For the next few months, Terry would be on an emotional roller coaster, uncertain of the direction that their relationship would or would not take.

My three months of training came to an end and it was determined that I was ready to be turned loose. There were of course calls that I had not yet experienced, but I was encouraged to not be afraid to ask for help and advice. In conversations over coffee, Terry had repeatedly told me that you never get to the point of knowing what to do in every situation, no matter how long you have been on the job. There would be twists and circumstances changing the way of how to proceed.

The first time I got into the cruiser alone I was excited but scared to death. I just prayed that I would be able to handle the calls sent my way. My heart pounded as dispatch radioed me for a call in my area, the first of many more to come.

Wayne continued to be the thorn in my side, constantly complaining to others on the unit (including our sergeant) of what I had or hadn't done. When we were assigned to the same area he would race to the calls to beat me there and then complain that he was stuck with all the reports. It felt that his number one priority was to make me look bad. Wayne had his followers, but thankfully there were some who would draw their own conclusions, John being one of them. From the start, he told me that he really didn't care what Wayne's opinion was; he would make up his own mind about me without Wayne's influence. Whenever we were paired up, I looked forward to the shift as he was fun to work with and had a great sense of humour. With all the negativity, he became a bright spot that I appreciated more than he knew.

Tracey continued to avoid me like the plague, and on the rare occasion that we were teamed up, conversation was awkward and trivial. For me the shift couldn't end soon enough. I still hoped that things would get better between us but I definitely had my doubts.

One day we were both dispatched to take a complaint call in our area, which she arrived at shortly before me. I volunteered to take the report but she said she would take it. At one point the complainant was arguing with what Tracey was saying, so I interjected with a comment to back her up. Without flinching, she stated, "Isana, shut up."

I was stunned, humiliated, and couldn't believe what had just transpired. It was rude and totally uncalled for, but more than anything it cut me to the core. I had nothing left to say to her.

Desperately, I tried to not let people's negative opinions and remarks get to me but they did. I would wake up during the night tossing and turning, rolling the scenes over and over in my head, wishing that someone would come to my defence and stand up for me. It seemed no matter what I did, it wasn't good enough. I was no longer the tough kid who was bothered by nothing. Rather, I was coming to the realization I never had been that tough; it had always hurt.

I could no longer pretend that it didn't.

It was a question I raised almost right from the start: how was I going to survive in this environment of hostility and still be okay at the end of it all? I didn't have an answer.

In April of 1996, Boomer accompanied me on my daily run as he always did. It was a beautiful day, and after the long winter, the warmth of the sun was welcome. About two miles out I noticed that Boomer was falling back. I urged him to keep up but he just kept falling farther behind. Finally, I stopped to wait for him, wondering what on earth was going on; he was always right there with me, never having a problem running my pace. When he saw that I was waiting for him he slowed to a walk, struggling just to keep moving forward. I went to him and as I did so he collapsed, appearing to have some form of seizure. There was not a thing I could do except comfort him and tell him it was okay.

After getting him home and giving him water he seemed fine, back to his old self. The only explanation I could come up with was that he must have overheated. Every spring I had his thick coat shaved down to make it cooler for him during the summer, so not wanting a reoccurrence I made an appointment for his annual shave, hoping that would solve the problem.

About two weeks later, I was startled out of sleep to the sound of him wheezing, struggling to breathe. I rushed to the back door where he slept and found him again in a seizure that had caused him to lose control of his bladder. Now I was really worried; obviously something was very wrong.

That day I got him in to see the vet, hoping for some explanation. After a brief examination the vet concluded that he must have epilepsy, assuring me that it was quite common with dogs and could be controlled with medication. I didn't waste any time, immediately giving him the prescribed dosage, hoping more than anything that it would work. It didn't, and a few days later he had another seizure. I again contacted the vet and he instructed me to increase the dosage; obviously he needed more than what had been prescribed.

As the days went by, I observed that all the pills were doing were putting him into a trancelike state. He was unsteady and unsure of his surroundings, and all the vet would recommend was higher doses. Finally, I had enough after helping him through yet another seizure. I took him in, demanding to see another vet, furious that his diagnosis had been based only on a presumption.

I was a mess, explaining to the new vet what had been going on, including the change in Boomer's appetite. I couldn't fill him up. He would devour his food as if he were starving. She assured me that she would get to the bottom of it but would need to do a blood analysis. I told her to do whatever it took; my dog was suffering and all I could do was stand by and watch, unable to fix him. It was the most helpless feeling in the world.

Not long after she called me with news that I wasn't remotely prepared for. Boomer, only seven years old, had cancer of the pancreas, which was playing havoc with his blood sugar levels, thereby causing the seizures. I was devastated, inconsolable, unable to comprehend that I was losing my best friend.

With all the heartbreaks and turmoil that I had gone through over the past few years, he had been the reason for me to keep going, to persevere, even to get out of bed in the morning. He was my constant and, indeed, my rock.

The vet further explained that his ravenous appetite would eventually subside to the point of not wanting any food at all. When this occurred it would be decision time. Nothing more could be done.

I don't even think it was a week later, when I was working midnights, that he lost all interest in food. Being new on the job, booking off sick would not have been a wise thing to do, so I forced myself to go in.

I couldn't concentrate, only thinking of what was happening to him at home and that he needed me there. I was paired up with Terry and he clearly saw my emotional state. Not long into our shift he told me we were going back to the station and that I needed to go home. He told me he would talk to the staff sergeant, explaining the circumstances, and would even make note of my condition in his notebook in the event that our superiors questioned it. "Furthermore," he told me, "to hell with the department. Take care of yourself, because the truth of the matter is that they don't give a damn." It was clear that he was talking from personal experience, and his support at that time was appreciated beyond words.

Having not eaten for a few days, Boomer's condition was deteriorating and I could no longer bear to see my big, black, gentle giant suffer any more. My decision was made.

In our last few moments together I told him that he had been my dream dog, everything that I had ever wanted. I thanked him for being such a good, obedient dog, always glad to see me no matter what mood I was in. I thanked him for all the joy and humour that he had filled my days with; above all I thanked him for his unconditional love.

I told him that I was sorry for the times that I had been way too hard on him, demanding perfection when I should have laid off. I told him that I was so sorry for having to leave him for three months and asked if he would please forgive me. Through my tears and sobs I told him that what I was most sorry for was that I couldn't make him better, and he didn't deserve to suffer anymore.

People who have never had the experience of forming that special bond with a pet might be skeptical of the non-verbal communication that exists. It is a silent exchange that is clearly understood by each. After saying what I needed to say, it was then that he looked at me with his big brown eyes. Our gazes locked, and it was as if he was staring straight into my soul. Simultaneously he lifted his paw, placing it gently on my knee. He understood, and there was nothing left to say.

On Friday, May 17th, I set Boomer free—free to run and play and jump in a world reserved for dogs that have touched the hearts of their owners, whose lives have been made richer because of them.

Chapter 32

It is said some lives are linked across time. Connected by an ancient calling that echoes through the ages. Destiny.
– Prince of Persia 1

Shiftwork was not easy. I had worked straight days, Monday through Friday, my entire life, and now my body was not adapting well to the change—specifically the midnight shift.

I was a morning person, preferring to go to bed early so that I could get up and have the entire next day to do whatever had to be done. For me, napping during the day was unheard of, probably in part a carry-over from how I had been raised: it simply wasn't allowed unless you were sick.

When the midnight shift rolled around it was all I could do to try to stay up until I left for work at 11:00 p.m. I would hope for a quiet night so I could pull over and park away from the public eye. For the most part this didn't happen, and by 4:00 a.m. my body was screaming for sleep. The shift ended at 8:00 a.m. (provided you were not sent on a last-minute call) so by the time I got home and gave myself some time to unwind, it was usually around 9:30 a.m. that I would crawl into bed, hoping to fall into a sound sleep.

I soon discovered that what I wished for was a far cry from reality. I would lie there exhausted, in a state of semi-sleep but conscious of sounds and very aware that I wasn't sleeping. By 11:30 or noon, I would give up and just get up, too tired to do anything except sit in a trance-like state, trying to will myself into motion.

I had no appetite. I was too starved for sleep but I would force myself to eat something, provided that it took no effort to make. At around 7:00 p.m. I would again climb into bed desperately hoping to get *some* sleep before having to leave again for work, but to no avail. Finally, at around 9:30 p.m., I could feel myself drifting off, unfortunately too late. At 10:00 p.m., on came my clock radio indicating that it was time to get up and do it all over again.

I tried everything to induce sleep: warm baths; sleepy-time tea; melatonin; warm milk and, as a last resort, low dosages of prescribed sleeping pills that only left a metallic taste in my mouth. Someone suggested that I stay up until one or two in the afternoon and then go to bed; that didn't work either.

Midnights became an endurance event and by the sixth night I was so fried I was nauseous. It was not only physically exhausting but mentally as well. Face it—most serious crimes are committed during the night when *most* people are sleeping. As a cop, that is when one needs to have their wits about them, as one never knows what could come down next. Mostly, it was only sheer adrenalin that got me through the night.

As summer was approaching thoughts of riding again in T.R.A.M. surfaced. I had missed last year's so I was eager to go back and face the challenge of a new route. My girlfriend Paula decided to come along with me, eager to experience it for the first time. Other than getting our butts conditioned to endure the long rides on not-so-comfortable bike seats, we were set.

As I progressed through my training regimen I recalled the things that kept drawing me back to T.R.A.M.: breathing in the fresh scent of morning dew as I packed up my tent, eager to get on the road, anticipating the warmth of the sun and the abundance of wildflowers adorning the roadsides. It would be a welcome change from the stress of my first year on the job. I even entertained the thought of possibly meeting someone special but quickly chastised myself for even considering the prospect of another long-distance relationship.

Time flew, and before we knew it we were there, gathering our registration packets and securing our tent spots for the night. As always, the organization of the event was impeccable. Paula and I had discussed and agreed that we would both ride at our own pace. She was one who would want to take her time, stopping to smell the roses; I on the other hand wanted the experience of hard physical exertion.

Sometimes history has a way of repeating itself in spite of what we may or may not intend or plan. Our first ride of the week was over, and Paula and I had joined up with a group gathered in a bar, relishing the taste of cold draught beer and sharing our experiences of the day. We were laughing, having a great time, when I noticed two gentlemen sitting at a table across from us. One of them was looking over at me with an amused look on his face. I didn't pay much attention to it until even Paula noticed and kiddingly stated, "I think he likes you."

Finally, I thought, *Hey, what the hell, why not?* and asked them if they wanted to join us. They were obviously also riding the T.R.A.M., so why not include them in the camaraderie of our group? Chairs were shuffled to accommodate them, and soon after they were engaged in conversation, fitting in with ease. He—Jerry was his name—zeroed in on me, and I was in no way protesting his advances. There was a spark between us of which we were both well aware. A business lawyer from Minnesota, he had done numerous other bike tours, but this was his first time on T.R.A.M. Our conversation continued as others from our group were dispersing and going their different ways. Even Paula decided to go and check out other venues, at least so she said. Once it was just the two of us he told me the reason I had gotten his attention was my laugh. He said it was infectious and he couldn't help but be amused and drawn in.

So began another long-distance relationship, with one drawback. He told me from the start that he was married but that his wife was preoccupied with her career and he with his, hence they were each living their own lives. My only question to him was, "Why stay married?" He didn't have an answer.

Getting together did not occur often. He was busy being a lawyer, and I, of course had the dilemma of shift work. We enjoyed each other's company, but I knew that as long as he was married the relationship wasn't going to go far. Due to his marital status, he conveyed to me that if I met someone single then I should pursue it; he would understand. However, on the local front, I had not met anyone in several years with whom I saw the potential of developing anything serious. After all, my last three relationships had all been long distance, so I wasn't holding my breath on that possibility.

In September, Jerry told me about an upcoming lawyer's convention that was going to be held in Boston the first week of October, and would I like to come along? He didn't have to ask twice, especially with plane fare and accommodations taken care of. The conference was booked at a large luxury hotel in the heart of Boston, a city that I had always aspired to visit due to the long history of the Boston Marathon. I didn't even have to arrange for time off work—I already had holidays booked for the time period that I would be away. I was ecstatic, counting down the days to our departure.

The last shift I worked before starting holidays was the dreaded midnights. I was teamed up with Terry who had to put up with my hyper anticipation of my upcoming trip. The hours dragged and I wished that it could just be quitting time, but most of all hoping that we didn't get stuck with a last-minute call.

At one point during the night, we met Roger for coffee, and our conversation turned to Boston. I told them that I fully intended to visit the famous "Cheers" bar, and did they want me to bring them back any mementos? Terry vouched for a ball cap and Roger didn't have any preference—whatever I picked out for him would be just fine.

Thankfully the night ended without any serious incidents, and most importantly, no last-minute call. Boston was waiting for me and I couldn't wait to meet her.

It is by far one of the most beautiful cities I have ever encountered. The old historical landmarks, rich with history, are intermingled with modern-day architecture. Horse-drawn carriages rumble over cobblestone streets followed by open two-tiered trolleys filled with curious tourists. Many parks buffer the busy streets, beautifully manicured and virtually litter free. Specialty shops are abundant, and the restaurants exquisite. Most of all, the people of Boston are warm and welcoming, proud to be called Bostonians.

The Cheers bar was everything I had hoped for—great atmosphere, great food and of course, refreshing cold draught beer. As promised, I found Terry a Cheers ball cap, and for Roger, a large glass mug bearing the Cheers logo.

While Jerry attended his conference I walked the streets of Boston, taking it all in, mesmerized by its uniqueness and vowing to someday return. In the evening, Jerry and I sought out fine dining establishments with no shortage of ones to choose from. The food and service was fabulous.

All too soon it came to an end with me returning to my life of shift work and the ongoing nitpicking of co-workers while Jerry went back to his mundane marriage and long work days filled with umpteen phone calls and countless meetings with clients and colleagues. Surely life had to have more in store for me than futile relationships that only left me feeling empty and more alone than ever.

My days of competitive running were seemingly becoming a thing of the past. The surgery on my ankle had left it susceptible to frequent joint pain and the inability to run strenuous workouts and long distances. Shift work was playing havoc with my role as a coach, so I even found myself needing to step away from what I had been committed to for so long. Circumstances beyond my control were slowly turning my life in a different direction, coaxing me along in spite of my resistance to change.

Not long after my trip to Boston, Terry's rapport with me at work started changing. He wasn't as serious, often joking around with me before going on the road and even calling me to meet for coffee during the shift. From what I understood, his relationship with Liz had not worked out. She had lied to him and used him, taking advantage of his generosity, exhibiting a nasty side that he had not noticed earlier on. He eventually came to the realization that their relationship had hit an impasse and it was time for Liz to move out and find her own place. Terry seemed resigned to the fact that it was over, but most importantly he was clear on the fact that he had given the relationship his best shot. It was indeed Liz who had sabotaged it. She had been on unfamiliar ground, either unwilling or unable to know how to accept the way that Terry had treated her—as an individual worthy of respect.

One day in the latter part of October it started out as any other. I was working the 4 - 12 shift, wondering as always with whom I was going to be paired, but really hoping that I would be left to work alone.

Terry and I normally arrived at work about the same time. I didn't like the feeling of running late, preferring instead to ease into it; I would read my messages and collect any information that I might need for the upcoming shift. The first thing I did was to check the schedule, relieved to see that I would be by myself.

Terry was in good spirits, kidding around and razzing me about something, but for what I don't recall. He too was working alone, but we had both been assigned to the same area so we agreed to meet for coffee as soon as we cleared from the station. I could feel that something was different between us. My intuition was working overtime and I just knew that our relationship was headed in a direction that neither of us had expected.

In the early evening I was doing radar in my area and had a vehicle pulled over. Terry drove up to check if everything was okay, a standard tactic when it was a single officer conducting a traffic stop. However, before driving away, he stated, "When you've cleared the vehicle meet me in the parking lot of the community centre."

I knew then without a shadow of a doubt that he was going to ask me out. I was giddy, excited, shocked, but not really, since the dynamics of our rapport with one another had definitely changed.

My intuition hadn't deceived me. That night he did ask me if I would be interested in going out with him, and with no hesitation I replied, "That would be great."

From that moment on we never looked back. The circumstances that led us to that night still astound me. When I first met Terry I had never imagined the two of us together; it just really never crossed my mind. Our interests and circle of friends were diversely different—he loved golf, I loved running. Most importantly, over the last several months I had observed what he was all about, long before becoming emotionally involved with him, and that for me was a first. It was Liz who showed me what Terry was made of, and as I had once stated to Roger, "She would be nuts to let him go."

All I can say with utmost sincerity is "Thank you, Liz, for doing just that." Finally I had found what I had been looking for my entire life—my soft place to fall.

PART VI

Chapter 33

God grant me the serenity to accept the things I cannot change;
courage to change the things I can;
and wisdom to know the difference.
– Serenity Prayer (Reinhold Niebuhr)

With Terry and I becoming an item, I knew I had to let Jerry know that it was time for him and I to part ways. He took the news harder than he or I expected, having fallen for me even more than he had anticipated. However, he remained true to his word, wishing me all the best, whimsically adding that if it didn't work out between Terry and me to please look him up. In my heart I knew it was over, in spite of whatever way the cards would play out. Thanks, Jerry, for the memories.

It wasn't long before I was spending my nights with Terry and only checking in at my house to pick up the mail, retrieve phone messages, and to ensure that everything was secure. Only Roger knew that we were seeing each other but it was inevitable that much sooner than later our secret would be out and we would be faced with the department's nepotism policy—a policy that prevented couples from working together. Splitting us up would mean different shifts, resulting in very little time together, something that neither one of us wanted. We knew it was only a matter of time.

Very early in our relationship, Terry introduced me to his parents, Bob and Louise. I am sure they were very skeptical of me, not wanting to see their son hurt again. However, I liked Terry's dad right from the start. He said what he thought and conversation came easy. Inevitably, during our visits, he would always ask us if we wanted a "smash"—his name for rye and water. Many times we really didn't want one, but knowing what it meant to him we would say, "Sure, why not?"

On the other hand, my relationship with Terry's mother did not come easy. Whenever we were out of earshot of Bob, she would incessantly complain about him and the way he treated her. If it wasn't Bob that she was expressing her resentment over, it would be Lynn, Terry's older sister, and if not her, then one of her sisters, Terry's aunts. Her bitterness was apparent and, as a result, conversation really never took place between us. It seemed that the only bright spot in her life was Terry's son Steven, whom she adored.

Terry had two children: Steven from his first marriage and Ashley from his second. He struggled with the fact that he had no contact with either one, feeling that both ex-wives had made it their priority to distance him from his kids. On the job, Terry had seen firsthand the results of parents fighting over custody of children, who were put in the middle of issues they had no control over. Having to listen to one or both parents degrade the other meant that, ultimately, it was the children who were hurt the most.

Not just once, but twice, Terry made the hardest decision he ever had to make: to not put them through this bitter dynamic, but rather to step back and hope for the day when they would be able to understand why.

In November, I celebrated my fortieth birthday, along with several longtime friends and, of course, Terry. I knew my friends were happy for me, but at the same time my relationship with them was undergoing change. For years, running had been the focal point that connected us, and now that I had to step back from running and coaching, we were losing the common ground that had cemented us together. I had also embarked upon a career that was not the average. Unless one had experienced working as a police officer, it would be very difficult for an outsider to understand what has to be dealt with on a daily basis; it only added another component that had not been there before.

Slowly, communication became sparse, and I was hurt when the phone stopped ringing, feeling abandoned by those who had been my adopted family. In retrospect, I know that it was never their intention to hurt me; through no fault of anyone our paths had diverged.

As anticipated, by early 1997 others in our unit had figured out that we were together, so the news quickly spread throughout the department. Desperately not wanting to be split up, we went on a mission to have the nepotism policy reviewed and dispensed with. Our police chaplain at the time, Father Chris, was on board with us trying to convince administration to take a different look at it. I researched other municipal police departments that allowed couples to work the same shifts and the results were overwhelmingly positive. Some couples preferred to work different shifts, especially where children were involved; we just wanted to have the choice. However, those in power at the time refused to look at the bigger picture, determined to remain in the old way of doing things and conjuring up a pile of "what-if" scenarios.

Now that they were well aware of our relationship, every day that I went to work I fully anticipated receiving word that I was being transferred. I would lie awake at night going over and over in my mind what I could say to make them see things differently; how could our relationship survive with so little time together; what about this, what about that? My thoughts were relentless, spinning me in circles and always bringing me back to the realization that I had no control over what they would decide. But for whatever reason things went on as they were with no word of any transfer, at least for the time being.

By early March, I began to question the validity of having a house that I was no longer living in but still paying the mortgage and monthly utility bills for. Tentatively, I brought it up with Terry, relieved to hear that he had been thinking the same thing. The real question was, was I ready to let go of what had been my safe haven, the first place where I had ever felt secure? In doing so I would be back at square one if it didn't work out between us. It was a big step, but deep inside I just seemed to know that it was time and it was right. There was no pressure at all from Terry, just his support, emphasizing that it was solely my decision and he would accept whatever I decided. The next day my home was up for sale.

During the winter months Terry had been invited to join a "fun-time" bowling league, an activity that years ago he had been active in. It was only once a week, so when work shifts allowed for it, he would bowl and I would watch. Another couple on his team came to do the same thing, only she (Barb) would bowl and he (John) would watch. They were fun to be around, and after bowling we would go to the lounge for a drink. Throughout our conversations we discovered that we both had grown up in the same city and her family still resided there. This was only the beginning.

The more we talked the more we discovered. I had in fact competed against her oldest sister, both of us members of the city's track and field club. Her face was still vivid in my mind, especially recalling her sad brown eyes. Their father was actively involved in the club, and I remembered him driving a few of us to a nearby city to try on various uniforms. Her mother was also very supportive, cheering us on as we ran our various events. The connections we discovered between us were uncanny.

There was another individual who had also been instrumental in forming the local track club. He was about the same age as Barb's father, and he too was very involved. When I asked her about him she replied, "You don't want to know."

He was good friends with her parents and was frequently in their home. They had a shared interest in developing the club, so it was not unusual to see him at the track, both to observe practices and helping out at organized meets.

As it turned out, he had more going on with her sisters than what her parents could ever have imagined. The sexual abuse was horrific and demented, forcing them into acts that no one should ever have to endure, let alone children. As with all pedophiles, he was a pro at convincing them that they could not tell—and they didn't, until it was too late. The damage had been done, leaving its mark, a life sentence of struggle.

Thankfully for Barb, her siblings had determined among themselves that they were not going to let the same thing happen to their little sister—and they succeeded.

Later, it was discovered that they weren't his only victims; no one will ever know how many there actually were. Looking back at my own vulnerability and insecurities during those years, I so easily could have played right into his hand if he had selected me as a target. Gratefully, I was spared.

In early summer of 1997 I was itching to get a puppy, thoroughly missing all the warmth and joy they add to a home. Terry liked dogs, but as a kid growing up he had never had one, so he could not relate to what I longed for. He wasn't crazy about the idea, but on the other hand he wasn't outright opposed; it was at least a starting point.

At about the same time, we had a roofing company come to re-shingle our roof. One of the workers, whom Terry had known from high school, asked me if we would be interested in buying one of his husky pups. He told me that the father was a purebred Malamute, and the mother a purebred Siberian husky that had just recently given birth to five puppies. My interest was evident, and before leaving he wrote down his address and invited me to drop by and have a look at them. I didn't need to be asked twice.

The next day we were working dayshift, and as it so happened, he lived in the area that I was working. Of course I made the time to drop in. His wife was at home with them and he had already told her that I more than likely would be coming by.

They were beyond adorable, but I was immediately drawn to one of the females; now the only obstacle was to convince Terry. Shortly thereafter he drove up to see me holding this little three-week-old black and white fur ball. My eyes said it all, but his reply lacked the enthusiasm I was hoping for. "Yeah, they're really cute, but Isana, what the hell are we going to do with a puppy?"

My power of persuasion paid off, and the next day I was back with my $100 cheque, payment for the puppy that yesterday had stolen my heart. It was official! In just a few weeks she would be coming home.

As passionate as I had been about running, Terry was close behind when it came to golf. Each year, he couldn't wait for the snow to be gone so he could get out and swing some clubs. This year was no different, and on his days off he was up early, eager to get out on the course.

I had nothing against him golfing, and why should I? He loved the game, he was a better than average golfer, and it was time spent with friends who shared the same interest. However, it was triggering old fears and insecurities: the part that said golf would supersede me and that my needs didn't matter; it was the old voices telling me that I didn't deserve to be valued, and that as far as being someone's priority, I belonged on the bottom rung. All of the relationships that I had been in had confirmed this, so why would this one be any different?

As I reflected, self-analyzing my inner dialogue, I concluded that it had nothing to do with Terry golfing but rather my own fear to allow myself to trust—to believe that his actions would back his words, to believe that, to him, I did indeed matter. I knew that I had to move past all the times I had been hurt, because if I didn't, it was inevitable that the past would just re-create itself, leaving me again with the belief that I didn't deserve love. It was my time to create something new.

Chapter 34

I choose you above all others to share my life with me. I want to love you for yourself in the hope that you will become all that you can be ... I take you...
– Marriage Vows of Isana & Terry

With a block of holidays already booked in July, we decided that would be a good time to bring home our new puppy. Casey, as we had named her, was so little and, like a typical puppy, irresistible.

We soon discovered on her first night home that she had a very healthy set of lungs. What started out as whimpers soon turned into full-volume yelps. I didn't care, as right from the start we bonded and I couldn't get enough of her.

Terry's parents did not know about her until we brought her over for the first time. Bob was in disbelief, exclaiming, "What the hell do you want a hound for?"

It didn't take long for both of them to become very attached to her, and if we didn't bring her on our visits, they were clearly disappointed. Soon Bob would question us as to why we hadn't brought the "hound."Any new puppy requires a lot of time dedicated to training and socializing them, with both people and other dogs. Casey was no different. She was smart, catching on quickly, but it wasn't long before her stubborn streak came to the surface. One night, in the early morning hours, I had let her outside to relieve herself, but this time instead of coming back to the door she decided it was play time, wanting no part of going back to her kennel. After that, much to her dismay, a leash became a valuable tool allowing me to reel her back inside.

All too soon our holidays were over and it was back to work. Leaving her was tough, as I much preferred her company to some of the people I had to work with. Little did I know that my preference to stay home would soon become a reality.

On August 8th, 1997, we were working our last 4 - 12 shift, still on the same unit and still not comprehending why they were permitting it. We weren't about to ask.

At 11:30 p.m., I was working alone in the downtown core, hoping for the shift to end before being dispatched to another call. No such luck. A call came in regarding a possible break and enter in progress. The area cars were already at another call, so dispatchers asked me to respond. I was nowhere close to where this was occurring and with it being a priority call, time was of the essence.

I activated my roof lights, picking up my speed. As I approached an intersection, westbound, I tried to recall if the middle of this intersection was still under construction. I looked for signs indicating as much but there were none. The light was green so I stepped down on the accelerator, the cruiser responding with a burst of speed.

The next thing I knew, my cruiser was airborne, and as it connected again with the roadway, the top of my head connected with the interior roof. The undercarriage landed on a protruding sewer pipe, bursting the radiator, and who knows what other damage ensued. I still tried to drive but I wasn't going anywhere.

A man came out of his residence asking me if I was okay, and I told him I was fine, at least I thought I was. He exclaimed that he had witnessed multiple times other drivers encounter the same thing, just not at the same rate of speed as I had.

I discovered that the pavement I was travelling on suddenly ended, dropping over a foot to the north/southbound graveled roadway. The man further went on to say that he had even called the city requesting signs to indicate the construction, but there had been no action taken on their part. He was adamant to witness on my behalf, even taking pictures of the intersection. Thankfully, because of him I was cleared of any wrongdoing. Before the cruiser could even be towed away, barricades were delivered and put in place.

With it being a workplace accident, I was required to attend the emergency department of the hospital to be checked out by a physician. Not exactly where Terry and I wanted to be at the start of our days off. The attending physician determined that I had sustained a minor whiplash and prescribed a muscle relaxant to relieve any soreness. Furthermore, he recommended that I be off work for one week but could after that return to full duties. I had no idea at the time that his diagnosis was way off the mark of what was really going on.

For the next few days I was sore and had limited neck movement. On August 11th, I saw my family doctor as per WSIB (Workplace Safety Insurance Board) instructions. He noted, after his examination, that I had diminished range of motion in my neck and muscular spasms in the trapezius and paracervical muscles. I had also advised him that I was experiencing frequent headaches. The x-ray report taken the night of the accident had come back showing reduction in disc height and degeneration in discs 4–7. He told me outright that he would not be approving my return to work anytime soon and that he would be referring me for physiotherapy.

For the next three months I attended the physiotherapy clinic, two to three times per week along with regular appointments at my doctor's office. Even with all the physiotherapy

I was receiving, my condition seemed to be worsening, and I experienced muscles spasms, joint dysfunction, referred numbness, and frequent headaches.

By late November, my doctor had also seen no substantial progress, which prompted him to write a letter to the WSIB physician. He was straight to the point requesting a MRI "expeditiously" and an assessment by a neurosurgeon in the very near future.

In December, my physiotherapist advised me that she would be discharging me from any more sessions. Her treatments were not making any difference and she felt there was no point in continuing; there was nothing more she could do. However, I finally got word that I was scheduled for an MRI, right after the New Year. All I could do was hope that it would show more than the x-ray had.

In spite of the discomfort I was in, I relished the time with Casey and the opportunity to be at home. I didn't miss midnights in the least, and was finally not feeling sleep deprived like before, but it was really hard to see Terry having to leave for work while I stayed at home. He didn't complain, but I knew how much he didn't want to go in. We had grown accustomed to working together and it had made going to work easier. Although it was not my fault, I still felt like I was letting him down.

Finally, on January 23rd, I met with the neurosurgeon, Dr. Farrell, for the first time. His reputation with patients and the medical field was impeccable and I liked him from the start. He had reviewed all of my doctor's notations and had my MRI results in hand.

After conducting his assessment of me he was straight to the point, stating that I was progressively becoming more disabled. Furthermore, I was showing signs of myelopathy, meaning damage to the spinal cord. What he told me next got my full attention. The MRI showed tiny bone fragments impinging on the spinal cord, and it turned out that what I had gone through in physiotherapy in the attempt to improve my mobility could have actually resulted in paralysis. The only way to correct the damage and prevent further problems would be surgery, fusing together discs C5–C7. He was clear that there were risks involved, but to not have it done would undoubtedly put me in greater jeopardy. After discussing it with Terry we decided that surgery really was my only option, giving the doctor the go-ahead to book a date for the procedure.

Soon after, I received confirmation that it was booked for March 3rd, only a few weeks away. I knew it had to be done, but it still did not dispel my fears and apprehension of what I would be up against—major surgery and a lengthy recovery.

On the morning of, shortly before being wheeled into the operating room, Terry was beside me and I could not hold back the tears. Dr. Farrell was also present, and what he did next was a testament to the kind of doctor he was. Taking my hand, he assured me that it would be okay, that I was in good hands, and I did not have to be afraid. He was a class act, exhibiting compassion when a patient needed it the most.

When it was all over he sought out Terry, informing him that it had gone well and that the surgery was a success. My recovery, however, was now up to me, and it was imperative that I adhere to the restrictions imposed over the next few months.

I found out after the fact that the other member of our family, Casey, did not cope well with my sudden absence. I had been with her every day for the last eight months and now I was nowhere to be found. On top of that, Terry was working day shifts, and in the evening he was at the hospital visiting me. She was in distress, making it clear that she did not like this change in her routine. In the morning, when Terry got up for work, he went to let her out of her kennel only to find her blankets covered in diarrhea and her huddled in the corner. It was not a good start to his day, with him desperately trying not to throw up as he gathered up her unsalvageable bedding. To his horror, he encountered it all over again the following morning; she was mortified and he was at his wits' end, ready to disown her. Thankfully, the next day I came home.

Over the next several weeks I worked hard at my recovery, adhering to the restrictions but remaining as active as possible. Running, of course, was not an option at this point, but thankfully walking was encouraged. Regular appointments had been scheduled with Dr. Farrell, and he was pleased with my progress, noting that the symptoms I experienced prior to surgery had diminished substantially. Other than minor pain, I was feeling great, slowly gaining more mobility and anxious to resume my physical activities.

Early in our relationship, Terry had made it clear that having gone through two divorces he was done with the institution of marriage. He made it clear that he was committed to our relationship, but marrying me was not going to be an option.

I, on the other hand, felt differently. We had been together for almost two years and I wanted him to be my husband and me his wife. I conveyed these feelings to him but I knew that it was not a subject that I should pursue. I had to accept that, for now, this was where he stood. The stark realization that I had to accept was that he might never be ready to get married again. I tried not to dwell on that possibility.

On Terry's days off we made a point of going out for breakfast, enjoying the change in routine. It was a Saturday in mid-August, and on our drive there I knew there was something up with him, but he wouldn't say what. However, as soon as we were seated he said to me, "I've made a decision."

The same intuition that had kicked in when I knew he was going to ask me out kicked in again, and I knew what was coming next. He told me that as our relationship progressed his position changed from "never again" to "let's get married." I felt like I had just won the lottery.

Having come to the conclusion that this was what we both wanted, we didn't see the point of putting if off. We wanted it simple, just the two of us along with my longtime friend Heather to stand up for me and Terry's best friend Greg to be his best man; no invitations, no guests, no gifts of things we didn't need. It went without saying who we wanted to marry us—Gord, a man who was not only a provincial judge but also our friend. When we asked him he readily agreed, honoured that we wanted him to perform the ceremony. He only had one stipulation—it couldn't be during duck hunting season.

On Friday, September 25, 1998, we were married on the number one tee blocks of the country club where Terry golfed. To this very day I have never had a moment of regret.

Chapter 35

The only way to make sense out of change is to plunge into it, move with it and join the dance.
– Alan Watts

Having progressed significantly since my surgery, it was inevitable that I would soon have to return to work in some capacity. Dr. Farrell, in his correspondence to the City's disability management consultant, stated clearly that a desk job was not recommended due to aching and numbing in the trapezius. He further advised that I be allowed a transition period of two to three months with fewer work hours (i.e., four hours per day) before resuming full-time police officer duties.

In spite of his recommendations, "they" seemed intent on relegating me to a desk for the two to three month period, insisting that it could be ergonomically set up for my particular needs. It was a fight to convince them that I needed active movement, not a sedentary position. Once again my family doctor backed me one hundred per cent.

It had been decided that when I did return to work, I would be assigned to another unit—one I had observed to be notorious for not accepting female officers. I had no idea how I was going to cope with what I would be up against.

During this time, Terry and I were out for supper, and an inspector was also at the same establishment. Before leaving he came to our table and told us that he was going to be reviewing the nepotism policy to see if changes could be made. I felt overcome with a flood of relief and a glimmer of hope that maybe things would soon be different.

In late November, as expected, I was sent to my new unit, beginning with four-hour shifts. I had been off work for a total of fifteen months. There had been changes and my confidence was lacking—not a good combination when I believed there were a few officers just waiting for me to slip up. Four hours felt like eight and I was alone with no alibi. There were two other females on the unit but they avoided me, looking out instead for their own survival.

Rumblings began from the get-go regarding my shortened work hours. Even the sergeant, after only one rotation, asked me when my hours could be increased. So much for a two to three month transition period. What made it even harder was being on totally different shifts than Terry. I felt isolated, struggling to stay afloat while constantly being pulled under by those who were supposed to have my back.

Numerous times I just couldn't face going to work and would book off sick, which also didn't help my case. One of the officers on the unit I had at one time considered to be a friend, so I approached him asking if we could please talk.

He refused, giving the excuse that it wasn't a good time; I soon discovered there was never a good time. I also came to the realization that when confronted face-to-face, these officers didn't have the balls to openly discuss what was going on. And yet, behind my back they had no problem rallying the troops against me.

After several weeks, my hours were increased to six-hour shifts, making going to work even harder. I should have been able to go to my sergeant to discuss my frustrations but he, knowing what was going on, seemed to prefer to turn a blind eye, caring more to be liked by the boys of his unit.

Several times I was dispatched to calls that, because of their nature, required two officers to attend. I would arrive and book off at the location, my back-up sometimes never showing up. I was fortunate to escape anything serious, but it was unnerving to know that my safety, with some of them, was not of their concern.

Every day that I went to work I longed to receive word that the nepotism policy had been reviewed and that change was on the way. Months had passed since the inspector had told us that he would be looking into it and I do believe that this was the only thing that kept me going during that time. Little did we know that he hadn't even begun to review it.

In the spring of 1999, I was working the 4 - 12 shift, but was to be off after my six hours. A report had to be submitted before I left, and by the time I completed it, my shift was over. I booked off with our communication centre, but shortly thereafter they advised me that one of the sergeants was ordering me to take a report from a civilian waiting in the front lobby. Its nature was not a priority and easily could have been taken by the officer working the front desk after his lunch break. When I reminded the sergeant that my shift was over, he told me that there was no one available to take it, so I had to do it, further adding, "So, does your neck just start to hurt when your six hours are up?"

I was beyond furious; I was seething. He was blatantly using his rank against me, knowing that if I refused he could have me charged under the Police Services Act with insubordination to a superior officer. He had me and he knew it.

This was the final straw. Ever since returning to work I had borne the brunt of ridicule and ostracism, all because of shortened work hours and, in my opinion, being the wrong gender. It didn't matter that I had undergone a spinal neck fusion and had worked my ass off to regain my physical conditioning. I had kept my mouth shut, hoping that it would get better, but after this I knew that it wasn't going to go away.

The next morning I went to the station to speak with the inspector who oversaw uniform patrol units. I told him what had transpired the evening before, and repeated the sergeant's remark to me, further trying to explain what I had experienced over the last few months. I tried to convey to him that I just couldn't do this anymore, but I didn't have to; it was already obvious to him that I could not go back to that unit. He told me that court section was short an officer, making that position a possibility. I didn't hesitate to say, "I'll take it."

So began my time in court section. It was straight days, Monday to Friday, weekends off. I felt like I had died and gone to heaven. The stress was gone and it was actually enjoyable to go to work, but most importantly it gave Terry and I more time together.

Sometime later, I found out that the sergeant who had made the sarcastic remark to me had been reprimanded by the inspector, as he should have been. However, it was logged in his memory bank, and down the road he would find a way to retaliate.

In late summer, the court sergeant asked me if I would be interested in staying on in court permanently. There were pros and cons to consider, but the biggest pro was that I didn't have to work midnights. Consequently, I conveyed to him that I would like to stay.

What I didn't know was that some officers working the road were complaining that I was just given the court position instead of applying and going through an interview process. I eventually caught wind of their grumbling but didn't think much of it. After all, I had been asked to stay, and that was good enough for me.

In early fall, as the weather changed, people I worked with were coming down with persistent colds and flu-like symptoms. Being in close quarters it was pretty hard to avoid catching the same ailment. In early November, just when I thought I was in the clear, I got hit hard, ending up with bronchitis, forcing me to miss several days of work. While I was off sick, Terry brought home a note that had been left in my mail slot. It was from the deputy chief, advising me that I was being transferred from court section back to the road and going to a new unit, effective in just a few days. I could hardly believe what I was reading and soon my disbelief turned to anger. If they never had any intention of keeping me in court, then why play the game of asking me if I wanted to stay?

I was furious and disheartened all at the same time. It was back to midnights and little time to spend with Terry. I would wake up during the night tossing and turning like a fish out of water, the frustrations swirling in my head like a merry-go-round I couldn't get off of. How was I going to endure midnights with no sleep? When would Terry and I get to spend quality time together? When was the nepotism policy going to be changed, or rather, would it ever be? How long could I live like this?

At least the officers on this unit, for the most part, were nothing like those I had encountered on the previous unit, so that stress was gone. However, my dilemma with midnights was not resolved. Even Terry, who had at one time experienced no difficulty in sleeping during the day, was now encountering insomnia. Between the two of us, we were booking off more nights than what we were going in for. I know it was a factor that did not endear me to members of my unit, and understandably so. However, I couldn't reconcile showing up for work having had no sleep, night after night. It wasn't just my safety that was at risk but theirs as well. I felt trapped between a rock and a hard place with nowhere and no one to turn to for a solution.

Over the past year, the Community Policing section of the department had been expanding. It was a mandated program in which selected officers were assigned to work the same neighbourhood on a continuous basis. Satellite offices were set up in each area, enabling the residents to report incidents or discuss concerns with the officer. Schools in each neighbourhood also utilized the officer to address issues pertinent to the students' needs. Hours were flexible and there were no midnight shifts.

As with any new initiative there were divided opinions on its effectiveness. The popular outspoken cops thought it was a joke, implying that those in these positions were no longer "real" police officers. From what I had observed it was quite the opposite, with the majority totally immersed in proactive rather than reactive policing. The officers in their respective areas handled many calls that otherwise would have been dispatched to officers on the road.

I hadn't really considered applying if a position were to become available, mostly because of the prerequisite of school involvement. The idea of having to do classroom presentations didn't really sit well with me. I believed I wasn't capable or competent enough to handle that task.

However, when two positions were posted in March of 2000, I reconsidered, primarily because there were no midnight shifts. Somewhat reluctantly I applied. After advising my sergeant that I had done so, he gave me his full support and encouragement. He had just completed my yearly evaluation that he had ranked "very good" in every area but one: my reliability in showing up for midnights, which was only fair. Consequently, he thought that this would be a perfect fit for me, highly recommending me for the position. Those of us who applied were all selected for the interview process. For the most part, interviews had been one of my strong suits but as I sat outside the inspector's office waiting to be called in, I struggled to control the nerves. Finally, I was summoned to enter. The interview was lengthy; question after question as each interviewer made notes, remaining stone-faced with little or no feedback.

When it was finally over I felt drained, not knowing if I had scored well enough to be offered the position. Later, I passed one of the interviewers in the hall and he pulled me aside stating that I had done very well and he was impressed. This was encouraging, but for now all I could do was wait and hope they all felt that way.

Terry and I had holidays booked during the first two weeks of April. Our flights and car rental were confirmed and we were looking forward to visiting friends that we hadn't seen in quite some time. Casey was booked in at her favourite boarding kennel, aka "Doggie Camp," so we were set, anxious to get away.

As the day of our departure came closer I still had not heard if I had been accepted for one of the positions. It was unnerving and I was beginning to have my doubts. Finally, on my last day of work, I mustered up my courage and went to see the inspector responsible for the selection process. I explained that we were going on vacation and tentatively asked him if it would be possible to know the outcome before we left. His reply was all I needed as he congratulated me on being one of the selected candidates. It couldn't have been a better sendoff for a much-needed break. I was on cloud nine!

Chapter 36

It's hard to play the game when you aren't given the rules.
– Unknown

Being away on vacation was just what the doctor ordered. Reuniting with old friends brought back all the good times we had shared, leaving us wishing that they could be closer. We visited where I had grown up, the streets I had lived on, and of course the high school track where I had run countless laps. It was surreal, sharing with Terry the places that had shaped the direction of my life so many years ago. The time flew and before we knew it we were headed home.

My new position began immediately upon returning to work, and for the first week I worked alongside the officer who was transferring to another area. There was a lot to take in and a lot to learn, but I was eager to take ownership of the area and claim it as mine.

Throughout the city there were eighteen areas that had their own neighbourhood officer. Mine had the highest number of schools: two high schools and four elementary. With the schools alone my work was cut out for me.

One sergeant, Pat, oversaw all of us, and I liked him from the start. He was easy to work with, always supportive, and ready to offer suggestions and help when asked.

Shortly after I started, another community position became available and I urged Terry to apply. Our offices would be in two different locations, so in compliance with the nepotism policy (which remained unchanged), we would not be working together, but we would be working the same shifts. If he was accepted we would actually be able to go to work together and come home together; it was all that we wanted.

Things finally seemed to be turning around for us. Terry applied and was accepted, all without even an interview.

My first priority in taking over the area was to become known to those who lived there. I made it a point to distribute flyers to every household, introducing myself, stating my objectives and what I hoped to accomplish as their neighbourhood officer. It took hours of walking from door to door but I was determined to complete the task, and I did.

Soon I was being flooded with calls requesting me to take reports of break-ins, vandalism to property, neighbour disputes, family disputes—it was endless. As if that wasn't enough, many times I had to drop what I was doing and attend to emergencies surrounding students at the high schools. Fights erupted, sometimes involving a dozen or more participants; there were students found with drugs; students dealing drugs; students racing cars down narrow residential streets; students threatening students. It even got to the point that the principals requested my presence during the lunch hours when students were outdoors. Regularly, I patrolled back lanes and found their hiding spots where they would get high before returning to afternoon classes. They weren't happy, never knowing when I would suddenly appear.

The principals, on the other hand, were more than appreciative of my availability and quick response. In a very short time, a positive rapport and a great working relationship developed between us.

The elementary schools had different issues that still required my attention. Teachers were calling, asking if I could come and give classroom presentations that covered a variety of topics: bullying, bike safety, dealing with peer pressure, drugs and violence. There was never a shortage of subjects to cover. Much to my surprise I discovered that I looked forward to doing these presentations. I was comfortable in the classroom and thoroughly enjoyed the interaction with the students.

I kept a regular tally of all the calls for service to my area when I wasn't there. Many of these I would follow up on, leaving my card for them to call me if they needed further assistance. I loved working alone and setting my own agenda, tackling problems specific to my area. I had found my niche in community policing.

At the start of every shift, officers would meet for coffee unless they were dispatched to a call. Neighbourhood officers were no different. Terry, myself, and another officer routinely met before going to our respective areas. However, there were still officers that decided to make it their business to complain about Terry and me. As a result, we were informed that we could meet other officers for coffee but not each other. We were expected to operate under a different set of rules without even knowing what the rules were. I don't even think they knew.

In our early days of Community Policing we were not dispatched to calls on the road due to the nature of our job. However, if we were free to take a call within our area, it was expected that we volunteer to take it rather than the officers on the road. For a select number, their griping about this issue was constant, whining to the dispatchers, "Why can't the neighbourhood officer take the call?"

Either they had no idea of what we were involved with throughout a shift or they simply didn't want to know, preferring instead to complain. It was an issue that wasn't going to go away, and the rift between neighbourhood and uniform officers would only continue to worsen.

With the expansion of the Community Policing Program, our sergeant became aware of the need for a community liaison officer to work in conjunction with various committees outside of the department. Several of these task forces were tackling problem areas that could benefit from police involvement. John, whom Terry and I had previously worked with, was selected for the position.

As a result, he was also given the opportunity to attend Ontario Police College to be trained as a D.A.R.E. (Drug Abuse Resistance Education) officer. The program had originated in the United States but was becoming widespread throughout Canada and was proving to be very effective.

The program was a thirteen-week course geared towards students at the Grade 5 and 6 levels. Each week, the D.A.R.E. officer would attend the class and present a forty-five minute lesson. Various group activities actively engaged the students, encouraging them to come up with solutions and ideas. Each lesson's goal was aimed towards giving the students the necessary tools to learn how to say no to drugs and violence in spite of pressure from their peers and other sources.

When John returned from the training, his enthusiasm regarding the D.A.R.E. program was evident. Soon he became involved in a number of schools with teachers and school administrators fully endorsing and supporting it, aware of its potential to steer kids in the right direction and create a lasting influence. Most importantly, the students loved it, eagerly anticipating "D.A.R.E. Day" with Constable John.

Rumours were beginning to circulate that our sergeant could possibly be transferred to another department. Other rumours indicated that our new chief wanted to cut back on the number of neighbourhoods by either eliminating or combining some. The uncertainty began to create dissension and rivalry between officers, with some trying to impress and look good to the chief so their area would be left intact.

Outside of work, other changes were transpiring for us. The house that I shared with Terry had been his house, not one that we had chosen together. On weekends, we enjoyed going to open houses just to see what was on the housing market, even looking at homes far outside of our price range. One thing led to another, and it wasn't long before we were referred to a house that was almost finished being built. Its location was only minutes from work, and traffic was limited to just the residents that lived there. It was a country-like setting surrounded by trees and a nearby river. As soon as we walked in we knew it was for us. The kitchen was exactly what I had wanted, spacious with ample counter space and cabinets. It even had a separate dining room for those special occasions.

After discussing our options we decided to put in an offer. It was accepted, and before we knew it our current house went up for sale and sold shortly thereafter.

In May of 2001 we moved into our home. The neighbours on the left, a really nice couple with three-year-old twins, had built the year before. On our right the property had been sold and construction had just begun; as of yet we had no idea who would be living there.

Our first priority was to fence the backyard so Casey could run free. She loved the size of her new quarters, much larger than the yard she had come from. It didn't take long for all of us to settle in and soon it became our safe haven, our sanctuary away from the drama of the workplace.

In the latter part of 2001, another sergeant, Bruce, was added to our section to help share the supervising responsibilities. I had always gotten along with him so I looked forward to his involvement. However, his added presence did not dispel the rumour that Pat, our other sergeant, was still going to be sent elsewhere.

My neighbourhood office was located in the rear of a building bordering a back lane, not visible from the street and not centrally located. I wanted something that people would take notice of and pass on a regular basis. Furthermore, I wanted to change the name of the zone to reflect more accurately the area that I served.

I ran these ideas past the members of my volunteer committee and they too were in agreement. After discussing this with both sergeants, I was given the go-ahead to try and find another location, provided it was rent free.

My chairperson came across unused office space in a hydro sub-station, directly across from one of my high schools. We checked it out, surprised to find that it was more than suitable. It had a kitchen, washrooms, and a large open upstairs room. The possibilities and potential of this newfound space were exciting. Coincidentally, I was already familiar with the hydro employee who oversaw the facility. There had been trouble with youth congregating on one side of the structure, littering, breaking beer bottles, and sometimes throwing items into the secured compound. With my office being located right there it could only help deter this kind of activity; it was a win-win for both of us.

The added exposure was a huge boost. People would drop in, commenting that they didn't even know they had a community officer. Others would come by and introduce themselves as the parents of some of the kids that I had given presentations to in the schools. Most of all there was one feeling that stood out from everything else: gratefulness for having an officer visible and readily available, allowing them to feel safer in their community.

One of the members of my committee volunteered to hold a craft day, once a month, for children in the area. It took off, with kids filling the large upstairs room, thoroughly enjoying the activities and interaction with their peers.

It also gave me the opportunity to meet parents as they dropped off their sons and daughters, allowing them to discuss any neighbourhood issues or concerns as well as any ideas they might have. I strongly felt that this was what community policing should be all about—establishing mutual trust and then working together to combat crime.

My first year and a half as a community officer was undoubtedly the most enjoyable and rewarding of my career. People from each segment of my involvement were vocal in their appreciation of my efforts, even voicing such to my superiors. However, as the saying goes, all good things must come to an end. Community policing was on the brink of a major change that, in my opinion, was not for the better.

Chapter 37

It is not the bruises on the body that hurt. It is the wounds of the heart and the scars on the mind.
– Aisha Mirza

In the spring of 2002, the rumour that Pat was leaving community policing came to fruition. I was upset to see him leave for several reasons: he had been instrumental in the growth and development of neighbourhood policing; he and Bruce were a good team, approachable with good common sense when it came to problem solving; I had their support with new initiatives that I was attempting in my area. However, there was one reason for my being upset that superseded all others—George, who would replace Pat.

Even though we had never worked together or exchanged words, I felt quite clear that our dislike for each other was mutual. He was also president of our police association, which put on meetings I rarely attended, due in part to him. I refused to endow him with accolades of how wonderful he was; instead I would rather have told him what I really thought. He struck me as loud and obnoxious, giving the impression that he wanted to be heard over everyone else. In my opinion, his ego was insatiable. I didn't trust him in the slightest, believing that he would do or say anything against someone if it served his purpose.

My gut feeling right from the start was that if he could find a reason to get me out of community policing, he would. I determined to tread lightly and try to stay below his radar without drawing unnecessary attention. I did my best to avoid him by only dealing with Bruce, but that was short-lived.

George appeared to me like a bull in a china shop, upsetting everything that had been in place and taking advantage of Bruce's passiveness and laid-back nature. His presence further intensified rifts that were already present between officers. Those who wanted to be on his good side embellished their comments of how great his ideas were, sucking up to ensure that they wouldn't be turfed out.

Within a very short time I was able to draw my own conclusion of where I stood with George—at the very bottom.

The whole dynamics of community policing changed when he came on board. Where before we had mostly been left alone to deal with issues specific to our neighbourhood, now we were being dispatched to calls, many not even in our area. We were pulled in every direction, and I felt overwhelmed in trying to take care of residents and schools that demanded my attention.

When I was first accepted into community policing, it was stressed that each neighbourhood was different and that it was our job to determine how best to serve these differences. What stood out in my area right from the beginning was the timeframe of break-ins to residences. It was a daytime crime, largely due to the high population of high school students. As a result, I worked more dayshifts than afternoon shifts, solely to tackle this problem. On top of this was the high demand for classroom presentations from my numerous schools.

With George now taking charge of approving shift changes, a few select officers who strove to be on his good side began complaining to him about my requests to switch my hours.

He clearly had the power to deny me these changes, which he often did, seemingly without regard or consideration for the needs of my area. I couldn't help but feel like I was letting my neighbourhood down.

On top of this added stress at work, in late July Terry's dad had been diagnosed with prostate cancer, requiring weeks of chemotherapy. His weight loss had been significant and he was so weak he could barely stand. It was difficult to watch him regress so rapidly, the cancer spreading to other organs. He was a proud man who had never relied on someone else for his personal care. It was this loss of human dignity that took away his desire to live, and it was evident he had given up.

Throughout the evening of October 25th we sat at his bedside watching him struggle for every breath, a terribly heart-wrenching thing to observe. Before leaving, we told him that we loved him and that it was okay for him to go, knowing that he would be unlikely to make it through the night.

Not long after falling asleep we got the call that Bob had passed. He had waited until he was alone so no one could witness his final moments, passing away shortly after midnight on October 26, 2002. As proud as he had lived he also chose to die—on his own terms.

I remembered Bob with fondness, and recalled his delight when we sat with him to share a "smash." Furthermore, I was surprised at how much I missed him for having only known him a few years. He had found a special place in my heart.

John continued to deliver the D.A.R.E. program and as a result more schools requested it. Along with his other responsibilities, John was unable to keep up with the increasing demand. I had talked at length with him about the program, excited about its content, hoping that one day I too could deliver it to my area schools.

John was informed that another D.A.R.E. course was going to be offered at Ontario Police College for officers to become trained and certified. He approached Bruce and suggested that I be sent for the training because of my degree of interest. Shortly thereafter, approval came from the chief for me to attend.

In December 2002, I attended the two-week course and received my certification to teach the program; I couldn't wait to get started. By February, I had my lesson plans prepared and ready to go, along with two of my schools on board.

From the outset, the kids' enthusiasm when I showed up for "D.A.R.E. Day," was beyond my wildest expectations. I felt privileged to be there, determined to give each lesson one hundred per cent; they deserved nothing less.

At the completion of the thirteen weeks, course guidelines suggested that the officer hold a special graduation, presenting each student with a personalized certificate. John and I decided to combine all of our classes and hold one large graduation ceremony, complete with dignitaries, parents, teachers and police; the impact of this, especially for the kids, would be enormous.

Even we were impressed, with over 200 students filling the bleachers of the university gymnasium. The support from parents and teachers was overwhelming. One of John's teachers prepared a speech, sharing from his perspective and observation the impact the D.A.R.E. program had on his students and the need for it to continue, describing it as "priceless." The chief also spoke, vowing to keep the DA.R.E. Program active in the schools. At the end of the ceremony, Bruce approached us, stating that he had no idea of what to expect but was really taken aback with the enthusiasm from all participants. He even told John and I how proud he was of us; that I won't forget.

It seemed that George was pulling us out of our areas to make up for shortfalls in other areas that were not even linked to community policing. In my opinion, he had no regard for plans and commitments that we had in place that now had to be changed or cancelled altogether. It made us look bad, giving the impression that other things were more important.

On top of this, a couple of neighbourhood officers who worked the same shift rotations as myself had decided to become my personal bullies. When I would get on the radio to contact our communications centre, one would key the mic so my transmission would not be heard; my pay stubs would continually disappear; cards or invitations put in my mail slot, I never received; in winter, we would start our vehicles to warm them up before going on the road—mine would be shut off. Again, I hoped it would just stop, but it didn't.

One morning over coffee, John told me that he had applied for a position at our community college to teach in the Police Foundations course. I would hate to see him leave but I truly hoped that he would get the job; he couldn't be more suited for the position, and for John it couldn't have come along at a better time.

As expected, some neighbourhood offices were being dissolved and combined with other areas adjacent to it; Terry's was one of them. He was now expected to police a neighbourhood double the size and achieve the same goal of reducing crime. For now my area was left alone, but I knew more changes were coming. All this uncertainty and having to deal with the playground bullies took its toll. I left for work feeling like I was going to vomit. I was caught between a rock and a hard place, loving what I *used* to do as a community officer, but now, under these conditions, everything had changed. I repeatedly asked myself, *How much longer can I take this?* But I had no answer.

Not long after applying to the college position, John told Terry and me that he had been selected to go through the interview process. With his personality and qualifications I was confident he would be selected, and sure enough, a week or so after his interview, he was informed that he was the successful candidate.

I was genuinely excited for him, but this news came at a time when I was feeling vulnerable, frustrated, and uncertain. John had been a support system for me from the very beginning, and now with him leaving, I felt more alone than ever. It went without saying that Terry always had my back—I knew that and, in fact, everyone knew it—but John had supported me as a friend, and I would miss him terribly.

Chapter 38

Dream: A gun right between my eyes. I look straight into the barrel. I am terrified.

Before John resigned in August 2003, he spoke with the inspector in charge of community policing about who would replace him as the community liaison officer. Since I was still the only other officer certified to teach the D.A.R.E. program, John recommended that I be given his position. The inspector agreed, emailing me of this, as well as noting the various committees I would need to contact.

Things happened quickly after that. At my monthly meeting with my volunteer committee, I introduced the officer who had been selected to be my replacement. I had mixed feelings because of the strong ties I had with the people in my neighbourhood, but on the other hand, I hoped this new position would put distance between George and myself.

Two days later, when I came to work, I read through my emails. George in particular had sent one to all of the community officers. I could hardly comprehend what I was reading. It stated who the new community liaison officer was going to be—not me but another neighbourhood officer. It outlined what her duties would be and went on to say that I would continue to present the DA.R.E. Program to two of my area schools and would remain where I was.

I was livid. Such audacity! How could he not have even the decency to communicate this to me face to face? When I asked him and Bruce what was going on, George stated they had discussed it and decided that another officer was a better choice for the position. When asked why this wasn't communicated to me prior to his email he really didn't have an answer. I did: I believed he did it with intention and purpose, not caring in the least about the impact it would have on me.

I spoke to the inspector, expressing my feelings on how this change in plans was communicated, and he agreed, stating it was wrong and should have been handled differently. I tried to explain the issues I was having with George but I felt brushed off, given the impression that he had more important things to take care of.

He did speak to George regarding the poor way it was communicated to me but it only made things worse. Being reprimanded did not sit well with George and I believed that eventually there would be payback.

With the startup of school in September there was an increasing need for my presence during the lunch hour. Several times I had to break up fights between students in nearby parks, usually drug or gang-related. Again, I was being torn in different directions, trying to accommodate the needs of my neighbourhood while being dispatched to calls and demands outside of my area. The only time I found solace was when I was delivering the D.A.R.E. Program.

It was common for each of our neighbourhoods to hold special projects with the objective to diffuse identified problem areas. One of mine was a popular bar that often exceeded the number of people allowed on the premises at any given time. In conjunction with the liquor control enforcer, we had in the past shown up, unannounced, which often resulted in charges being laid under the Liquor Control Act. Due to the volatile nature when dealing with intoxicated individuals, other community officers were also included in the project.

Unknown to me, during my days off, George arranged to target this bar and went ahead, organizing it with the officers in the area adjacent to mine. Repeatedly, George was questioned if he had notified me of what was taking place, since it was my area. He assured them that I would be notified.

I wasn't, finding out after the fact what had transpired. I asked George why I hadn't been contacted and he stated that Bruce was supposed to call me. Bruce had no idea what he was talking about.

I was at my lowest point. George appeared to be winning the quest to make me look bad in the eyes of my superiors and there was nothing I could do about it. I was not given the opportunity to speak or to defend myself.

Then, in early December, we received news that seemed too good to be true: George was being transferred out of community policing. The word "elated" doesn't come close to describing the relief I felt. Finally he would go away, which couldn't help but make things better. For the first time in a long time, I breathed easier.

Shortly before Christmas, both Terry and I were at the station submitting reports. It was a busy 4 -12 shift and calls were getting backed up on the road. George was there, and out of the blue announced that he was teaming us up, and for the rest of the shift we were working the road. It didn't matter that we had previously been ordered never to meet for coffee; here we were once again working together. It was like old times, but what we didn't know was that it would be the last time.

Christmas came and went, ushering us into 2004. Every year, each officer is required to undergo refreshment training in defensive tactics, conducted by a qualified training officer. Ours had been scheduled for Sunday, January 11th during our 4 -12 shift.

We were gathered in the training room when our trainer, who was also a community officer, asked us if we had heard the latest news. He went on to tell us that George was not being transferred after all but was staying in neighbourhood policing.

I felt like I had been kicked—*hard*—and nausea enveloped me. My light at the end of the tunnel suddenly turned dark and menacing, a place where I just couldn't go. I was defeated. I went through the mechanics of changing and getting ready to begin the next segment of training, repeating to myself, "I can't do this anymore. I just can't. I'm done. I need an out."

Terry later relayed to me his conversation with a few other officers as they made their way to the garage where our "scenarios" would play out. Recently, in another province, there had been a fatal shooting of an officer during a training exercise. They had been at their gun range, playing out takedowns of "bad guys." One officer had been called away to respond to an emergency, quickly exchanging the training pistol for his actual service revolver. Upon returning to the range he was rushed to resume, forgetting to switch back to the training pistol. His partner was playing the bad guy, pointing his gun at the officer. The officer responded, firing shots, fatally shooting his partner in the head. Terry had stated, "I hope nothing like that happens here."

Before beginning, our training officer removed our live rounds from our revolvers, adapting our guns to fire paint pellets. Each gun was carefully inspected to ensure the proper ammunition was intact. Raincoats were provided to protect our clothing from the dispersed paint upon impact. Terry and

I were selected to role-play the first scenario and I opted to take the lead role.

The other officers were on the sidelines looking on, two of them being the officers who had harassed and bullied me for months. There they were, arms crossed, whispering comments between themselves, just waiting for me to screw up so I could be the brunt of their mockery. I just wanted it to be over. It was 1930 hours.

The training officer was playing the role of an individual who had a warrant out for his arrest. We had located him in an area of high crime. He hid in the shadows, hard to make out. We were on foot and I called out to him, "Mark, it's the police and we would like to have a word with you."

Suddenly from behind one of the pillars I saw him move, simultaneously with the sharp crack of a shot fired. Immediately I felt a sharp, searing pain in my left hand, consciously thinking that it sure didn't feel like a paint pellet. My next thought was to suck it up and keep going because "they" were watching. After "killing" him, I stated, "I've been shot."

My hand was dripping blood and I couldn't grasp anything. Mark took me to the sink, holding it under the running water, and I saw the bullet fully embedded in the web between my thumb and forefinger. He pulled it out, setting it on the side of the sink.

As soon as my hand was bandaged up, Terry drove me to the emergency department of the hospital to have it treated. We were still under the belief that I had been shot with a paint pellet, even though thoughts in the back of my mind were screaming otherwise, thoughts that I smothered before they could surface.

The next day, we had to go to the station to file the necessary forms for a workplace accident, along with the doctor's report. It was then that we learned the truth.

I had been struck with a .32 caliber plastic bullet that travels at 800 feet per second. Our actual live rounds that we carry in our service revolvers travel at 900 feet per second, not significantly faster. The bullet that had been removed from my hand and placed on the side of the sink was gone—and it never resurfaced.

Before leaving the station, we were in the neighbourhood office, along with the inspector. Terry asked him if he could have some "compassionate" time off, considering that I had been shot. His response? "Only if *you* had shot her."

The training officer, to the best of my knowledge, was never questioned or reprimanded as to why his gun was loaded with incorrect ammunition. There was never an investigation, and the entire episode was swept under the carpet like it never transpired. Furthermore, he never apologized or showed any remorse for what he had done.

I was left only with the stark realization that if the bullet had impacted my neck instead of my raised hand, it could have been fatal, and these pages would never have been written.

I was in for a very long road ahead, unaware that my desperate plea for needing an out had indeed been heard.

PART VII

Chapter 39

Dear God, I hurt. Please hold me. Amen.
– Richelle E. Goodrich

In the days that followed the shooting, I was on autopilot, frequently gazing at my bandaged hand and watching my entire forearm turn into various shades of black and blue. The doctor who initially treated me had stated in his report that I would be off work for a period of five to seven days. However, when I saw my family doctor on January 19th, he couldn't have disagreed more.

He was in utter disbelief when I relayed to him what had occurred and expressed his disgust in the way it was handled—or rather, *not* handled. From a physical standpoint there was swelling and limited movement. If I attempted to grasp anything, the pain was intense. In his report he recommended that due to the nature of my injury I should remain off work, also adding that he believed there would likely be permanent internal damage.

I was determined to continue delivering the D.A.R.E. Program to my three classes. We were only halfway through and I was not going to let them down. Though not aware of it at the time, they became my little therapists with their infectious positive energy. Their classrooms also provided me an atmosphere of safety that I did not feel elsewhere; feeling the need to hide would only worsen as time went on.

In the fall of 2003, we had booked and paid for an all-inclusive trip to the Mayan Riviera in Mexico for the last week of February. It couldn't have come at a better time. The resort where we stayed featured a labyrinth, which encourages the ancient practice of "circling to the centre." One was encouraged to walk slowly, following the intricate pathways and to turn one's thinking inward, asking for clarity and insight. Its purpose was to calm those who were dealing with change and transition, offering a self-alignment tool to help put one's life in perspective.

As I walked its paths, I pleaded for peace and the ability to accept whatever the outcome would be regarding work. I visited this labyrinth several times, wanting to feel and absorb its energy, wishing that it could continue to resonate deep inside of me.

We had a choice of several excursions, but there was one in particular that captivated me—the opportunity to swim with dolphins.

It was an experience that touched me deeply and I felt the magic of these spectacular beings. They exhibited power and freedom, gentleness, and intelligence. I didn't want to leave.

When we returned home, my anxiety escalated with the pressure to return to work in some capacity. I was avoiding the police station, not even wanting to drive by. When I was forced to go there I entered through back entrances, climbing back stairwells, avoiding other officers as much as possible. It was on one of these occasions I learned that another officer had been assigned to my area, complete with business cards that endorsed him as the neighbourhood officer. I could only assume that he was in and I was out.

My doctor had already picked up on much more than the physical injury, that being the psychological effect it was having on me. He even sent a letter to the chief requesting that they take the heat off of getting me back to work. His letter was never acknowledged.

In April, it was arranged that for a few hours each day, I would interview the people listed as references on police application forms. I dealt specifically with the head of human resources, submitting my findings and reports to him. For the most part, I worked from home, only attending the station when I absolutely had to.

On one occasion I went to hand in some completed paperwork. As per my usual, I was headed towards the rear door, not aware that the Emergency Tactical Unit was on the other side involved in a training exercise. As I approached there was suddenly a series of shots fired. I froze. I couldn't breathe, my body paralyzed with fear. I tried to brush it off but it wasn't going away.

Our physiotherapist who Terry and I saw on a regular basis was also seeing the signs of PTSD (Post Traumatic Stress Disorder). On April 10th, he sent a letter to my WSIB caseworker stating: "Although I am not fully qualified to make this call, I do recognize elements of PTSD. This should be investigated by the proper health professionals."

His recommendation went unheeded.

I finished up with my remaining D.A.R.E. classes and decided to combine all of them for a joint graduation ceremony. I asked John to be my MC and he readily agreed. I sent a letter to the chief requesting, if possible, that he attend. He declined, forwarding my letter to the inspector who also declined. Then it was sent to George. In plain view Terry saw it on his desk with a line drawn through the letter and written across it in bold letters—"NOT!"

There was no representation from the police department. In spite of what appeared to be a blatant lack of support, it was a huge success.

The ultimate insult occurred on April 29th when I was handing in reports to the head of Human Resources. He stated that he didn't know what this was all about, but George had gone to the chief requesting that he order me to report to him every morning at 8:00 a.m. The chief had agreed and had told him to inform me.

I was becoming undone to the point of total collapse. I was barely able to handle just the few times I had to physically attend the station, but now, every day, having to report to George? I believed it was all about control, nothing else.

I somehow made it home and it was there that I fell apart. Terry was desperate, knowing I needed major help, but to whom could we turn? And then he knew.

On March 9, 1993, at 1520 hours, Terry and another officer were dispatched to a local park. They were to investigate the contents of a garbage bag that some girls had found behind a retaining wall. They had told the call taker that it felt "fleshy" when they poked at it.

What Terry was about to discover forever changed his life. The contents were those of a newborn baby boy, the umbilical cord still intact, but clearly with no sign of life. He went through the motions of taking the report, questioning the girls, doing a thorough investigation before beginning his days off.

It was the following morning that he knew something was very wrong. He drove aimlessly, not even remembering where he had gone, but found himself walking through the back door of the police station. An officer saw him walk in and immediately knew something was terribly wrong, ushering him into the lunchroom. When an inspector came in, one whom Terry respected, he broke down, sobbing, unable to hold it together.

He was referred to Don, a doctor in psychology who diagnosed him with PTSD; it was Don who gave him the help and support that he needed.

Now, seeing me in distress, he drove to where Don lived. His wife was there and she assured Terry that she would contact him to call us ASAP. Within a very short time he called.

I believe that certain people cross our paths at crucial times and in a very real way become our angels on earth. Without a doubt, Don was one of those people.

He told Terry that I was not to return to work under any conditions. He would contact the appropriate people and advise them that I was now under the care of my doctor and himself. He would handle it and I was not to worry.

So began my journey with Don. Years earlier, he had been there for Terry and now he would be there for me—I just didn't know to what extent his involvement would turn out to be.

Chapter 40

Dream: I was in a hallway with nowhere to go. A group of men had me trapped, forcing me into a room. They all sat around a big table and I knew I was there to be tortured. I scream but no one hears me. I wake up terrified, unable to move.

Following my initial appointment with Don, he diagnosed my condition as chronic/severe. He had given me a series of questions related to PTSD, and according to the Post-traumatic Stress Scale, I had recorded sixteen symptoms out of a possible seventeen. In Don's words, "The road ahead is going to be long."

To add insult to injury, I soon discovered that certain officers felt it was their duty to ostracize me from the ranks. If they saw me in public it was like I wasn't there. If Terry and I were together, they would greet him but would intentionally ignore me.

This only added to my frustration and guilt, feeling that there must be something inherently wrong with me as to why I just couldn't "suck it up" and get back to work. I felt like a bad little girl who was being punished, my distorted perception actually allowing a part of me to believe that I deserved it. I learned to keep my head down and avoid eye contact. I was no longer a "real" cop but rather a huge failure.

The wound in my hand had healed well, however it ached constantly and I could not grip anything without experiencing sharp pain. On June 8, 2004, I was sent to Toronto for an assessment from the WSIB Hand Specialty Program. Based on their results they recommended I attend a hand-strengthening program three times per week, for a period of eight weeks.

My hand, however, was the least of my worries. When I returned home from Toronto, I was summoned to testify in court where other officers would be present. This sent me in a downward spiral, anxiety taking over, desperately wanting to run and hide.

Don tried to intervene by writing a letter to the court sergeant, pleading my case, but it went nowhere. I had no choice. If I didn't attend I knew with certainty that they would have me charged under the Police Services Act for refusing to obey an order and neglect of duty.

Court was set for Monday, June 14th, 10:00 a.m. On the Sunday, in desperation, I phoned our friend, the judge who had married us. He was aware of what I was going through and volunteered to phone the Crown Attorney to see if he would be willing to give me a call so that I could explain to him my situation.

Not long after, he called. I tried so hard to make him understand, but his response was sarcastic and belittling, undermining what I was going through. He told me that all he could do was speak to the presiding judge in the morning; if the judge agreed that I was not required, he would call and let me know.

Needless to say, I didn't sleep, anxious thoughts bombarding me throughout the night. There was no call in the morning to excuse me. Terry assured me he would be there, no matter what, to give me his support.

When I approached the stand I noticed two sergeants from the station seated in the courtroom, sergeants who had nothing to do with the case or court involvement. I could only assume they were sent there to make sure I showed up. Their presence only added to my stress level and I have no idea how I made it through the hearing. It was like I was on remote and someone else was talking through me.

When I was finally free to leave court, Terry walked me to the parking lot where I fell apart, sobbing, shaking, wanting to throw up.

It didn't end there. The following day, Terry booked off sick, feeling that I needed him at home. He was right.

When he returned to work on the Wednesday he read a message from George that had been sent on Tuesday, first thing in the morning. It had stated that he wanted Terry to report to him immediately. Now, upon reading this, Terry went to see what it was all about. George informed him that the inspector wanted to see him upstairs, now.

Two inspectors were present, questioning him as to why he hadn't responded to George's message from the day before. He explained that he had booked off sick and did not get the message until today. Then they proceeded to question him as to why he was at court on Monday when he had no business there. Terry stated, straight to the point, "I was there to support my wife."

With that they told him that he was being transferred out of Community Policing back to Uniform Patrol, effective immediately.

Not long after this had all transpired we ran into the judge who had presided over the case. He apologized profusely, stating that if he had known my circumstances at the time, he would certainly have excused me from having to testify. The Crown Attorney never consulted him prior to the trial as he had told me he would. Obviously, he had never intended to.

Throughout the summer, I saw Don on a regular basis, often reduced to tears when discussing "them." Every day I would see police cruisers slowly drive by our house for no apparent reason. I felt spied on, almost like they were trying to catch me doing something that I wasn't supposed to, whatever that was. All it did was increase my anxiety and guilt.

In September 2004, Don wrote to my WSIB caseworker stating that the nature and severity of PTSD had not lessened or improved, and in his opinion he did not think that I would ever be able to return to my workplace.

As a result, it was decided that I would be assessed in Toronto by a team of doctors from the Psychological Trauma Program. Appointments were set up for over the course of two days, October 26th and 27th. Initially, they were not going to cover the cost of having Terry come with me but again, Don came through. He convinced them of my need and the importance of having Terry there for support. Thankfully, they complied.

By the end of the two-day period I was exhausted from question after question that covered my entire life: rehashing childhood abuse right up to the present day. I so wanted all of it to just go away, but it was far from over.

A month or so later, we received their analysis regarding the interviews and tests that had been conducted.

They agreed with Don regarding the severity of my PTSD and the high anxiety I exhibited when discussing the workplace. Their final conclusion was that they believed it to be unreasonable to expect me to return to the department, in any capacity. It was also their recommendation that a plan be devised, sooner rather than later, to return me to the workforce, even if retraining in another field was required.

The decision was made. I wasn't going back.

Chapter 41

There is a crack in everything; that's how the light gets in.
– Leonard Cohen

I was numb. Relieved in one sense that I wasn't going back, but at the same time the question that was paramount in my mind was, *What the hell am I going to do?*

I was forty-eight years old and had absolutely no desire or interest to go back to school. When I opted to change careers and become a police officer, that was supposed to be it, finishing my work career as a cop. This wasn't supposed to happen. What frustrated me the most was that "they" had done this to me—and now *I* was the one who had to pay? It just wasn't fair.

WSIB did not waste any time in getting a plan in motion. Clearly, their goal was to get me back to work—somewhere.

It was known as LMR—Labour Market Re-entry Program. I was assigned to Cheryl, a caseworker from the Employment Services division of Ontario March of Dimes. Her job was to find out where my interests lay and how my skills could work in conjunction with them. If my skills or qualifications were lacking, then retraining would be required; I wouldn't have a choice. All of her findings were forwarded to WSIB for their feedback and approval.

In my first meeting with Cheryl, I expressed my frustration and feeling that I was being forced into something that I just didn't want to do. She empathized but it didn't change what she was mandated to do—get me back to work.

On January 25, 2005 I was sent to undergo a psycho-vocational assessment that lasted most of the day. The results were intended to assist in narrowing down where I would best be suited, taking into account my strengths and weaknesses.

Also considered in the vocational pursuit was the average hourly rate of pay, depending on the profession. At the time, I was earning just under $31.00/hour as a first-class constable. Nothing else out there was even close. One thing was becoming very apparent: to obtain a job anywhere near my current salary, earning a degree or diploma in something would be necessary.

The thought of being forced back to school just added more stress, anxiety, and feeling like what I wanted, or didn't want, just didn't matter. Decisions were being made for me, and if I didn't comply or cooperate, WSIB would simply cut me off.

I continued to see Don, breaking down frequently. He constantly assured me to take it one step at a time—he wasn't going anywhere and he would continue to represent my best interests. For now, I had to jump through the hoops they threw at me. I had no idea how long I could keep this up, feeling I had no control over the direction of my life.

One work option I discussed with Cheryl was the possibility of working with youth. I had loved presenting the D.A.R.E. Program, but who would hire me to do something similar, especially at a higher-than-average wage? Pressure was being put on me to do a work placement of some kind, even in a volunteer capacity. It was during one of my sleepless nights that an idea was forming in my head.

What if I put together a program for youth, similar to the D.A.R.E. Program, but with the style and curriculum created by me? I knew the issues that were relevant and important for kids at the Grade 5/6 levels; it would be just a matter of gathering information and putting it all together. This, of course, would take some time; my hurdle now would be to convince Cheryl to treat this project as a placement.

In our next meeting, I ran my idea by her, explaining that my goal would be to eventually present it in classrooms. After some discussion she agreed, much to my relief. She believed this new direction could be the basis for work as a life skills coach, but the question still loomed: Who would hire me? I tried to put that thought aside, just relieved that for now I had bought myself some time.

I delved into it, spending many hours putting the material together. The end result was a series of eight lessons covering a variety of topics, all of which pertained to challenges they faced on a daily basis. Each lesson's main focus was incorporated into a workbook along with exercises designed to portray real-life scenarios. The next challenge was in how I would get it into the schools to present it.

I sent out samples and cover letters to contacts I had made while on the job, but their feedback was not what I wanted to hear. To go into the schools independently to work with youth, I would require a diploma or degree in social work. My days of freely coming and going into schools as a police officer were over; now I required a piece of paper. It wasn't fair.

I needed to be under the umbrella of an organization that already had the school board's approval to be there. Fortunately, Darrell responded to the information I had sent him. He was a social worker employed with an organization that provided services for low-income families living in the intercity area. Also included in his responsibilities was involvement with elementary students in the same geographical vicinity. He believed that what I had put together would greatly benefit students at the Grade 5/6 level.

It became clear right from the outset this would not be a paid position. Darrell himself was hired on a short-term contract; its continuation was totally dependent on whether or not funding was available. I still agreed to do it knowing that the kids in this area of the city needed it more than anyone. Some of their situations were unimaginable.

However, as excited I was to present it, it was not going to fulfill the mandate of getting me back to work. The reality of having to go back to school was becoming glaringly clear.

Between Cheryl and my WSIB caseworker, it was decided that my best option for obtaining work would be to enroll in the social work program at the community college. I met with the head of the department who was very encouraging and pleasant, but my heart was not in it, even though some of the courses appeared somewhat interesting.

I was beyond anxious at the prospect of now *having* to return to school. Again Don intervened, strongly recommending that I be allowed to start slowly, perhaps with just one course at the outset.

It was decided that in January 2006, I would take the English/Grammar course that was mandatory for all first-year students. I did not have to attend class for this but could work on it independently from home. As well, I would present my lessons along with Darrell at two of the intercity schools. Following completion of the first course, I was expected to complete another elective before enrolling full-time in September 2006.

Nightmares continued to disrupt my sleep and I would often wake myself up by screaming out. My mind would start reeling with the worry and anxiety of returning to school, squelching any hope of falling back to sleep.

I continued to go for my runs with Casey, trying to avoid main thoroughfares where police cruisers were very likely to pass by us. On the outside, it appeared as though there was nothing wrong with me, but the inner turmoil was building, not dissipating. I was vulnerable and edgy, constantly looking over my shoulder, waiting for whatever was going to happen next.

As per the plan, I gathered the textbooks and lesson material that I was to begin working on, my confidence severely lacking.

Again, the one bright spot was when I was in the classroom presenting my program. The kids loved it and the teachers were fully engaged and supportive. Darrell and I worked well together. I took charge of the teaching aspect while he participated in discussions and helped out with group activities.

My afternoons were mostly devoted to working on the course. After each lesson was a quiz that I had to complete and turn in to the Distance Education department for marking. I was always apprehensive of the results. I was scoring well but felt like it was just a fluke, certain that I would totally mess up on the final. With just this one course taking up so much of my time I couldn't help but wonder how I would ever handle a full course load. The self-doubt and pressure that I was putting on myself consumed me. Feeling like a failure as a cop only exacerbated my inner belief that I was sure to fall short of what was expected of me.

As the end of March approached, my anxiety level was heightened with pressure from WSIB to complete this course and get on to the next. I had no warning as to what was about to unfold.

It was a Sunday evening and Terry had taken me out for supper. Throughout our meal we talked about the pressure I was feeling and the uncertainty of the future. Suddenly I became detached from my surroundings and Terry's voice sounded like it was coming from far away. I heard myself talking but it wasn't my voice. It came from deep down, a place of desperation and hopelessness as I heard it speak out, "I have no choice, I can't do this. I have to go back, I have to go back." (Meaning, back to the police department.)

Terry was afraid, having never seen me like this, hearing a voice that wasn't mine and having no idea what to do. Once in the car I became silent but went into something like a trance, staring into nothing.

Terry somehow got me into the house where it continued. I heard myself letting out deep moans, still trance-like, bent over, rocking back and forth. He was desperate and phoned one of our neighbours, Leanne, to please come over—he needed help. He phoned Don, leaving a message to call him immediately. I was falling apart and he didn't know what to do. He phoned the nurses' registry for them to forward a message to our family doctor to call us ASAP.

After some time, Leanne and Terry's voice became audible and my own voice returned. I was exhausted. At some point while Leanne was there, Terry took all of my course material off of my desk and concealed it so I wouldn't be inclined to keep at it. He had decided that enough was enough.

The next morning, I remember looking in the mirror, feeling like I was looking at a stranger, not knowing who she was. Don had been out of town, but when he got Terry's message he immediately made arrangements to see me, along with Terry. Once I was in his office my body went into uncontrollable tremors and my voice was barely audible. He determined, as had Terry, that I could no longer continue on this plan. I had also seen my family doctor who as well observed the tremors and inability to pull it together. In joint consultation, they agreed that returning to school was not going to work and I was to stop immediately. Don advised Cheryl and WSIB of this latest development and that my condition was fragile. It was time to back off.

They had come very close to having me hospitalized and, without Terry's support, I undoubtedly would have been. He was my rock that brought me back. I discovered through this experience that the mind indeed is a fragile thing. If pushed to the limit without heeding the warning signs, inevitably it will break. I know that without the intervention from Don and my doctor the outcome would have been very different.

Chapter 42

In three words I can sum up everything
I've learned about life.
It goes on.
– Robert Frost

There were only a few weeks remaining in the schools to complete the lessons, and with Darrell's help I made it through. He was supportive and understanding, willing to complete it himself if it was too much for me to handle. I thanked him for offering but it was where I needed to be. The department had cancelled the D.A.R.E. Program, even with two other officers recently certified.

I did not understand. Why cancel a program that was so necessary and had proven itself to be effective? I felt compelled to replace what had been taken away. These kids deserved the right to learn how to cope with the challenges of their world. I vowed to finish what I had started. It was only right.

The stress of our situation had also impacted Terry. He felt helpless, unable to fix what I was dealing with, and all he could do was stand by and support me as best he could. In one of our sessions with Don he stated that when at work, his mind was not on the job; he was anxious and sleep deprived. More often than not, he was booking off sick during midnight shifts, unable to function properly. Don strongly suggested that he take some time off on stress leave and refuel, so to speak. We didn't need to have our lives complicated even more by something happening at work because of Terry's mind focused elsewhere. At first, the insurance company rejected Terry's application to be off on short-term disability (STD). However, between Don and our doctor's input, it was enough to grant him nine weeks off, time that he so needed.

Soon we would be met with another challenge. Prior to being off on STD, Terry had undergone an x-ray and a series of MRI scans due to an incident of his head hitting the door-frame of the cruiser. He was experiencing some neck pain, so as a precaution scans were conducted. Each of them came back showing an "unknown mass" adjacent to his shoulder blade. Consequently he was referred to a neurosurgeon for his analysis, finally getting an appointment for early September. We were both concerned; each of us not wanting to vocalize our fear of the possibility that it could be malignant.

The mass was in a precarious position: behind the shoulder blade and positioned alongside the spinal cord. It would require two surgeons, one to open the chest cavity and the second to remove the tumour.

A few days after signing the consent forms we were informed that the surgery would take place on October 12, 2006. As the day drew nearer I grew more anxious thinking of all that could go wrong, but not admitting my fears to Terry. Instead, I shared my worries with Gord, our judge friend to whom we had increasingly grown close.

On the day of, two friends sat with me as the hours crawled by: Gord and Barb, both doing their best to distract me from my vigilant scrutiny of the waiting room's clock. The surgeon had promised to let me know how everything had gone but failed to do so, only adding to the intensity of my anxiety. Finally, hours later, the nursing staff informed me that Terry had been taken to the intensive care unit to be closely monitored for the next twenty-four hours. The crucial part was over, leaving ahead the long road to recovery. Terry's goal was simple: recover in time for next year's golf season.

A few weeks later we received the news that we had waited and hoped for: the tumor was benign.

In the days following his surgery Terry complained of a persistent raspy sensation in his throat. At first we thought it was from the oxygen tubes inserted during surgery, but nothing was alleviating it. Weeks later, it still persisted, so he attempted to make an appointment with the surgeon who had removed the tumour, but was declined, and we had no idea why. Finally he was referred to an ENT (ear, nose, and throat) specialist for consultation.

After the initial examination, Terry was informed that during surgery his vocal cord had been nicked, resulting in paralysis. Since the equipment necessary to repair it was not available locally, he would have to be sent to Toronto to have the specialist there perform the procedure. The doctor explained to Terry that a stent would be inserted alongside the vocal cord, giving it support, and would then be "tuned" to the proper frequency. For now it was a matter of waiting for a date when the procedure could be carried out. In retrospect, it was no wonder that the surgeon responsible refused Terry's request for an appointment: he did not want to take responsibility for his slipup.

For the past several months, Don had continued to monitor my progress, or rather lack thereof. It was becoming very apparent to him that I was truly a casualty of the workplace. My symptoms of PTSD persisted and he felt they were likely to remain. His belief of where my condition was at compelled him to write a letter in January 2007 to my WSIB caseworker. He stated that I was not going to be capable of returning to work; training, re-training, and employment of any kind was out of the question. He further stated that he blamed the department for the way they had handled (actually, the way in which it was *not* handled) the incident. What he observed was a highly anxious, moderately-to-severely depressed, vulnerable and fragile victim of the workplace. In his opinion, a decision regarding my future needed to be made.

On February 26, 2007 I was sent to see a psychiatrist. All of Don's documentation had been sent prior to my appointment for his review. For two hours I was questioned on matters that I was sick and tired of, issues from my childhood right up to the present, all of which had been documented in previous appointments with other psychologists and psychiatrists. I prayed that this would be the end of it, but for now we just had to wait.

Arrangements were finally made for Terry to see the specialist in Toronto. The procedure was booked for May 12th—one day before his forty-seventh birthday. We could only hope that the results would be a great birthday present.

We arrived early at the clinic to begin all the pre-op preparations. I immediately liked his surgeon. She was young, energetic, and straightforward with the facts of what she was going to do and what to expect afterwards. One thing she made clear: although Terry's voice would sound normal, he would be limited in the ability to raise his voice. The damage had been done and the vocal chord itself was irreparable.

The procedure did not take long; the stent was in place, and amazingly Terry's voice was back to normal. However, for the next twenty-four hours he was not allowed to talk, so it was a quiet birthday celebration. We were just relieved and thankful for the positive outcome.

We couldn't help but wonder, was this surgical error an actual blessing in disguise? In order to work on the road as a cop, it is imperative that one be able to shout out police commands that can be heard loud and clear. Seemingly for Terry, this would no longer be possible. He was burnt out from working twenty-five years as a frontline officer, desperately wanting to be off the road. This perhaps could be the solution to more of a behind-the-scenes position. We would just have to wait and see.

As summer approached, I found myself still on hold and uncertain what "they" were deciding about my future. All I knew was that the report sent to WSIB from the psychiatrist that I had seen in February confirmed Don's analysis of my condition. What I wasn't aware of was that all of the reports and documentation from my file were now in the hands of a consulting psychologist for WSIB. His mandate was to do a full review of all the reports, taking everything into account and drawing his own conclusion of where to go from here. Ultimately, his decision would be final.

On July 31, 2007, I was at home with Casey and Terry was golfing. As per usual I walked to the corner to pick up our mail, immediately noticing a letter from WSIB addressed to me. Instantly, I was overcome with anxiety, dreading what was written and certain that it wouldn't be good. Now what were they going to make me do? I opened the envelope, wishing desperately that Terry were home with me, hesitating to read its contents.

I read it quickly, trying to brace myself for the bad news. I read it again and then again, believing that there had to be a catch. Obviously, I had to be misunderstanding the words that I read.

In the letter, my caseworker explained that all of the psychological and psychiatric reports in my claims file had been sent to a WSIB psychologist for review in order for him to reach a conclusion regarding my level of disability. After reviewing all of the clinical evidence, his opinion was that I was totally disabled and incapable of participating in a return-to-work program or LMR (Labour Market Re-entry) activities.

Furthermore, in regards to my level of disability and my age taken into account, I was considered to be unemployable in the general labour market. However, I would continue to receive a full LOE (Loss of Earning) benefit.

Anxiously, I waited for Terry to get home to read the letter and verify that yes, I was interpreting it correctly. I kept my guard up, afraid that if I let myself believe what I had read my hopes would be shattered.

For three and a half years, I had gone through hell—decisions being made for me over which I had no control. Suddenly, I was given the hope of being able to reclaim my life. Still, I knew that nightmares would persist and that the PTSD would always be there, just under the surface, waiting for the next trigger to yank me back into its clutches.

Chapter 43

To forgive is to set a prisoner free and discover that the prisoner was you.
–Philip Yancey

Apart from the many stressors that had impacted our lives, 2007 presented other challenges that gave me the opportunity to make a choice—the choice to hang on to past resentments or to let them go.

In early November 2006, my brother informed me that our mother had been hospitalized and her condition was dire. In so many words he stated that if I had anything to say to her, now would be the time.

I had not seen or spoken to either her or my father since attending my niece's wedding in 1995. It was a decision that was right for me, choosing to live my life without their involvement. However, now knowing that her time was closing in, I needed to make a choice. Would I let her die without hearing from me or would I acknowledge her existence?

I did not hate her, but on the other hand the word "love" was not a fit. I could not conjure up a feeling that wasn't there and in fact never had been. I felt no bond with my mother and was therefore not experiencing sadness in knowing she was dying.

It didn't seem right—after all, she was my *mother*, so shouldn't I feel *something*?

In spite of the hurt and pain experienced as a child, largely in part from her actions and also lack thereof, I needed to let it go. She had done her best but was simply not equipped to deal with what life had handed her. I did have things to say to her, in part for her benefit but also for mine. I wanted a clear conscience, having no regrets of ever thinking, *I should have...*

I told Ron that I would be writing her, and he asked if I would mind if Ken, (a friend of his and also an Anglican minister) could assist in reading it to her, a bit at a time, allowing her to process it as she was able. That was fine with me.

On November 10th, I sent her my final words:

> *I am writing this note for the purpose of having it read to you. First of all, I want you to know that it is okay for you to go. I am okay. I am in a wonderful, loving relationship with a man who loves and respects me deeply. Life for the most part is good. When I reflect on my childhood I am filled with various emotions. I am angry. I am sad. I am disappointed. I remember never feeling good enough. I remember feeling guilt and shame for who I was. I felt abandoned and that I just did not matter. That was then and this is now.*
>
> *Yes, those same feelings do at times creep in and I remember. However, I have used that experience to become who I am today. I am an honest person. I am a very loving, giving, and caring person. I feel deep empathy for people who suffer unnecessarily due to the circumstances they are in. I am passionate about protecting children and giving them reason to believe that they are special, unique, and valued.*

I am a good person. My life has been a journey and will continue to be until it is my time to cross over.

Your time to go appears to be soon. You can be at peace. It is okay for you to go. Let the light embrace you and do not be afraid.

Ken did present this to my mother and afterwards he sent me a letter. He told me that my words gave her the opportunity to face hard questions and profound issues that they discussed in length, again and again. He also stated, "Know that she is sorry." In her words, "Very sorry for the wrongs to my daughter Frances."

On January 3, 2007 my mother passed on. I believe my father, who had suffered from Alzheimer's disease, somehow knew that his wife was gone. On February 5th, only thirty-three days later, he too passed on.

I chose not to attend their funerals. It would not have been appropriate considering the fractured dynamics between my older brother and sister; rather it would have been a distraction, unfitting for the event. Besides, I had already said my goodbyes, holding no regret.

Not even a month had passed since my father's death when I began to notice the presence of a crow that was larger than most, appearing to follow me. Over the winter I regularly dropped birdseed on the shoulder of the road for the resident wildlife and I noticed that he was now helping himself to the handouts.

I began to play a game with him (it just seemed like he was a male!) dropping extra treats on our driveway whenever I would leave for a run with Casey. When I returned I would drop a few more. It became a ritual, so every time I went outside he was never far away, waiting to swoop down and make his claim.

One spring day, I sat on the deck relishing the warmth of the sun when suddenly I saw a flash of black as the crow swept in, landing on the railing only a few feet away. I was fascinated. He stared directly at me and I was drawn in to his jet-black penetrating eyes.

In a soft voice I talked to him and he just sat there, unafraid. Slowly I got up and went inside to retrieve some treats then slowly came back onto the deck. With that he flew to the roof of the garage and continued to watch me. Carefully, I placed the treats on the deck railing, then returned to my chair. As soon as I was seated he returned, tentatively taking each treat one at a time, being sure to keep a watchful eye on me before flying away.

Native legend states that the crow is very mystical and able to bring messages to the living from ancestors in the spirit realm. He is believed to be a Watcher, acting as a messenger between the physical and spiritual worlds. I have no idea if he was sent or if this was his purpose in "choosing" me. That part didn't matter. This was only the beginning of an extraordinary bond that developed between him and I; the encounters still yet to unfold would become memories that would always be held close to my heart.

In August, our doctor gave Terry the okay to return to work, provided it wasn't a frontline position. He had recovered well from his surgeries, but just as the ENT surgeon had predicted he was unable to shout out in a loud voice. Consequently, he was given a job in the Records department, inputting information to the database. Not overly exciting, however he was relieved to be off the road and working straight days, Monday to Friday.

One day he was conversing with the court sergeant who advised him that a position would soon be opening up for a court security officer. Terry expressed that he would very much like to be considered for the job. With only five years to go before retiring, it would be a perfect position to end his career on. As soon as the job was posted Terry applied, hoping for the best.

A few weeks later he received the good news that he had been accepted and was to begin on September 24, 2007. Finally it seemed like things were turning around for us.

With the start of school, Darrell and I were back presenting my material to three intercity schools. It provided me with the feeling that I was making a positive contribution, something that I really needed to experience after what I had gone through.

One day, however, I received a call from an inspector for whom I had a lot of respect. He apologized for what he was about to ask me, explaining that he had to follow up on information that he had received.

Apparently an officer reported that I was going into the schools doing presentations and assumed that I was being paid for my time. To work outside of the police department, officers needed approval to do so, and if they didn't, there would be negative ramifications.

I explained that no, I was not being paid. Rather, I was volunteering my time to present a program that I had devised for Grade 5/6 students. He was genuinely interested in what I was doing and wished me all the best. Again, he apologized for having to call me.

Why could I not just be left alone? Why did some officers feel it was their duty to tell on me, not unlike children in a schoolyard? This was just one aspect. Cruisers continued to slowly drive by our house keeping tabs on what I was or wasn't doing. It felt like they were hoping to catch a glimpse of the "freak." Sadly, part of me believed that I was just that.

As winter set in and temperatures dropped my crow was nowhere to be seen. I missed his frequent visits, hoping that he was okay and had just chosen to winter in a warmer climate. I couldn't blame him.

Terry and I also decided to take a break from the harsh winter and booked an all-inclusive trip to Punta Cana in the Dominican Republic for the first week of February. I couldn't wait to get away, desperately needing a reprieve from meddling cops that continued to make us their business.

Our break was everything we had hoped for: warm ocean waters and miles of white sand beaches. As I let the ocean surf bob me from one wave to the next, I envisioned it also washing away the stress of the last four years.

What we didn't know was that this was only an intermission. Another storm was brewing.

Chapter 44

Be leery of silence. It doesn't mean you won the argument. Often, people are just busy reloading their guns.
– Shannon L. Alder

After arriving home we began to sift through the pile of mail that had accumulated in our absence. What stood out from everything else was a large, thick manila envelope from WSIB. I assumed that since my case had been decided upon, they were simply providing me with a copy of my entire claims file. I was correct on that account, but the cover letter that accompanied it brought me to my knees.

It read that the police department was appealing the decision of WSIB to declare me disabled and unable to return to work as stated in their letter of July 31, 2007. Furthermore, the department wanted a copy of my entire file, which they could not obtain without my consent. Also, I needed to inform WSIB if I had representation, and if so, who—or would I be representing myself? Finally, I had only thirty days to respond.

I was in disbelief, lambasted with the reality that indeed it wasn't over, and that I was back in the throes of emotional and psychological upheaval. I had assumed that WSIB had the final word, totally unaware that the department had six months to appeal their decision. The letter of appeal was dated January 23, 2008, one week short of the six-month deadline.

Terry and I consulted with Don as he observed me regress right back into the hole I had desperately tried to claw my way out of. Again he assured me that he would have my back in whichever way the appeal would proceed.

Time was of the essence and it was imperative that I find a lawyer to take my case. I knew with certainty that there was no way I could represent myself.

I contacted Gord, updating him and asking for his advice as to whom I should contact. He too was dumbfounded that the department was appealing, considering its action to be that of harassment more than anything else. After some consideration, he gave me the name of a lawyer who he felt would be very competent, even suggesting that I inform this individual that he had advised me to call him.

Hesitantly I contacted the lawyer's office, briefly explaining to his secretary the reason for my call and the need to speak with Keith ASAP. She stated she would pass my message on and my request for him to contact me.

Nervously I waited, hoping and praying that he would return my call. I knew that even if he did call me back that would only be the first step; to actually take my case would be the challenge.

Thankfully, he called and I explained my situation. He stated that he was cutting back on his hours, however he would refer my case to his colleague, Tom and would assist him where needed. Keith did request a copy of my entire case file along with a letter outlining the background and course of events leading up to the department's appeal.

I was overwhelmed with gratitude and relief, turning everything over to them on February 21, 2008, thereby meeting the thirty-day deadline.

After reviewing my file, Terry and I met with Keith and Tom for the purpose of clarifying some of the events that had taken place. Before leaving Tom stated to me, "I don't often say this to clients for fear of giving them false hope; however, in regards to your case, they don't stand a chance."

For the next two years and nine months they were words that I would cling to.

One morning in early March, as I was about to pour our first coffee of the day, a familiar greeting erupted from the railing of our deck. I looked out, and there he was in all of his black brilliance, strutting back and forth as if he'd never been away. I was delighted to see my crow, and it certainly seemed like the feeling was reciprocated with frequent visits and him seemingly content to just hang around. However, not everyone was thrilled to see him back—in particular the neighbours that had moved in beside us.

In the beginning, all of us had gotten along, enjoying block parties and socializing over cold beers. When anyone needed help there was always someone nearby more than willing to lend a hand.

Eventually, the true colours of Cathy and Frank emerged, turning from what we had thought were ideal neighbours into nothing less than neighbours from hell. With no one else directly beside them we bore the brunt of their hostility; a shared driveway only exacerbated matters.

Every spring, we hung a large wind chime underneath our eaves close to the corner of our house. Warmer weather also meant the resurrection of our backyard fire pit, enjoying the fire's ambiance and the relaxation it provided. They decided they didn't like either, frequently calling the police about the wind chime and the fire department regarding our evening fires. Apparently, the wind chime was too loud and the fires (in her words), made their house smell like a teepee. The return of "my" crow only fueled their animosity, with their anger escalating as summer progressed.

Our focus, however, had turned towards Casey. Over the winter she had developed a limp to the point that I had to leave her behind when I went for a run. We still brought her to the golf course where she could run free, but her limp was progressively more noticeable. I assumed she had a strained tendon and that rest would remedy the situation, but it didn't.

Our concern mounted when one night in late April she limped up from her bed in the basement to our bedroom, whining in pain, her eyes pleading for us to help her. It was heartbreaking to watch her and devastating to not be able to fix her.

For a while she seemed to be improving, but in May she took a turn for the worse. Clearly, something was terribly wrong. We brought her to our vet who examined her and took x-rays, hoping that they would show the source of her discomfort. As we waited with Casey for the results, I had a sick feeling in my gut that things were not good. When the vet came in her face verified what I already knew.

The x-rays revealed a mass in her shoulder as well as her lungs. Our beautiful, sweet husky, who had never been sick a day in her life, was now stricken with cancer, a disease that takes far too many, regardless of age, gender, or species.

The vet prescribed drops that would alleviate her pain, but that evening, when we struggled to empty the syringe of liquid into her throat, we stopped. Clearly, she wanted no part of it and we knew then that we were putting off the inevitable. Casey had been a dog full of life and personality, stubborn as hell but with a sweetness that was infectious and endearing. To keep her alive was not for her benefit; it was only for ours, and we could not do that to her. She just didn't deserve to have her suffering prolonged.

Early the next morning we took her to the golf course, long before anyone else was there. It had been her favourite place to run free, smelling all the wonderful scents and just doing what dogs love to do. It would be a short jaunt today, only down the last fairway and back, but it was our farewell gift to her.

It ended far too soon, and our hearts broke with the finality of it all. I will never forget the look on her face as we climbed the last hill to the clubhouse. She stopped and looked straight at me, her expression clearly that of gratitude.

Casey was one week shy of turning eleven years old when we bid her adieu. As with all pets, if one is open to it, they become part of your family; they own you as much as you own them, forever staking their claim to a place in your heart.

The days that followed were gut wrenching, anticipating her presence but knowing she wasn't coming back. Even the crow sensed the change, hanging out more frequently and for longer periods of time. In a strange way his presence was consoling and powerful.

Our neighbours were unrelenting, seemingly determined to provoke us in whatever way they could. Countless times the police would be at our door responding to their complaints. Where before we were on speaking terms and visiting in their home, they now accused us of drinking all of their alcohol and that they would have to ask us to leave. We were blamed for vandalism to their property as well as hosting loud obnoxious parties, drunk every night.

Of course our "good" neighbours stood up for us, stating that Cathy and Frank were the problem, but it solved nothing.

Finally they found a sergeant that was more than willing to take action on behalf of their complaint of our wind chime, a sergeant that disliked us as much as we him; the sergeant that I had reported on years earlier and was reprimanded for his comments towards me. He had not forgotten.

At around 10:30 a.m. on July 26, 2008, I was in the kitchen when our front doorbell rang. Terry was golfing so I went to see who was there. As soon as I opened the door I knew there was trouble. It was him, advising me that he was charging me with disturbance, i.e., the wind chime was chiming. I was beyond furious, sick and tired of Frank and Cathy's relentless harassment—and now this, all because of a wind chime? His deliberate smugness fueled a spark deep inside and I so wanted to drive my fist square into the smirk on his face. He stood there representing all of the officers that had harassed, bullied, and belittled me over the years, and it was all I could do to restrain myself.

At the time, I had no way of knowing that the charge would never reach the courts. The section that he had charged me with was obsolete, but that wasn't enough to deter him. He returned a couple of weeks later and charged me under another section that was current. Mysteriously, the paperwork that was necessary for the case to proceed vanished. Terry was suspect and even questioned regarding it, but he had nothing to do with its disappearance, nor did he have any knowledge of who might have destroyed it. I would just love to thank whoever decided to take such action.

While this incident was still unresolved, I had an encounter with my crow that to this day resonates deep within:

Casey had only been gone a short while and I missed her something fierce. I had just finished a run and, as per my custom, I would walk to the corner and back to cool off and catch my breath. Crow, of course, was close by and I tossed him a couple of treats. I reached the corner, turned around, and was headed back towards our driveway. It was then that my crow flew up from behind me and ever so gently grazed the top of my head as he floated by.

I was stunned, struggling to comprehend what had just transpired. It was nothing less than the gentlest caress, a priceless gift from one of nature's own.

Chapter 45

Sometimes good things fall apart
so better things can fall together.
– Marilyn Monroe

In August, Terry and I decided to go south of the border for a few days to get some reprieve from Frank and Cathy and to escape the emptiness without Casey. She had been gone for almost three months and I was still grieving her absence. Gord encouraged us to get another dog, even offering to buy us whatever breed we wanted, but it didn't feel right. To get another dog so soon felt like we were discounting her importance with a quick replacement. No dog could ever replace the special place she held in my heart.

Our trip started out as any other, with me in the driver's seat and Terry content to be the passenger. It was a beautiful summer day and we couldn't wait to take in the view and atmosphere from our hotel on the lakefront. But as we began to drive through the small towns scattered along the way, every dog we saw being either walked or run was a husky. My tears obliterated my view of the road as I struggled to get a grip on my emotions. Terry offered to drive but all I could say was, "I'm fine!" (Yeah, right!) God, I missed her.

Finally we arrived, and after settling in I told Terry that I was going to go and sit by the boardwalk to take in the sounds and beauty of sun and surf.

Not even five minutes later I looked down the boardwalk, and walking towards me was an older couple with a malamute in tow, identical markings as Casey. As they continued to approach I could not hold back the tears, overcome with her loss. They must have thought I was some piece of work when I blubbered out, "Can I pat your dog?"

I explained the reason for my state after which ensued a lengthy conversation. The dog was their son's and they were taking care of it while he was away. They relayed that dogs had always been a part of their family, believing that every kid should have the opportunity to grow up with one. In parting, she gave me a hug and said, "I feel like I've known you for a long time, not for just the past ten minutes."

Her final words however, struck home: "You need to get yourself another dog."

Shortly after I went back to our room and told Terry about the nice couple I had met with the malamute, lamenting that I wished he too could have met them and the beautiful dog.

One of our favourite places to go, just a short walk from our hotel, was an outdoor patio for happy hour. During the summer it is a buzz of activity with tourists congregating from near and far. We had just been served our drinks when I spotted the man with the malamute. I exclaimed to Terry, "There they are!"

I got up and made my way to where he was, asking if he would mind bringing over the dog to meet Terry. As we were talking, a waitress came to our table, also in admiration of the big black and white beauty. She went on to say that a lady had been there last week with two litters of husky pups, all with blue eyes and absolutely adorable. Pulling out a slip of paper, she wrote down the lady's phone number, and without hesitation handed it to me saying, "You should give her a call."

It was uncanny, the coincidences glaringly blatant. I made the call.

The owner of the puppies was out of town but arrangements were made for her mother to meet us the next day at her daughter's residence. Both Terry and I couldn't wait to see them, but how would we ever be able to choose?

That night I dreamt that one of the puppies was silvery grey in colour, having one blue eye and one brown.

The next day when we were brought to the barn where all the puppies were, sure enough there was the puppy that had been in my dream—but we were quickly informed that he wasn't for sale; her daughter had decided to keep him.

Nine-week-old puppies from two litters were all over me, climbing at my legs, vying for attention and begging to be picked up. We had decided to pick a female, thankfully distinguishable with their pink collars, but now we were faced with a dilemma—which one?

My attention was drawn to one in particular. She was a light golden brown, very sociable and playful, but not aggressively so. As soon as I picked her up she snuggled against me, proceeding to lick my face and neck. My heart melted.

Do dogs choose us or do we choose them? This time, I believe, she found us. We had no intention of bringing home a puppy, but sometimes you just can't ignore what the universe sends your way. We named her Copper, born on June 23, 2008—exactly one month after Casey passed.

Our drive home was uneventful, with her sleeping most of the way. However, her first night away from her littermates was a different story. As soon as the lights went out her chorus of despair kicked in. Toys and a ticking clock did nothing to appease her; she was traumatized and determined to tell the world.

At 4:00 a.m. I got up to take her outside, hoping that some fresh air would help. When I came back inside I glanced out our front window, startled to see two cops walking across our front lawn. I couldn't believe it—Frank and Cathy had called the police because of our puppy, now another item to target. Were they ever going to just back off? It did not appear likely.

I had forgotten how much work it is to train and raise a puppy. I was exhausted, having to always be one step ahead of her need to relieve herself. With Terry at work, the responsibility fell on me, and there were times I felt overwhelmed. Right from the start it was evident that she was one clever little puppy, catching on quickly to commands, knowing that treats were the reward for obeying. Her blue eyes were captivating and her love of play quickly endeared her to us. Our family, once again, felt complete.

September 25th would mark our tenth wedding anniversary. We had and were still going through hard times, but the one thing that had remained constant was our love and commitment to each other. Hence we decided to gather our friends to celebrate with us as we renewed our vows. Gord was more than willing to "marry" us again on the number one tee blocks of the country club. It was a special time for both of us and I again had never felt or been so loved.

As we had grown closer to Gord over the past few years our relationship had also grown with his partner, Leslie. We frequented each other's houses for dinner and to celebrate special occasions. During one of my conversations with Leslie, I told her about a book I had read by Shirley MacLaine regarding her experience of walking the El Camino de Santiago (Camino: a word meaning "road" or "a path of travel")—an ancient pilgrimage comprising a 805 km (500 miles) trek from the border of France to the centuries-old cathedral in Santiago de Compostela, Spain.

I was intrigued from the outset, hungry to read more accounts of others who had hiked the trail and what their purpose had been in doing so. Without hesitation Leslie said, "Let's go there and do it!"

Over the next several months we would plan out our route and the timeframe of when to go. We would not have the time to hike all 805 km (500 miles) so we decided that we would start in Ponferrada, Spain and hike the last 220 km (137 miles) to Santiago. Gord thought we were nuts but was fully supportive, as was Terry. I couldn't wait to experience it for myself.

The year 2009 was ushered in along with Gord and Leslie, toasting our proposed trip to Spain and to good friends and good health. But one never knows what is waiting around the bend.

In March, Leslie and Gord were on their way to the Caribbean for two weeks of sun and relaxation when their trip came to a halt in the Toronto airport. Terry was at work when I received the call from a mutual friend informing me that Gord had suffered a stroke while waiting for their connecting flight. I was stunned, asking if he was okay; where had they taken him, was there anything we could do?

Terry too was shocked and we were more than ready to fly to Toronto if Leslie needed us. As it was, Gord's daughter lived nearby so she was able to be there for Leslie and her dad.

Leslie was a mess but she kept us informed of test results and what the plan of action would be. Thankfully, he had been rushed to a renowned cardiac facility and was receiving the best of care; however, it would still be a long road to recovery.

Consequently, with our trip to Spain only a few weeks away, Leslie would have to bow out, and understandably so.

The question now posed was whether I would choose to go alone. Terry was leery of me traveling by myself, but if I still wanted to go he would support my decision. My heart said yes, so I continued to move ahead with plans.

Over a year had passed since the police department had appealed WSIB's decision, and neither my lawyer nor I had heard anything. Tom's advice was to just let it be; the longer they prolonged it, the better it would look for us. However, without knowing what the outcome would be, I felt like my life was on hold. They controlled the deck, and all I could do was wait for whatever cards they decided to play.

Our neighbour's behaviour was becoming more bizarre and irrational, with Frank even trying to entice Terry to a physical fight at the end of our driveways. Our home that had once been our safe haven was no more.

The final straw was when I discovered a bluish-green liquid in the snow by our fence in the backyard. It was Copper that had drawn my attention to it as she was sniffing it out. My suspicion was that it was antifreeze, and if Copper had ingested it, it could have been fatal. We couldn't prove it, but our gut feeling was that our neighbours were responsible for its presence. Any attempt to hurt our dog was crossing a line that would not be tolerated. Enough was enough.

Shortly before my trip to Spain our house went up for sale. It was time to move on before Terry or I did something that would not be retractable.

My travel dates to Spain were booked and confirmed, flying out on April 29th and leaving Santiago for home on May 14th. A few days before I was scheduled to leave there was a breakout of the swine flu and people were cautioned not to travel. I was an emotional wreck pondering, *Do I go or do I stay?*

Part of me wanted to take the easy way out, giving in to my fears and reasons for opting out. But I knew that if I were to succumb to that I would never forgive myself, always wondering what I had missed out on. I was so close to packing it all in.

At the airport I was in tears. Along with Terry, Leslie was there, and even Gord came along to see me off and wish me well. Leslie promised to be with me every step in spirit as I hiked along. I hugged Terry goodbye, not wanting to let go. But it was time, my time to go and embrace the mystery of the Camino.

PART VIII

Chapter 46

Follow your heart … it will guide you correctly. Miracles happen every day if you are open to it. Angels will find you and you will find them. Experience a community of people helping people. It's YOUR journey … there is no right or wrong way. Just follow the yellow arrows … and you will see direction. Total freedom … pause, think, dream …It is a privilege to be called to the Camino.
– Unknown

Once we were on our way I settled myself down, preparing for the long hours in the air with many connections: flight to Ottawa then Ottawa to Frankfurt, Frankfurt to Barcelona and finally, Barcelona to Santiago de Compostela. I arrived on April 30th, 2:20 p.m., totally exhausted from the six-hour time change and I couldn't help but wonder, *What the hell was I thinking?*

Everything I required for the next two and a half weeks was contained in my backpack: thirty pounds of gear that would be with me every step of the way. It was heavier than what I had wanted but mornings would be cool so I needed the extra clothing that could be peeled off as the temperatures rose.

Once in Santiago airport I looked for signs indicating the location of taxi service. Abruptly, I found myself immersed in an unfamiliar culture and language that I was only vaguely knowledgeable of. I hoped that my high school Spanish would help me out but I wasn't feeling overly confident. Climbing into a waiting cab, I gave the driver the name of the hotel to take me to—Hesperia Peregrino—hoping that my reservation was still intact.

Entering the lobby I was relieved to see that it was clean and modern, complete with a bar and restaurant. As I produced my passport to the hotel clerk she smiled and asked "Camino?" "*Si,*" I replied.

Soon she handed me my room number and key and relief swept over me knowing that I had a bed to sleep in. My plan was to spend the following day securing a bus ticket to Ponferrada and to acquaint myself with the cathedral square—the destination that I would be hiking towards.

In Barcelona, between flights, I had purchased an international calling card that would be my link to Terry. Although he was six hours behind and not expecting him to be home, I decided to call and at least leave a message that I had arrived. I went through the directions on the card, step by step but for whatever reason it would not connect me. It was so frustrating. I had barely arrived and already I missed him terribly.

I decided to familiarize myself with the area around the hotel and get an idea of where I would be heading tomorrow. The area I was in was old with a rundown appearance but the countryside was spectacular. I tried to get directions to a phone or an internet café but no one seemed to understand. Finally, I located a phone room and a place to send emails. It was dark and dingy and the worker spoke no English. My attempt to call Terry was unsuccessful and I could not get connected. Then I tried to email him, not realizing beforehand that it would be a Spanish keyboard, not English. It seemed to take forever to find the right keys to form some sort of message that would be legible. I had no idea if it had even sent—I could only hope.

On my way back to the hotel I came across a payphone and made another attempt with the calling card but again, no connection. I tried to hold back the tears but without success. I had followed the directions exactly as they were laid out so why wasn't it working? The fact that I hadn't slept for practically two days didn't help matters. All I wanted was to hear Terry's voice.

Arriving back at the hotel I decided to order something to eat in the restaurant so I took a seat. I saw workers in the back but no one came to my table. After several minutes I gave up, not realizing that food was not served until 8:00 p.m. It was only four o'clock.

I retraced my steps to where I had seen a café, hoping that there would be something that I could order. The waiter didn't speak any English however part of the menu was in English. I ordered a bun with ham and cheese, accompanied with tomato, lettuce and onion on the side. A *cerveza* (beer) along with it, went without saying. The ham was greasy and I was quick to discover that one needed strong jaws to bite through the tough, hard buns. The beer was great.

Back at the hotel, I picked up a map of Santiago from the lobby, hoping to get my bearings for where I would be headed tomorrow. I tried to convince myself that things could only get better. I would figure out the calling card and I would secure a bus ticket to Ponferrada.

I woke up shortly after 8:00 a.m. from a restless sleep. It was Friday, May 1st, Spain's "May-Day." I was still tired, wanting to sleep but there were more pressing matters: I had to find the tourist information office and most importantly call Terry.

After having breakfast I started out, walking towards where I thought I would find the information centre. While en route I asked people for directions, even the *policía* but no one spoke

English and they could only point me in a general direction. I felt like I had been walking in circles but finally I found what I was looking for and fortunately the worker spoke English. However, she informed me that she couldn't help me with a bus reservation to Ponferrada, suggesting that I use the internet. Of course there was no internet available at this location. Panic was setting in. Today was a holiday so businesses were closed; furthermore, the time that I told Terry I would call him was only one and a half hours away.

By the time I found my way back to the hotel I only had fifteen minutes to spare. I tried again from a payphone, the recording repeatedly informing me that the number was not recognized. I went to the front desk of the hotel, tears flowing uncontrollably as I handed the clerk my calling card saying, "*No entiendo!*" (I don't understand!)

I was now in full meltdown and strangely enough had acquired the full attention of front desk staff. The clerk took my card and from what I could understand, contacted an operator. Several minutes later she handed me the phone with Terry on the line. Words wouldn't come, only sobs of relief to finally hear his voice.

After our conversation I handed her back the phone while she handed me the correct sequence of numbers needed to use my card. I couldn't thank her enough but she wasn't finished with me yet.

She, in conversation with another worker, called the bus station to reserve me a seat only to find out that reservations had to be made seven days in advance. *No problema!* Next thing I knew they called a cab to drive me to the bus station where I could purchase my ticket. When the driver arrived they instructed him to wait for me until I had my ticket in hand and to then drive me back.

Not long after, I returned, ticket in hand. I made two new friends that day who I will never forget and they undoubtedly will never forget me.

Now I could relax and enjoy the rest of the day. Casually I walked back to the downtown area where I had previously passed a Pizza Hut. I let myself indulge, savouring the taste of familiar food.

With camera in hand, I continued on passing historical statues and ancient cathedrals. I spotted a sign and arrow pointing towards the *Turisto* Information Centre. Earlier, I had obviously walked miles out of my way. There were several outdoor cafés so I picked one and ordered a cold beer. The sun was warm, I had my ticket, I had talked to Terry and tomorrow was yet to unfold.

I was already awake before the wake-up call, anxious to be on my way. After a quick shower I reorganized my backpack with the essentials near the top, hoping that I had packed what I would need. At 6:25 a.m. the hotel clerk called me a cab and twenty minutes later I was at the bus station. It was still dark with no sign of other people or buses. Finally the bus pulled up and I took a seat; I was the only passenger.

Soon we were under way and a few others boarded at selected stops before leaving Santiago. It would take three and a half hours to reach Ponferrada so I settled back and took in the magnificent scenery. At some points I saw hikers with backpacks and realized they were on the Camino. It felt surreal knowing that soon I would be one of them.

We reached the bus station on the outskirts of Ponferrada at 10:35 a.m. There were no signs so I began walking towards what appeared to be a downtown area. I had no idea of where I was going so finally I stopped a young man and asked if he spoke any English. He replied, "A little bit."

His "little bit" was actually a lot! I explained that I needed to find the *Albeque de Pelegrino* which means a hostel for pilgrims, the name given to those that walk the Camino. He was somewhat familiar with its location but told me that it was quite a distance from where we were. However, if I didn't mind waiting for him to run a quick errand, he would drive me there. Boy, had I lucked out.

When we arrived I saw other hikers, one in particular that stood out. He was limping and his feet were bandaged—blisters had taken their toll. The young man came in with me to help out with translating if required. It was.

Each pilgrim has the choice to register wherever they begin the Camino and are issued a *Credencial del Peregrino* meaning, pilgrim credential. An official fills out the date and location of where one begins including their name, country and passport identification number. As one passes through each village this credential is stamped with the name and date; all to verify and hold proof that one did indeed walk the path of the Camino.

We were told that the man who could issue me my credential was somewhere on the grounds wearing blue overalls. Finally we located him and after several translations back and forth I had my credential stamped with "Ponferrada 02 MAYO 2009." I was officially registered as a *peregrino.*

The young man continued to go out of his way to help me, even going part of the way to a hotel fairly close by. As we walked he told me that someday he too would walk the Camino but wasn't ready yet. Before we parted I thanked him profusely for all his help. He was a gift and I never even learned his name.

Soon after, I entered the lobby of the Hotel El Castillo and told the clerk that I needed a room for one night. In English, she informed me that because of the holiday they were booked solid with no rooms available. My heart sank wondering now what? As I stood there the phone rang and after a brief conversation in Spanish she hung up and proceeded to inform me that I had a room—the caller had cancelled his reservation.

Between the young man that I just happened to come across and now this, a room becoming available at precisely the right time, was only the beginning of "coincidences" that I would encounter every step of the way. After all, it was the Camino.

Chapter 47

Memory: I am sitting in a café drinking a cold beer. My feet are throbbing but I'm doing my best to ignore the discomfort. A radio is playing in the background and then I realize the artist is singing in English. I listen to the words that describe life, filled with uphill battles and mountains to climb. Speed is not what's important; rather the importance lies in embracing the challenge. My eyes fill with tears, the words too powerful to ignore.

For the rest of the afternoon I took in the beauty of Ponferrada—snow-capped Pyrenees Mountains on the horizon and a spectacular twelfth century castle that had been declared a national monument. I was in the heart of the old city centre with the path of the Camino winding through it. In one of the shops I purchased a walking stick to assist me with the varying terrain that I would encounter; it would prove to be invaluable.

I sat sipping cold beer, a warm breeze fanning me as I observed Camino pilgrims making their way along. Tomorrow I would be among them.

Later on I called Terry, trying to describe how my experiences of the day had miraculously fallen into place. He cautioned me to be careful tomorrow and not to push too hard; he knew me well.

I did not get the night's sleep that I had hoped for. Partygoers carried on all night, seemingly oblivious to the fact that some people needed to sleep. A couple of times someone actually tried to get into my room, obviously too intoxicated to realize it wasn't theirs. Finally, at 7:00 a.m. I got up and showered, hoping that the water would erase my grogginess.

After my breakfast of toast and coffee I checked out, hoisted my backpack into place, and ensured that the laces of my hiking boots were tied securely. It was May 3rd, 8:35 a.m. as I officially began my Camino experience, bidding farewell to Ponferrada.

My goal was to reach Cacabelos, a 15.1 km (9.2 mile) hike. It was a beautiful sunny day and by the time I reached the outskirts of Ponferrada, I had to remove my fleece jacket and lower leg portions of my zip-offs. As people passed me and I passed others the phrase *buen camino* was exchanged. Even the locals were quick to acknowledge our presence by wishing us a good Camino.

I was surprised at the number of people on bicycles, wondering how they would ever manage the steep rocky trails that undoubtedly lay ahead. I was content to walk. I also observed and was amazed at the number of older hikers—like *old*, just trekking along with intent and purpose. I listened to people conversing in diverse languages, many of which I couldn't identify.

It struck me how everyone here had their own story of why they had come and what they hoped to achieve. What was mine? As each day passed it would become clear.

I was surprised at the primitive conditions of the locals' homesteads, largely in part resembling third world countries. Oxen were used to plough the fields while the farmers trailed behind. Much of the land was used to harvest grapes, tedious backbreaking work. It was a sharp contrast to Spain's modern cities that lacked for nothing.

The first hint of hot spots started to develop on the outside of both toes with about five kilometers (three miles) left to go. The trail had been manageable but now the downhill portions were becoming increasingly painful. I tried to transfer my weight to the walking stick, striving to relieve the pressure, hoping that I could reach Cacabelos before they became full-blown blisters.

As I drew closer to Cacabelos, signs advertised discount rates for pilgrims if they stayed at Hotel Villa de Cacabelos. Many pilgrims opted to stay at the hostels that accepted only those walking the Camino; certainly a cheaper option, but I preferred the privacy of my own room and shower. I just prayed that a room would be available.

With less than a kilometer to go I felt the skin separate where blisters had formed. I hobbled on, looking for more signs that would direct me to the hotel. Finally, I located it and limped to the front desk. A wonderful, friendly lady greeted me and urged me with gestures to remove my backpack; my discomfort was evident and required no translating. Thankfully a room was waiting for me.

Gingerly, I removed my hiking boots and socks, bloodstains and all. They didn't look good. What concerned me the most was that tomorrow's walk was 24 km (15 miles), considerably longer than what I had walked today.

As I stood in the shower letting the water wash away grime and sweat, I tried to figure out why I had developed blisters. My hiking boots were well broken in and I had even worn two pairs of socks. All I could do was treat the existing blisters and hope that no more developed.

After cleaning up I went to the hotel bar and ordered a cold one, instantly refreshed. I found out that the restaurant only served breakfast so I would have to walk to the town center to find something to eat. Thankfully, I had packed comfortable sandals that my feet welcomed.

Later I called Terry and relayed my blister predicament. I could tell he was concerned but there was nothing he could do; just to hear his voice was, for now, enough. Tomorrow was another day, and really, all I had to do was walk. How difficult could that be? With certainty I would find out.

Just before turning out the light to get some much-needed rest, I reviewed my itinerary for the upcoming days:

May 4th: Cacebelos to Vega de Valcarce, 24 km (15 miles)

May 5th: Vega de Valcarce to O Cebreiro, 11.8 km (7.3 miles)

May 6th: O Cebreiro to Triacastela, 22.5 km (14 miles)

May 7th: Triacastela to Sarria, 19 km (11.8 miles)

May 8th: Sarria to Portomarin, 22 km (13.9 miles)

May 9th: Portomarin to Palas de Rei, 25 km (15.5 miles)

May 10th: Palas de Rei to Melide, 14.5 km (9 miles)

May 11th: Melide to Arzua, 14.3 km (8.8 miles)

May 12th: Arzua to Pedrouzo, 19.3 km (11.9 miles)

May 13th: Pedrouzo to Santiago de Compostela, 19.2 km (11.9 miles)

I had allowed for one extra day, for whatever unknown predicament might occur, otherwise this was the plan. I turned off the light and fell into a troubled sleep.

In the days that followed, the condition of my feet progressively deteriorated. Shortly before I reached Vega de Valcarce on May 4th, the pads of my feet behind all my toes split open; it was excruciating. I had brought bandages and other items to treat blisters, but nothing was helping. As my feet perspired the bandages and tape would come loose, creating even more of a problem.

May 5th marked the shortest day, however it was all uphill, bringing us to the highest elevation of the Camino—1292 metres (4240 feet). Many parts of the trail were very narrow with loose rocks, and every time my feet would slip, it was agonizing. The final 4.5 km (2.8 miles) climbed straight up, but in spite of the sweat and burning in my legs and feet, the scenery on this portion of the Camino couldn't help but take your breath away.

However, what goes up must come down—such was the nature of the route to Triacastela. The trail switched back and forth precariously close to the edge of what would certainly be a disastrous fall. My arm ached from leaning hard on my walking stick as it slammed into loose rocks that more often than not slipped from under it.

I stopped in the village of Alto do Poio to rebandage my feet, and as soon as I was again under way, I approached the entrance to a cattle barn just as a herd decided to exit. I had nowhere to go, forced to the side of the narrow path, struggling to avoid eye contact with the ones possessing horns; God knows what they could do to a hurting *peregrino*. Just to add insult to injury one of the stragglers decided to swat me with its shit-covered tail. Lovely!

When I finally reached Triacastela, I asked a few locals in Spanish, "Where is the hotel?"

My pilgrim's guidebook clearly showed that there was a hotel here but no one knew its whereabouts. I had no alternative but to stay at the pilgrim's hostel—a room that housed twelve bunk beds with shared shower and washroom facilities. In spite of my misgivings it was very clean and well run. I was impressed.

A large portion of the trail to Sarria on May 7th was through forests with difficult declines on wet, mucky and slimy rocks. My feet burned with every step, and within the first kilometer I felt one of my bandages let go. I was angry and wailed out loud to the universe, "Can't I have just one fucking day to walk with no pain?"

It was a constant struggle just to put one foot in front of the other. I felt like a tortoise, slowly dragging myself across unforgiving terrain towards my destination.

Earlier, I had decided to use up my one extra day in Sarria, hoping that it would give my feet a chance to recover for what remained in the trek towards Santiago. I didn't want to dwell on the stark realization that Sarria was just under the halfway mark to Santiago—I had a long way to go.

I checked in at Hotel Alfonso IX, directly on the path of the Camino. Sarria is a beautiful modern city with amenities that had not been available after leaving Ponferrada.

It is a city that welcomes and caters to the thousands of pilgrims who pass through.

At the *farmacia* (pharmacy) I loaded up on several boxes of blister pacs, hoping and praying that they would suffice.

Ready or not it was May 9th and time to get back on the trail that led to Portomarin. The first few kilometers weren't too bad, and for a brief time I thought my feet would be okay. It was short-lived. There were few landmarks to indicate how far I had walked and what distance remained. All I knew was that my feet were deteriorating quickly and there was not a thing I could do about it. I forced myself to focus, to ensure that I walked the shortest route possible and avoid any extra steps. But in doing so I missed a yellow arrow and ended up in farmland with no hikers in sight. I had no choice but to retrace my steps and hope to find the turn that I had missed.

I came undone, sobbing, every step, agonizing. I was forced into the grim reality that my feet were trashed, and in spite of my determination to will them better, it wasn't going to happen. Portomarin would mark the end of my Camino.

Words could not describe my disappointment. I felt like I had let down everyone at home who had been pulling for me. But most of all I had let myself down. I was someone who had run marathons and countless miles. Here, all I had to do was walk and I couldn't even do that. I felt like a quitter, unworthy to be called a *peregrino*. So much for *buen camino*.

After beating myself up I started to reflect on my Camino experience, slowly absorbing the dynamics of my journey.

Finding and following the yellow arrows was a feat unto itself that demanded one stay present and focused. They could be located anywhere: on sides of buildings, on poles, on rocks, on pavement, on fences. When my mind wandered or my focus shifted to the pain I was experiencing, sure enough, that was when I would miss the arrow.

Interestingly, every time I went off course, either a local or another hiker would get my attention and point me in the right direction. Coincidence? I don't think so.

As stated earlier, after Chad's death I took time to redefine my belief regarding the relationship of human beings with God or a higher power, or however one wishes to describe such an entity. I have come to believe that our true essence is not our physical body but rather one's soul—the infinite, spirit form of who we really are. The fact that I experienced so many "magical" coincidences was a powerful reminder of my connectedness to something far bigger than myself, a connection that is shared by every living being.

I am a person who likes to plan ahead and have all my ducks in a row, so to speak. While on the trail I never knew where I would be spending the night or if a room would even be available. This was my biggest challenge—to rely on the universe to provide me with exactly what I needed. I had learned early in life not to trust anyone or anything. To have to let go of that control was terrifying, certain to be disastrous. Miraculously, the right place was always there waiting for my arrival.

I mused over the number of people who impacted my journey in a powerful way.

There were two men from Norway that I had met on Day 2. Both were retired and they had started in Leon, a distance of 325 km (210 miles) from Santiago. They offered me valuable advice and in Vega de Valcarce, where they also spent the night, we shared a bottle of wine and toasted the Camino. Our paths wouldn't cross again.

A trio of a man and two women from France were my greatest supporters, cheering me on as they watched me tackle the difficult terrain, refusing to succumb to the blisters. The last time I saw them was when I was waiting for the bus to take me back to Santiago. They hurried over, knowing from my expression that I was done. The man gave me a big hug and I broke down. We didn't speak the same language, but their heartfelt empathy and compassion were understood perfectly, no dictionary required.

On May 6th, after reaching Triacastela, I went to make sure of the route for the next day, but I was confused. There were two yellow arrows for the Camino—one to the right, the other to the left. Two women approached me and I found out they were from Holland. Verbally, we couldn't communicate, but between gestures they told me that the arrow to the right was a shorter route, one that they too would take.

The next day they caught up to me on the roughest part of the trail. I was close to tears from the pain and they were really concerned for my well-being. One of them offered me a pill and urged me to take it, so I did. They indicated that it was about twelve kilometers (7.5 miles) to Sarria but there was a café four kilometers (2.5 miles) from where we were, where they would wait for me.

When I arrived it was obvious that they had told the owner that a hiker would be arriving who was in trouble. The owner asked if she could call me a taxi to take me the rest of the way to Sarria but I declined. I had come to walk the Camino and if I had to crawl my way there, so be it. The two women gave me a hug and a thumbs-up as I resumed my walk. Their genuine concern touched me deeply.

In Sarria, I met a couple from Germany who were staying at the same hotel as myself. Their English was limited but they conveyed that this was their third time walking the Camino. They had divided the entire 805 km (500 miles) into three sections and this was their final trek.

At breakfast I saw them just prior to leaving for Portomarin; they asked me if I was going to continue and I assured them that I was. They wished me luck. Fairly early into the walk I caught up to them at a café and they asked me how I was doing. "So-so," I replied, but I think they knew the truth of my condition.

As I wrote earlier, this was the day that I missed the yellow arrow and had to retrace my steps. The last stretch to Portomarin crossed a wide river after which there was no clear direction of where to go. I was physically and emotionally depleted, simply running on empty. I turned to look behind me and spotted the German couple proceeding to climb steep steps. I motioned to them, and she stopped and waited saying, "Bravo!"

Once again synchronicity of events had led to perfect timing. They told me that they had reservations at Pousada de Portomarin, which I never would have located on my own. I waited with his wife in the town centre while he went to check in and ask if there was a room available for me, which of course there was.

Later, after talking to Terry, and coming to the realization that I was done, our paths crossed again as they headed to dinner. I broke down. She touched my arm and in her broken English said, "How do you say it, but your health is more important. You need to stop."

With a farewell hug I thanked them and promised that their kindness would not be forgotten. *Buen Camino.*

As I waited for the bus back to Santiago, an Irish couple who had offered me their help earlier left me with words that I hung on to: "You accomplished a lot of distance—your credential is stamped to Portomarin and that can't be taken from you. Don't beat yourself up. You did what you could and beyond. Come back and pick up where you left off."

As the plane took off leaving Santiago far behind, I vowed to do exactly that.

Chapter 48

Everything that happens to you is a lesson.
Everyone you meet is a teacher.
There are no exceptions and it happens all your lifetime.
– Unknown

It was a long flight home, and my feet ached, but there was nothing sweeter than to see my beloved Terry waiting for me after I cleared customs. I was home.

It took many weeks for my feet to heal, even losing some toenails in the process. I resumed my runs with Copper with the crow always nearby to welcome us when we returned.

With our house up for sale, the harassment from our neighbours escalated. It was summer, and normally I would have been outside fussing over my flower gardens, but I had had enough of their glares and sarcasm. Instead, I remained in the backyard out of sight, praying that the house would sell quickly.

Darrell, who had assisted me in the intercity schools, told me that his position was no longer going to be funded, so he had found other employment. Hence my days of school presentations came to an end. I would dearly miss the interaction with the kids, but it was time to move on.

Finally, in the fall of 2009, we received an offer on our house that allowed us to pursue the purchase of a home we had been interested in for several months. It had everything we wanted and we could not understand why it hadn't sold. I could only conclude that it was waiting for us.

Our closing date was set for November 17th and I hadn't seen my crow for about two weeks prior. Snow had come early, so I assumed he had left to fly off to wherever he spent his winters. He was my only regret in leaving that house. I had never had such a unique experience with a wild animal and more than likely never would again. He was a gift and I would miss him dearly.

On the other hand, getting away from Frank and Cathy felt like a giant weight had been lifted off of us. Nevertheless I had to ask myself, *What was my part in contributing to the circumstances that evolved?*

They had triggered old issues and insecurities of not being able to stop or control people who spoke unfairly of me or told lies about me. I wanted to fight back, wishing that someone would come to my defence and make them go away. They had recreated how I had felt as a child and "Frances" was pissed off, wanting revenge.

Consequently, me reacting to their antics only fueled the fire. Did this excuse their actions? Of course not, but I had to take ownership for my reaction to their behaviour.

It didn't take long for Terry and I to adapt to our new surroundings. The lot size was much bigger than what we had come from, which provided Copper plenty of room to expend her endless energy. Our new location was a few miles away from the city, allowing us the pleasure of many places to walk, bike, or run, free of traffic. Most importantly, our neighbours were friendly and amiable. We could finally relax.

However, the appeal process from the police department still lingered in the back of my mind, leaving me uncertain and anxious regarding the final outcome.

In early spring, my lawyer contacted me with new information. The department had hired a consultant to review my case and her findings were not in my favour. I was devastated, feeling that what I had gone through had been trivialized and downplayed, even implying that I had made it all up. Again, Don supported me. He reviewed her findings and discovered that she was not even qualified to render an opinion. He assured me that if required, he would gladly testify on my behalf.

Not long after, I was told that a hearing had been set for November 17, 2010—one day after my birthday. Although it was several months away, the anxiety of knowing that I would have to face and be questioned by "them" left me feeling small and intimidated. I had no idea of how I would ever get through it.

With Gord's condition now stabilized it was taken for granted that when I returned to Spain to finish the Camino, Leslie would join me. We even decided that after completing the walk we would treat ourselves to a few days at a resort in Malaga, taking in the beauty of the Mediterranean. Making plans to return was a positive distraction from the impending hearing that crept ever closer.

Exactly one month before the hearing, we had gone out for supper, and when we returned home there was a message from my lawyer to call him. I had no idea why he would be calling on a Friday evening; it had to be important.

I was stunned as I began to process what he told me. Was he sure? He stated that WSIB had contacted him to advise that the department had withdrawn its appeal. There would be no hearing. I was elated, but still wary that there had to be a catch. It was too good to be true, and in part it was. He explained that although they withdrew this appeal, they could still reappeal in the future; however, he didn't think it likely. I still needed to know that the possibility existed. It wasn't fair that they could essentially hold me hostage indefinitely, but they could.

After the initial shock and relief, Terry and I discussed it. We both believed that the individual behind the appeal was the chief. He did not like to be questioned or criticized for what he had or hadn't done. Both my doctor and Don were very blunt in their correspondence to him regarding the department's handling, or lack thereof, regarding the incident surrounding the shooting.

He had officially retired in July, a few months previously, which left the appeal process in the hands of the new chief. Our theory was that the chief now in office had more pressing issues to deal with and therefore decided not to pursue it. I could only hope that we had it right.

As the winter months closed in, Spain was on my mind. Leslie was excited and looking forward to, as she described it, a vacation. However, the more we discussed it, a nagging uncertainty was forming in the recesses of my mind. I tried to ignore it, but it was increasingly demanding that I pay attention and put my concern into words.

Finally, in early December, I discussed with Terry the realization that I had come to: I needed to return to Spain and complete my journey as I had begun it—alone.

In retrospect, Gord's stroke cleared the way for me to go the first time without Leslie. As much as I had looked forward to going together, we were never intended to. Having experienced the dynamics of the Camino, it was clear to me that we were not on the same page as to what we wanted to gain from the experience. Terry couldn't have agreed more.

I didn't view it as a vacation but rather a time to turn my attention inward without the distraction of having to consider another person's likes or dislikes or compromising what I needed. My entire life I had put other people's feelings and wants above my own, believing that they mattered more. I also went along with others for fear that if I didn't I would be rejected, something that I would go to extremes to avoid. I knew with certainty what I had to do. The dilemma was how.

About a week before Christmas the four of us met for supper. I could not put off telling Leslie of my decision to go without her; it wouldn't be fair. I knew she would not take the news well but I didn't foresee her reaction being as hostile as it turned out.

I seized the opportunity when she brought the subject of Spain into our conversation at which point I said, "Leslie, I have a favour to ask of you."

I went on, trying to explain my position and urging her to meet up with me in Malaga after I finished.

Both Terry and I witnessed a side of Leslie that we had never seen. She made no attempt to understand where I was coming from but declared, "How dare you do this to me!" I had fully expected her to be disappointed—who wouldn't be? But I never anticipated what I felt to be a personal attack.

I was crushed. Her words had cut deep, leaving me feeling despicable and selfish. I struggled, knowing I had done what was right for me, but feeling like crap for what I had done to her.

Slowly a realization began to take shape. I had struck a deep chord in Leslie that was much more than just this incident. Whatever was the real underlying issue was hers. I only sparked a reaction that was probably based on a multitude of incidents that fed the root of her pain.

My analysis went further. I looked back at all the people throughout my life who had "wounded" me, each becoming a story that I continued to compile and stack together, its contents filled with recurring themes: rejection, not good enough, please like me, don't leave me.

By the time I encountered the select few officers that had decided to make my life miserable, I reacted to a history of insecurities and pain. Together we triggered each other's issues, all of us reacting, all of us choosing to join the dance.

Chapter 49

The willow is my favourite tree. I grew up near one. It's the most flexible tree in nature and nothing can break it—no wind, no elements, it can bend and withstand anything.
– Pink

On May 21, 2011, I boarded the plane to return to Spain—this time to complete the Camino. As I settled into my seat, a man across the aisle from me was reading our local paper and I couldn't help but notice the heading to an article. It read, "Camino a spiritual trek." I was overcome with the coincidence and assurance of knowing that I was exactly where I was supposed to be.

It was surreal, returning to Santiago and entering the hotel where I had had my meltdown. It didn't feel like two years had passed.

When I booked into the hotel in Portomarin, I was given the exact same room that I had stayed in earlier. I couldn't help but recall my disappointment and the painful condition of my feet. But this was now and I was ready. I had replaced my hiking boots with hiking shoes and refined the contents of my backpack, lightening the load by a good ten pounds. The next morning I would be on my way and I couldn't wait.

Each day I took it all in, relishing the solitude and the beauty that surrounded me. Again, whenever I needed something, it was there. Friendships were made along the trails, people coming together just to walk.

Two people in particular were a testament of forgiveness and moving on. The man was a young Israeli Jew, having served in the army and no doubt had witnessed atrocities. The woman was older than him and from Germany, and it was on the Camino that their paths crossed. They developed a friendship, free from the hatred that had consumed and destroyed thousands of people before them. It was beautiful and powerful and I was blessed to witness it.

This time I made it to Santiago, tired but blister-free. My credential was stamped with all the villages and centers that I had passed through, validating that I had indeed walked the Camino. In recognition of this I received my *Compostela* (certificate), dated May 29th, 2011.

I decided to attend the pilgrim's Mass, held each day at noon in the cathedral. The cathedral itself is a historical masterpiece. During the twelfth century, detailed carvings depicting Christ, the Apostles, and St. James were carved into the ancient stone. Over the years, millions of pilgrims have ascended the stairs leading into the interior, and now I was one of them.

I took a seat on the worn benches and watched people meeting and hugging those that they had met along the way. It was emotional to witness as I too had experienced the same. The Mass was simple but incredibly moving. I hardly understood a word, but the energy that permeated throughout required no translation. I was reluctant to leave, wanting to soak up everything I saw and felt.

My experience of walking the Camino has remained with me, a constant reminder that what appears to be negative can actually be positive. Would I go again? Absolutely. Unfortunately, my relationship with Leslie was over. She remained angry, unwilling to reconcile our differences, and even our relationship with Gord deteriorated. That hurt the most. Gord had been there for me through some of my darkest days. He had married us twice. He had been Terry's golfing buddy, but even that ended. Most of all, I felt like I had lost a mentor, and I missed him a lot.

In 2012, I was faced with the fact that my running days were over. Physically I just couldn't do it, and x-rays taken of my hips confirmed that I was a candidate for a hip replacement. My right hip was the worst, preventing me from performing simple everyday tasks, and even walking down or up an incline was excruciating.

My identity for so many years had been that I was a *runner,* and one to be reckoned with. It was difficult to let go of an activity that had been my escape from inner turmoil, my drug of choice. A lot of sadness and anger had been pounded into the ground as I ran mile after mile, trying to convince myself that I had to count for something. I had to grieve the loss of what I had so depended on to survive.

In my transition of acceptance, I began to realize that my life had shifted. I had faced my demons of the past and even forgiven wrongs that had been committed. Now I was stronger, freer, more grounded into who I had become.

At times I am still tempted to replay all my past hurts and judge those who wounded me as terrible, insensitive human beings. But it weighs heavy and only feeds my illusion that I am more righteous than they. Every human being, without exception, chooses their own journey of life, holding full responsibility. To keep blaming "them" only keeps one stuck.

Life is a mystery that sometimes doles out unimaginable hardships that seem insurmountable and cruel. In short, life is difficult. As long as I am breathing I know that the universe will put in my path lessons to inspire and challenge my growth. Nothing ever goes away until it has taught us what we need to learn. I will fall down and maybe even get lost for a while, but eventually I will crawl my way back and keep going.

As long as I am alive, I am a work in progress—unfinished.

Epilogue

I stand in front of a mirror staring at the reflection before me, noticing lines and imperfections, testament to the years that I have lived. My fingers trace many scars that range from my head to my feet, each with their own story to tell.

My focus wanders back to my eyes and I gaze intently into them. And then I see her. She's still there, ready to come out at any given moment.

I smile at her and remember . . .

She was the feisty one, the scrapper, and the one who wouldn't back down. She took the punishments, remaining defiant, refusing to break. She also took the abuse, storing with it shame and humiliation.

She picked up the rocks, drilling them as hard as she could at the bullies and authority figures that abused their power, screaming at the world to take notice. She never gave up and she never backed down.

However, as I continue to look at her, I see what lay beneath her roughness: the little girl who only wanted to be accepted and loved for who she was. The little girl who would curl into a ball when rejected or when cruel words were spoken against her. She was much more sensitive than what she would ever admit to. I knew that about her.

Today, I honour her. I honour her tenacity, her strength and her spirit, her wildness. She endured much and learned many skills of how to survive in a hostile world. I tell her, "It's okay now. We're safe and we don't have to fight anymore." But she's always ready, sometimes pleading to pick up and throw rocks and fight back and defend what is right—and sometimes she does. I gently remind her, "Let it go."

There are still times when harsh words or actions trigger her and she wants to hide and run away and escape.

That's when I remind her that it's my turn now to protect her, to hold her close, to tell her she's loved, to reassure her that it's okay. And sometimes, I fail her.

There are days that I take her deep into the woods or to a quiet spot where there is water, with the sounds of birds and rustling creatures. Nature was always her solace. I marvel at her endless curiosity to explore and learn. She is so special.

I come back to my image in the mirror and I acknowledge my journey thus far, grateful, thankful for all who have shared it with me.

Printed in Canada